# THE
# LEVIATHAN

# Great Books in Philosophy Series
## (Social and Political Philosophy)

Aristotle, *The Politics*

Mikhail Bakunin, *The Basic Bakunin: Writings, 1869–1871*

Edmund Burke, *Reflections on the Revolution in France*

John Dewey, *Freedom and Culture*

John Dewey, *Individualism Old and New*

John Dewey, *Liberalism and Social Action*

G. W. F. Hegel, *The Philosophy of History*

G. W. F. Hegel, *Philosophy of Right*

Thomas Hobbes, *The Leviathan*

Sidney Hook, *Paradoxes of Freedom*

Sidney Hook, *Reason, Social Myths, and Democracy*

John Locke, *Second Treatise on Civil Government*

Niccolo Machiavelli, *The Prince*

Karl Marx, *The Poverty of Philosophy*

Karl Marx (with Friedrich Engels) *The German Ideology,* including *Theses on Feuerbach* and *Introduction to the Critique of Political Economy*

Karl Marx/Friedrich Engels, *The Economic and Philosophic Manuscripts of 1844* and *The Communist Manifesto*

John Stuart Mill, *Considerations on Representative Government*

John Stuart Mill, *On Liberty*

John Stuart Mill, *On Socialism*

John Stuart Mill, *The Subjection of Women*

Charles de Secondat Montesquieu, *The Spirit of Laws*

Friedrich Nietzsche, *Thus Spake Zarathustra*

Thomas Paine, *Common Sense*

Thomas Paine, *Rights of Man*

Plato, *Laws*

Plato, *The Republic*

Jean-Jacques Rousseau, *The Social Contract*

Mary Wollstonecraft, *A Vindication of the Rights of Men*

Mary Wollstonecraft, *A Vindication of the Rights of Women*

See the back of this volume for a complete list of titles in Prometheus's Great Books in Philosophy and Great Minds series.

# THE
# LEVIATHAN

# THOMAS HOBBES

**PB** Prometheus Books

59 John Glenn Drive
Amherst, New York 14228-2197

320.1
Hobbes

Published 1988 by Prometheus Books
59 John Glenn Drive, Amherst, New York 14228-2197
716-691-0133. FAX: 716-691-0137.

Library of Congress Catalog Number: 88-60150
ISBN 0-87975-445-1

Printed in the United States of America on acid-free paper

THOMAS HOBBES was born the son of a cleric on April 5, 1588, in the town of Malmesbury in the county of Wiltshire, England. He was schooled in the Scholastic tradition at Oxford, and from the time he received his bachelor of arts degree in 1607, Hobbes served as a private tutor to various wealthy nobles in England and France. This career offered him access to well-stocked libraries and provided the opportunity to travel throughout Europe. During the next forty years, Hobbes would meet such famous people as Galileo, Descartes, and Gassendi, whose ideas were to influence him greatly.

In 1640, during one of the many periods of political turmoil he was to witness, Hobbes wrote a short work on the *Elements of Law, Natural and Politique,* which supported absolute monarchy. When the political tide turned in favor of the anti-royalists, Hobbes escaped to Paris. While there, he was to write *De cive* in 1642, a work that expanded his political theory. When Civil War broke out in England, Hobbes sought to bring his political philosophy to the English audience with the publication of *Leviathan* in 1651. This work was to be his most powerful restatement of absolute government grounded on a compact between the ruled and a sovereign authority that would protect the citizenry and secure peace. Since his political philosophy supported neither the divine right of a monarchy based upon succession nor the independent authority of the church, Hobbes was viewed with suspicion by both royalists and the ecclesiastical community.

Hobbes returned to England in 1651, after an eleven year exile, and took up residence in London. After the Restoration in 1658, he lived on a modest pension from King Charles II and continued to write. In 1668 he wrote *Behemoth,* a history of the Civil War, but it was suppressed in manuscript until 1682 when it was published posthumously. Having borne the brunt of political in-fighting for many years, Hobbes finally retired to the town of Hardwick, where he died on December 4, 1679, at the age of 91.

# Contents

# THE INTRODUCTION

NATURE (the Art whereby God hath made and governes the World) is by the *Art* of man, as in many other things, so in this also imitated, that it can make an Artificial Animal. For seeing life is but a motion of Limbs, the begining whereof is in some principall part within; why may we not say, that all *Automata* (Engines that move themselves by springs and wheeles as doth a watch) have an artificiall life? For what is the *Heart*, but a *Spring*; and the *Nerves*, but so many *Strings*; and the *Joynts*, but so many *Wheeles*, giving motion to the whole Body, such as was intended by the Artificer? *Art* goes yet further, imitating that Rationall and most excellent worke of Nature, *Man*. For by Art is created that great LEVIATHAN called a COMMON-WEALTH, or STATE, (in latine CIVITAS) which is but an Artificiall Man; though of greater stature and strength than the Naturall, for whose protection and defence it was intended; and in which, the *Soveraignty* is an Artificiall *Soul*, as giving life and motion to the whole body; The *Magistrates*, and other *Officers* of Judicature and Execution, artificiall *Joynts*; *Reward* and *Punishment* (by which fastned to the seate of the Soveraignty, every joynt and member is moved to performe his duty) are the *Nerves*, that do the same in the Body Naturall; The *Wealth* and *Riches* of all the particular members, are the *Strength*; *Salus Populi* (the *peoples safety*) its *Businesse*; *Counsellors*, by whom all things needfull for it to know, are suggested unto it, are the *Memory*; *Equity* and *Lawes*, an artificiall *Reason* and *Will*; *Concord, Health*; *Sedition, Sicknesse*; and *Civill war, Death*. Lastly, the *Pacts* and *Covenants*, by which the parts of this Body Politique were at first made, set together, and united, resemble that *Fiat*, or the *Let us make man*, pronounced by God in the Creation.

To describe the Nature of this Artificiall man, I will consider

First, the *Matter* thereof, and the *Artificer*; both which is *Man*.
Secondly, *How*, and by what *Covenants* it is made; what are the *Rights* and just *Power* or *Authority* of a *Soveraigne*; and what it is that *preserveth* and *dissolveth* it.
Thirdly, what is a *Christian Common-wealth*.
Lastly, what is the *Kingdome of Darkness*.

Concerning the first, there is a saying much usurped of late, That *Wisedome* is acquired, not by reading of *Books*, but of *Men*. Consequently whereunto, those persons, that for the most part can give no other proof of being wise, take great delight to shew what they think they have read in men, by uncharitable censures of one another behind their backs. But there is another saying not of

late understood, by which they might learn truly to read one
another, if they would take the pains; and that is, *Nosce teipsum*,
*Read thy self*: which was not meant, as it is now used, to countenance, either the barbarous state of men in power, towards their
inferiors; or to encourage men of low degree, to a sawcie behaviour
towards their betters; But to teach us, that for the similitude of the
thoughts, and Passions of one man, to the thoughts, and Passions of
another, whosoever looketh into himself, and considereth what he
doth, when he does *think, opine, reason, hope, feare*, &c, and upon
what grounds; he shall thereby read and know, what are the
thoughts, and Passions of all other men, upon the like occasions.
I say the similitude of *Passions*, which are the same in all men,
*desire, feare, hope*, &c; not the similitude of the *objects* of the Passions, which are the things *desired, feared, hoped*, &c: for these the
constitution individuall, and particular education do so vary, and
they are so easie to be kept from our knowledge, that the characters
of mans heart, blotted and confounded as they are, with dissembling,
lying, counterfeiting, and erroneous doctrines, are legible onely to
him that searcheth hearts. And though by mens actions wee do
discover their designe sometimes; yet to do it without comparing
them with our own, and distinguishing all circumstances, by which
the case may come to be altered, is to decypher without a key, and
be for the most part deceived, by too much trust, or by too much
diffidence; as he that reads, is himself a good or evil man.

But let one man read another by his actions never so perfectly,
it serves him onely with his acquaintance, which are but few. He
that is to govern a whole Nation, must read in himself, not this, or
that particular man; but Man-kind: which though it be hard to do,
harder than to learn any Language, or Science; yet, when I shall
have set down my own reading orderly, and perspicuously, the pains
left another, will be onely to consider, if he also find not the same
in himself. For this kind of Doctrine, admitteth no other Demonstration.

# LEVIATHAN

## PART I.—OF MAN

### CHAP. I

#### *Of* Sense

Concerning the Thoughts of man, I will consider them first *Singly*, and afterwards in *Trayne*, or dependance upon one another. *Singly*, they are every one a *Representation* or *Apparence*, of some quality, or other Accident of a body without us; which is commonly called an *Object*. Which Object worketh on the Eyes, Eares, and other parts of mans body; and by diversity of working, produceth diversity of Apparences.

The Originall of them all, is that which we call Sense; (For there is no conception in a mans mind, which hath not at first, totally, or by parts, been begotten upon the organs of Sense.) The rest are derived from that originall.

To know the naturall cause of Sense, is not very necessary to the business now in hand; and I have elsewhere written of the same at large. Nevertheless, to fill each part of my present method, I will briefly deliver the same in this place.

The cause of Sense, is the Externall Body, or Object, which presseth the organ proper to each Sense, either immediatly, as in the Tast and Touch; or mediately, as in Seeing, Hearing, and Smelling: which pressure, by the mediation of Nerves, and other strings, and membranes of the body, continued inwards to the Brain, and Heart, causeth there a resistance, or counter pressure, or endeavour of the Heart, to deliver it self: which endeavour because *Outward*, seemeth to be some matter without. And this *seeming*, or *fancy*, is that which men call *Sense*; and consisteth, as to the Eye, in a *Light*, or *Colour figured*; To the Eare, in a *Sound*; To the Nostrill, in an *Odour*; To the Tongue and Palat, in a *Savour*; And to the rest of the body, in *Heat, Cold, Hardnesse, Softnesse*, and such other qualities, as we discern by *Feeling*. All which qualities called *Sensible*, are in the object that causeth them, but so many several motions of the matter, by which it presseth our organs diversely. Neither in us that are pressed, are they any thing else, but divers motions; (for motion, produceth nothing but motion.) But their apparence to us is Fancy, the same waking, that dreaming. And as pressing, rubbing, or striking the Eye, makes us fancy a light; and

3

pressing the Eare, produceth a dinne; so do the bodies also we see, or hear, produce the same by their strong, though unobserved actions. For if those Colours, and Sounds, were in the Bodies, or Objects that cause them, they could not bee severed from them, as by glasses, and in Ecchoes by reflection, wee see they are; where we know the thing we see, is in one place; the apparence, in another. And though at some certain distance, the reall, and very object seem invested with the fancy it begets in us; Yet still the object is one thing, the image or fancy is another. So that Sense in all cases, is nothing els but original fancy, caused (as I have said) by the pressure, that is, by the motion, of externall things upon our Eyes, Eares, and other organs thereunto ordained.

But the Philosophy-schooles, through all the Universities of Christendome, grounded upon certain Texts of *Aristotle*, teach another doctrine; and say, For the cause of *Vision*, that the thing seen, sendeth forth on every side a *visible species* (in English) a *visible shew, apparition,* or *aspect,* or *a being seen;* the receiving whereof into the Eye, is *Seeing.* And for the cause of *Hearing,* that the thing heard, sendeth forth an *Audible species,* that is, an *Audible aspect,* or *Audible being seen;* which entring at the Eare, maketh *Hearing.* Nay for the cause of *Understanding* also, they say the thing Understood sendeth forth *intelligible species,* that is, an *intelligible being seen;* which comming into the Understanding, makes us Understand. I say not this, as disapproving the use of Universities: but because I am to speak hereafter of their office in a Common-wealth, I must let you see on all occasions by the way, what things would be amended in them; amongst which the frequency of insignificant Speech is one.

## CHAP. II

### *Of* IMAGINATION

THAT when a thing lies still, unlesse somewhat els stirre it, it will lye still for ever, is a truth that no man doubts of. But that when a thing is in motion, it will eternally be in motion, unlesse somewhat els stay it, though the reason be the same, (namely, that nothing can change it selfe,) is not so easily assented to. For men measure, not onely other men, but all other things, by themselves: and because they find themselves subject after motion to pain, and lassitude, think every thing els growes weary of motion, and seeks repose of its own accord; little considering, whether it be not some other motion, wherein that desire of rest they find in themselves, consisteth. From hence it is, that the Schooles say, Heavy bodies fall downwards, out of an appetite to rest, and to conserve their nature in that place which is most proper for them; ascribing appetite and

Knowledge of what is good for their conservation, (which is more than man has) to things inanimate, absurdly.

When a Body is once in motion, it moveth (unless something els hinder it) eternally; and whatsoever hindreth it, cannot in an instant, but in time, and by degrees quite extinguish it: And as wee see in the water, though the wind cease, the waves give not over rowling for a long time after; so also it happeneth in that motion, which is made in the internall parts of a man, then, when he Sees, Dreams, &c. For after the object is removed, or the eye shut, wee still retain an image of the thing seen, though more obscure than when we see it. And this is it, the Latines call *Imagination*, from the image made in seeing; and apply the same, though improperly, to all the other senses. But the Greeks call it *Fancy*; which signifies *apparence*, and is as proper to one sense, as to another. IMAGINATION therefore is nothing but *decaying sense*; and is found in men, and many other living Creatures, as well sleeping, as waking.

The decay of Sense in men waking, is not the decay of the motion made in sense; but an obscuring of it, in such manner, as the light of the Sun obscureth the light of the Starres; which starrs do no less exercise their vertue by which they are visible, in the day, than in the night. But because amongst many stroaks, which our eyes, eares, and other organs receive from externall bodies, the predominant onely is sensible; therefore the light of the Sun being predominant, we are not affected with the action of the starrs. And any object being removed from our eyes, though the impression it made in us remain; yet other objects more present succeeding, and working on us, the Imagination of the past is obscured, and made weak; as the voyce of a man is in the noyse of the day. From whence it followeth, that the longer the time is, after the sight, or Sense of any object, the weaker is the Imagination. For the continuall change of mans body, destroyes in time the parts which in sense were moved: So that distance of time, and of place, hath one and the same effect in us. For as at a great distance of place, that which wee look at, appears dimme, and without distinction of the smaller parts; and as Voyces grow weak, and inarticulate: so also after great distance of time, our imagination of the Past is weak; and wee lose (for example) of Cities wee have seen, many particular Streets; and of Actions, many particular Circumstances. This *decaying sense*, when wee would express the thing it self, (I mean *fancy* it selfe,) wee call *Imagination*, as I said before: But when we would express the *decay*, and signifie that the Sense is fading, old, and past, it is called *Memory*. So that *Imagination* and *Memory*, are but one thing, which for divers considerations hath divers names.

Much memory, or memory of many things, is called *Experience*. Againe, Imagination being only of those things which have been formerly perceived by Sense, either all at once, or by parts at severall times; The former, (which is the imagining the whole object, as it was presented to the sense) is *simple Imagination*; as when one imagineth a man, or horse, which he hath seen before. The other is *Compounded*; as when from the sight of a man at one time, and of a horse at another, we conceive in our mind a Centaure. So when a man compoundeth the image of his own person, with the image of the actions of an other man; as when a man imagins himselfe a *Hercules*, or an *Alexander*, (which happeneth often to them that are much taken with reading of Romants) it is a compound imagination, and properly but a Fiction of the mind.   There be also other Imaginations that rise in men, (though waking) from the great impression made in sense: As from gasing upon the Sun, the impression leaves an image of the Sun before our eyes a long time after; and from being long and vehemently attent upon Geometricall Figures, a man shall in the dark, (though awake) have the Images of Lines, and Angles before his eyes: which kind of Fancy hath no particular name; as being a thing that doth not commonly fall into mens discourse.

The imaginations of them that sleep, are those we call *Dreams*. And these also (as all other Imaginations) have been before, either totally, or by parcells in the Sense.   And because in sense, the Brain, and Nerves, which are the necessary Organs of sense, are so benummed in sleep, as not easily to be moved by the action of Externall Objects, there can happen in sleep, no Imagination; and therefore no Dreame, but what proceeds from the agitation of the inward parts of mans body; which inward parts, for the connexion they have with the Brayn, and other Organs, when they be distempered, do keep the same in motion; whereby the Imaginations there formerly made, appeare as if a man were waking; saving that the Organs of Sense being now benummed, so as there is no new object, which can master and obscure them with a more vigorous impression, a Dreame must needs be more cleare, in this silence of sense, than are our waking thoughts.   And hence it cometh to passe, that it is a hard matter, and by many thought impossible to distinguish exactly between Sense and Dreaming.   For my part, when I consider, that in Dreames, I do not often, nor constantly think of the same Persons, Places, Objects, and Actions that I do waking; nor remember so long a trayne of coherent thoughts, Dreaming, as at other times; And because waking I often observe the absurdity of Dreames, but never dream of the absurdities of my waking Thoughts; I am well satisfied, that being awake, I know I dreame not; though when I dreame, I think my selfe awake.

And seeing dreames are caused by the distemper of some of the inward parts of the Body; divers distempers must needs cause different Dreams.   And hence it is, that lying cold breedeth Dreams of Feare, and raiseth the thought and Image of some fearfull object (the motion from the brain to the inner parts, and from the inner parts to the Brain being reciprocall:)   And that as Anger causeth heat in some parts of the Body, when we are awake; so when we sleep, the over heating of the same parts causeth Anger, and raiseth up in the brain the Imagination of an Enemy.   In the same manner;

as naturall kindness, when we are awake causeth desire; and desire makes heat in certain other parts of the body; so also, too much heat in those parts, while wee sleep, raiseth in the brain an imagination of some kindness shewn. In summe, our Dreams are the reverse of our waking Imaginations; The motion when we are awake, beginning at one end; and when we Dream, at another.

The most difficult discerning of a mans Dream, from his waking thoughts, is then, when by some accident we observe not that we have slept: which is easie to happen to a man full of fearfull thoughts ; and whose conscience is much troubled; and that sleepeth, without the circumstances, of going to bed, or putting off his clothes, as one that noddeth in a chayre. For he that taketh pains, and industriously layes himself to sleep, in case any uncouth and exorbitant fancy come unto him, cannot easily think it other than a Dream. We read of *Marcus Brutus*, (one that had his life given him by *Julius Cæsar*, and was also his favorite, and notwithstanding murthered him,) how at *Philippi*, the night before he gave battell to *Augustus Cæsar*, hee saw a fearfull apparition, which is commonly related by Historians as a Vision: but considering the circumstances, one may easily judge to have been but a short Dream. For sitting in his tent, pensive and troubled with the horrour of his rash act, it was not hard for him, slumbering in the cold, to dream of that which most affrighted him; which feare, as by degrees it made him wake; so also it must needs make the Apparition by degrees to vanish: And having no assurance that he slept, he could have no cause to think it a Dream, or any thing but a Vision. And this is no very rare Accident: for even they that be perfectly awake, if they be timorous, and supperstitious, possessed with fearfull tales, and alone in the dark, are subject to the like fancies; and believe they see spirits and dead mens Ghosts walking in Church-yards; whereas it is either their Fancy onely, or els the knavery of such persons, as make use of such superstitious feare, to passe disguised in the night, to places they would not be known to haunt.

From this ignorance of how to distinguish Dreams, and other strong Fancies, from Vision and Sense, did arise the greatest part of the Religion of the Gentiles in time past, that worshipped Satyres, Fawnes, Nymphs, and the like; and now adayes the opinion that rude people have of Fayries, Ghosts, and Goblins; and of the power of Witches. For as for Witches, I think not that their witchcraft is any reall power; but yet that they are justly punished, for the false beliefe they have, that they can do such mischiefe, joyned with their purpose to do it if they can: their trade being neerer to a new Religion, than to a Craft or Science. And for Fayries, and walking Ghosts, the opinion of them has I think been on purpose, either taught, or not confuted, to keep in credit the use of Exorcisme, of Crosses, of holy Water, and other such inventions of Ghostly men. Neverthelesse, there is no doubt, but God can make unnaturall Apparitions: But that he does it so often, as men need to feare such things, more than they feare the stay, or change, of the course of

Nature, which he also can stay, and change, is no point of Christian faith. But evill men under pretext that God can do any thing, are so bold as to say any thing when it serves their turn, though they think it untrue; It is the part of a wise man, to believe them no further, than right reason makes that which they say, appear credible. If this superstitious fear of Spirits were taken away, and with it, Prognostiques from Dreams, false Prophecies, and many other things depending thereon, by which, crafty ambitious persons abuse the simple people, men would be much more fitted than they are for civill Obedience.

And this ought to be the work of the Schooles: but they rather nourish such doctrine. For (not knowing what Imagination, or the Senses are), what they receive, they teach: some saying, that Imaginations rise of themselves, and have no cause: Others that they rise most commonly from the Will; and that Good thoughts are blown (inspired) into a man, by God; and Evill thoughts by the Divell: or that Good thoughts are powred (infused) into a man, by God, and Evill ones by the Divell. Some say the Senses receive the Species of things, and deliver them to the Common-sense; and the Common Sense delivers them over to the Fancy, and the Fancy to the Memory, and the Memory to the Judgement, like handing of things from one to another, with many words making nothing understood.

The Imagination that is raysed in man (or any other creature indued with the faculty of imagining) by words, or other voluntary signes, is that we generally call *Understanding*; and is common to Man and Beast. For a dogge by custome will understand the call, or the rating of his Master; and so will many other Beasts. That Understanding which is peculiar to man, is the Understanding not onely his will; but his conceptions and thoughts, by the sequell and contexture of the names of things into Affirmations, Negations, and other formes of Speech: And of this kinde of Understanding I shall speak hereafter.

## CHAP. III

### Of the Consequence or TRAYNE of Imaginations

BY *Consequence*, or TRAYNE of Thoughts, I understand that succession of one Thought to another, which is called (to distinguish it from Discourse in words) *Mentall Discourse*.

When a man thinketh on any thing whatsoever, His next Thought after, is not altogether so casuall as it seems to be. Not every Thought to every Thought succeeds indifferently. But as wee have no Imagination, whereof we have not formerly had Sense, in whole, or in parts; so we have no Transition from one Imagination to another, whereof we never had the like before in our Senses. The reason whereof is this. All Fancies are Motions within us, reliques of those made in the Sense: And those motions that immediately succeeded one another in the sense, continue also together after Sense: In so much as the former comming again to take place, and be prædominant, the later followeth, by coherence of the matter moved, in such manner, as water upon a plain Table is drawn which way any one part of it is guided by the finger. But because in sense, to one and the same thing perceived, sometimes one thing, sometimes another succeedeth, it comes to passe in time, that in the Imagining of any thing, there is no certainty what we shall Imagine next; Onely this is certain, it shall be something that succeeded the same before, at one time or another.

This Trayne of Thoughts, or Mentall Discourse, is of two sorts. The first is *Unguided, without Designe,* and inconstant; Wherein there is no Passionate Thought, to govern and direct those that follow, to it self, as the end and scope of some desire, or other passion: In which case the thoughts are said to wander, and seem impertinent one to another, as in a Dream. Such are Commonly the thoughts of men, that are not onely without company, but also without care of any thing; though even then their Thoughts are as busie as at other times, but without harmony; as the sound which a Lute out of tune would yeeld to any man; or in tune, to one that could not play. And yet in this wild ranging of the mind, a man may oft-times perceive the way of it, and the-dependance of one thought upon another. For in a Discourse of our present civill warre, what could seem more impertinent, than to ask (as one did) what was the value of a Roman Penny? Yet the Cohærence to me was manifest enough. For the Thought of the warre, introduced the Thought of the delivering up the King to his Enemies; The Thought of that, brought in the Thought of the delivering up of Christ; and that again the Thought of the 30 pence, which was the price of that treason: and thence easily followed that malicious question; and all this in a moment of time; for Thought is quick.

The second is more constant; as being *regulated* by some desire, and designe. For the impression made by such things as wee desire, or feare, is strong, and permanent, or, (if it cease for a time,) of quick return: so strong it is sometimes, as to hinder and break our sleep. From Desire, ariseth the Thought of some means we have seen produce the like of that which we ayme at; and from the thought of that, the thought of means to that mean; and so continually, till we come to some beginning within our own power. And because the End, by the greatnesse of the impression, comes often to mind, in case our thoughts begin to wander, they are quickly again reduced into the way: which observed by one of the seven wise men, made him give men this præcept, which is now worne out, *Respice finem*; this is to say, in all your actions, look often upon what you would have, as the thing that directs all your thoughts in the way to attain it.

The Trayn of regulated Thoughts is of two kinds; One, when of an effect imagined, wee seek the causes, or means that produce it: and this is common to Man and Beast. The other is, when imagining any thing whatsoever, wee seek all the possible effects, that can by it be produced; that is to say, we imagine what we can do with it, when wee have it. Of which I have not at any time seen any signe, but in man onely; for this is a curiosity hardly incident to the nature of any living creature that has no other Passion but sensuall, such as are hunger, thirst, lust, and anger. In summe, the Discourse of the Mind, when it is governed by designe, is nothing but *Seeking*, or the faculty of Invention, which the Latines call *Sagacitas*, and *Solertia*; a hunting out of the causes, of some effect, present or past; or of the effects, of some present or past cause. Sometimes a man seeks what he hath lost; and from that place, and time, wherein hee misses it, his mind runs back, from place to place, and time to time, to find where, and when he had it; that is to say, to find some certain, and limited time and place, in which to begin a method of seeking. Again, from thence, his thoughts run over the same places and times, to find what action, or other occasion might make him lose it. This we call *Remembrance*, or Calling to mind: the Latines call it *Reminiscentia*, as it were a *Re-conning* of our former actions.

Sometimes a man knows a place determinate, within the compasse whereof he is to seek; and then his thoughts run over all the parts thereof, in the same manner, as one would sweep a room, to find a jewell; or as a Spaniel ranges the field, till he find a sent; or as a man should run over the Alphabet, to start a rime.

Sometime a man desires to know the event of an action; and then he thinketh of some like action past, and the events thereof one after another; supposing like events will follow like actions. As he that foresees what wil become of a Criminal, re-cons what he has seen follow on the like Crime before; having this order of thoughts, The Crime, the Officer, the Prison, the Judge, and the Gallowes. Which kind of thoughts is called *Foresight*, and *Prudence*, or *Providence*; and sometimes *Wisdome*; though such conjecture, through the difficulty of observing all circumstances, be very fallacious. But this is certain; by how much one man has more experience of things past, than another; by so much also he is more Prudent, and his expectations the seldomer faile him. The *Present* onely has a being in Nature; things *Past* have a being in the Memory onely, but things *to come* have no being at all; the *Future* being but a fiction of the mind, applying the sequels of actions Past, to the actions that are Present; which with most certainty is done by him that has most Experience; but not with certainty enough. And though it be called Prudence, when the Event answereth our Expectation; yet in its own nature, it is but Presumption. For the foresight of things to come, which is Providence, belongs onely to him by whose will they are to come. From him onely, and supernaturally, proceeds Prophecy. The best Prophet naturally is the best guesser; and the best guesser, he that is most versed and studied in the matters he guesses at: for he hath most *Signes* to guesse by.

A *Signe*, is the Event Antecedent, of the Consequent; and contrarily, the Consequent of the Antecedent, when the like Consequences have been observed, before: And the oftner they have been observed, the lesse uncertain is the Signe. And therefore he that has most experience in any kind of businesse, has most Signes, whereby to guesse at the Future time; and consequently is the most prudent: And so much more prudent than he that is new in that kind of business, as not to be equalled by any advantage of naturall and extemporary wit: though perhaps many young men think the contrary.

Neverthelesse it is not Prudence that distinguisheth man from beast. There be beasts, that at a year old observe more, and pursue that which is for their good, more prudently, than a child can do at ten.

As Prudence is a *Præsumtion* of the *Future*, contracted from the *Experience* of time *Past*: So there is a Præsumtion of things Past taken from other things (not future but) past also. For he that hath seen by what courses and degrees, a flourishing State hath first come into civil warre, and then to ruine; upon the sight of the ruines of any other State, will guesse, the like warre, and the like courses have been there also. But this conjecture, has the same incertainty almost with the conjecture of the Future; both being grounded onely upon Experience.

There is no other act of mans mind, that I can remember, naturally planted in him, so, as to need no other thing, to the exercise of it, but to be born a man, and live with the use of his five Senses. Those other Faculties, of which I shall speak by and by, and which seem proper to man onely, are acquired, and encreased by study and industry; and of most men learned by instruction, and discipline; and proceed all from the invention of Words, and Speech. For besides Sense, and Thoughts, and the Trayne of thoughts, the mind of man has no other motion; though by the help of Speech, and Method, the same Facultyes may be improved to such a height, as to distinguish men from all other living Creatures.

Whatsoever we imagine, is *Finite*. Therefore there is no Idea, or conception of any thing we call *Infinite*. No man can have in his mind an Image of infinite magnitude; nor conceive infinite swiftness, infinite time, or infinite force, or infinite power. When we say any thing is infinite, we signifie onely, that we are not able to conceive the ends, and bounds of the thing named; having no Conception of the thing, but of our own inability. And therefore the Name of *God* is used, not to make us conceive him; (for he is *Incomprehensible*; and his greatnesse, and power are unconceivable;) but that we may honour him. Also because whatsoever (as I said before,) we conceive, has been perceived first by sense, either all at once, or by parts; a man can have no thought, representing any thing, not subject to sense. No man therefore can conceive any

thing, but he must conceive it in some place; and indued with some
determinate magnitude; and which may be divided into parts; nor
that any thing is all in this place, and all in another place at the
same time; nor that two, or more things can be in one, and the
same place at once: For none of these things ever have, or can be
incident to Sense; but are absurd speeches, taken upon credit
(without any signification at all,) from deceived Philosophers, and
deceived, or deceiving Schoolemen.

## CHAP. IV

### *Of* SPEECH

THE Invention of *Printing*, though ingenious, compared with the
invention of *Letters*, is no great matter.   But who was the first that
found the use of Letters, is not known.   He that first brought them
into *Greece*, men say was *Cadmus*, the sonne of *Agenor*, King of
Phænicia.   A profitable Invention for continuing the memory of
time past, and the conjunction of mankind, dispersed into so many,
and distant regions of the Earth; and with all difficult, as proceeding
from a watchfull observation of the divers motions of the Tongue,
Palat, Lips, and other organs of Speech; whereby to make as many
differences of characters, to remember them.   But the most noble
and profitable invention of all other, was that of SPEECH, consisting
of *Names* or *Appellations*, and their Connexion; whereby men
register their Thoughts; recall them when they are past; and also
declare them one to another for mutuall utility and conversation;
without which, there had been amongst men, neither Common-
wealth, nor Society, nor Contract, nor Peace, no more than amongst
Lyons, Bears, and Wolves.   The first author of Speech was *God*
himself, that instructed *Adam* how to name such creatures as he
presented to his sight; For the Scripture goeth no further in this
matter.   But this was sufficient to direct him to adde more names,
as the experience and use of the creatures should give him occasion;
and to joyn them in such manner by degrees, as to make himself
understood; and so by succession of time, so much language might
be gotten, as he had found use for; though not so copious as an
Orator or Philosopher has need of.   For I do not find any thing in
the Scripture, out of which, directly or by consequence can be
gathered, that *Adam* was taught the names of all Figures, Numbers,
Measures, Colours, Sounds, Fancies, Relations; much less the names
of Words and Speech, as *Generall*, *Speciall*, *Affirmative*, *Negative*,
*Interrogative*, *Optative*, *Infinitive*, all which are usefull; and least
of all, of *Entity*, *Intentionality*, *Quiddity*, and other insignificant
words of the School.
   But all this language gotten, and augmented by *Adam* and his
posterity, was again lost at the tower of *Babel*, when by the hand

of God, every man was stricken for his rebellion, with an oblivion of his former language. And being hereby forced to disperse themselves into severall parts of the world, it must needs be, that the diversity of Tongues that now is, proceeded by degrees from them, in such manner, as need (the mother of all inventions) taught them; and in tract of time grew every where more copious.

The generall use of Speech, is to transferre our Mentall Discourse, into Verbal; or the Trayne of our Thoughts, into a Trayne of Words; and that for two commodities; whereof one is, the Registring of the Consequences of our Thoughts; which being apt to slip out of our memory, and put us to a new labour, may again be recalled, by such words as they were marked by. So that the first use of names, is to serve for *Markes*, or *Notes* of remembrance. Another is, when many use the same words, to signifie (by their connexion and order,) one to another, what they conceive, or think of each matter; and also what they desire, feare, or have any other passion for. And for this use they are called *Signes*. Speciall uses of Speech are these; First, to Register, what by cogitation, wee find to be the cause of any thing, present or past; and what we find things present or past may produce, or effect: which in summe, is acquiring of Arts. Secondly, to shew to others that knowledge which we have attained; which is, to Counsell, and Teach one another. Thirdly, to make known to others our wills, and purposes, that we may have the mutuall help of one another. Fourthly, to please and delight our selves, and others, by playing with our words, for pleasure or ornament, innocently.

To these Uses, there are also foure correspondent Abuses. First, when men register their thoughts wrong, by the inconstancy of the signification of their words; by which they register for their conceptions, that which they never conceived; and so deceive themselves. Secondly, when they use words metaphorically; that is, in other sense than that they are ordained for; and thereby deceive others. Thirdly, when by words they declare that to be their will, which is not. Fourthly, when they use them to grieve one another: for seeing nature hath armed living creatures, some with teeth, some with horns, and some with hands, to grieve an enemy, it is but an abuse of Speech, to grieve him with the tongue, unlesse it be one whom wee are obliged to govern; and then it is not to grieve, but to correct and amend.

The manner how Speech serveth to the remembrance of the consequence of causes and effects, consisteth in the imposing of *Names*, and the *Connexion* of them.

Of Names, some are *Proper*, and singular to one onely thing; as *Peter*, *John*, *This man*, *this Tree*: and some are *Common* to many things; as *Man*, *Horse*, *Tree*; every of which though but one Name, is nevertheless the name of divers particular things; in respect of all which together, it is called an *Universall*; there being nothing in the world Universall but Names; for the things named, are every one of them Individuall and Singular.

One Universall name is imposed on many things, for their similitude in some quality, or other accident: And whereas a Proper
Name bringeth to mind one thing onely; Universals recall any one
of those many.

And of Names Universall, some are of more, and some of lesse
extent; the larger comprehending the less large: and some again
of equall extent, comprehending each other reciprocally. As for
example, the Name *Body* is of larger signification than the word
*Man*, and comprehendeth it; and the names *Man* and *Rationall*,
are of equall extent, comprehending mutually one another. But
here wee must take notice, that by a Name is not alwayes understood, as in Grammar, one onely Word; but sometimes by circum-
locution many words together. For all these words, *Hee that in his
actions observeth the Lawes of his Country*, make but one Name,
equivalent to this one word, *Just*.

By this imposition of Names, some of larger, some of stricter
signification, we turn the reckoning of the consequences of things
imagined in the mind, into a reckoning of the consequences of
Appellations. For example, a man that hath no use of Speech at
all, (such, as is born and remains perfectly deafe and dumb,) if he
set before his eyes a triangle, and by it two right angles, (such as
are the corners of a square figure,) he may by meditation compare
and find, that the three angles of that triangle, are equall to those
two right angles that stand by it. But if another triangle be shewn
him different in shape from the former, he cannot know without a
new labour, whether the three angles of that also be equall to the
same. But he that hath the use of words, when he observes, that
such equality was consequent, not to the length of the sides, not to
any other particular thing in his triangle; but onely to this, that
the sides were straight, and the angles three; and that that was all,
for which he named it a Triangle; will boldly conclude Universally,
that such equality of angles is in all triangles whatsoever; and register his invention in these generall termes, *Every triangle hath its
three angles equall to two right angles*. And thus the consequence
found in one particular, comes to be registred and remembred, as
an Universall rule; and discharges our mentall reckoning, of time
and place; and delivers us from all labour of the mind, saving the
first; and makes that which was found true *here*, and *now*, to be
true in *all times* and *places*.

But the use of words in registring our thoughts, is in nothing so
evident as in Numbring. A naturall foole that could never learn
by heart the order of numerall words, as *one*, *two*, and *three*, may
observe every stroak of the Clock, and nod to it, or say one, one, one;
but can never know what houre it strikes. And it seems, there
was a time when those names of number were not in use; and men
were fayn to apply their fingers of one or both hands, to those things
they desired to keep account of; and that thence it proceeded, that
now our numerall words are but ten, in any Nation, and in some
but five, and then they begin again. And he that can tell ten, if he

recite them out of order, will lose himselfe, and not know when he has done: Much lesse will he be able to adde, and substract, and performe all other operations of Arithmetique. So that without words, there is no possibility of reckoning of Numbers; much lesse of Magnitudes, of Swiftnesse, of Force, and other things, the reckonings whereof are necessary to the being, or well-being of man-kind.

When two Names are joyned together into a Consequence, or Affirmation; as thus, *A man is a living creature*; or thus, *if he be a man, he is a living creature*, If the later name *Living creature*, signifie all that the former name *Man* signifieth, then the affirmation, or consequence is *true*; otherwise *false*. For *True* and *False* are attributes of Speech, not of Things. And where Speech is not, there is neither *Truth* nor *Falshood*. *Errour* there may be, as when wee expect that which shall not be; or suspect what has not been: but in neither case can a man be charged with Untruth.

Seeing then that *truth* consisteth in the right ordering of names in our affirmations, a man that seeketh precise *truth*, had need to remember what every name he uses stands for; and to place it accordingly; or else he will find himselfe entangled in words, as a bird in limetwiggs; the more he struggles, the more belimed. And therefore in Geometry, (which is the onely Science that it hath pleased God hitherto to bestow on mankind,) men begin at settling the significations of their words; which settling of significations, they call *Definitions*; and place them in the beginning of their reckoning.

By this it appears how necessary it is for any man that aspires to true Knowledge, to examine the Definitions of former Authors; and either to correct them, where they are negligently set down; or to make them himselfe. For the errours of Definitions multiply themselves, according as the reckoning proceeds; and lead men into absurdities, which at last they see, but cannot avoyd, without reckoning anew from the beginning; in which lyes the foundation of their errours. From whence it happens, that they which trust to books, do as they that cast up many little summs into a greater, without considering whether those little summes were rightly cast up or not; and at last finding the errour visible, and not mistrusting their first grounds, know not which way to cleere themselves; but spend time in fluttering over their bookes; as birds that entring by the chimney, and finding themselves inclosed in a chamber, flutter at the false light of a glasse window, for want of wit to consider which way they came in. So that in the right Definition of Names, lyes the first use of Speech; which is the Acquisition of Science: And in wrong, or no Definitions, lyes the first abuse; from which proceed all false and senslesse Tenets; which make those men that take their instruction from the authority of books, and not from their own meditation, to be as much below the condition of ignorant men, as men endued with true Science are above it. For between true Science, and erroneous Doctrines, Ignorance is in the middle. Naturall sense and imagination are not subject to absurdity. Nature it selfe cannot erre: and as men abound in copiousnesse of language; so they become more wise, or more mad than ordinary. Nor is it possible without Letters for any man to become either excellently wise, or (unless his memory be hurt by disease, or ill constitution of organs) excellently foolish. For words are wise mens counters, they do but reckon by them: but they are the mony of fooles, that value them by the authority of an *Aristotle*, a *Cicero*, or a *Thomas*, or any other Doctor whatsoever, if but a man.

*Subject to Names*, is whatsoever can enter into, or be considered in an account; and be added one to another to make a summe; or substracted one from another, and leave a remainder. The Latines called Accounts of mony *Rationes*, and accounting, *Ratiocinatio*: and that which we in bills or books of account call *Items*, they called *Nomina*; that is, *Names*: and thence it seems to proceed, that they extended the word *Ratio*, to the faculty of Reckoning in all other things. The Greeks have but one word λόγος, for both *Speech* and *Reason*; not that they thought there was no Speech without Reason; but no Reasoning without Speech: And the act of reasoning they called *Syllogisme*; which signifieth summing up of the consequences of one saying to another. And because the same things may enter into account for divers accidents; their names are (to shew that diversity) diversly wrested, and diversified. This diversity of names may be reduced to foure generall heads.

First, a thing may enter into account for *Matter*, or *Body*; as *living, sensible, rationall, hot, cold, moved, quiet*; with all which names the word *Matter*, or *Body* is understood; all such, being names of Matter.

Secondly, it may enter into account, or be considered, for some accident or quality, which we conceive to be in it; as for *being moved*, for *being so long*, for *being hot*, &c; and then, of the name of the thing it selfe, by a little change or wresting, wee make a name for that accident, which we consider; and for *living* put into the account *life*; for *moved, motion*; for *hot, heat*; for *long, length*, and the like: And all such Names, are the names of the accidents and properties, by which one Matter, and Body is distinguished from another. These are called *names Abstract*; because severed (not from Matter, but) from the account of Matter.

Thirdly, we bring into account, the Properties of our own bodies, whereby we make such distinction: as when any thing is *Seen* by us, we reckon not the thing it selfe; but the *sight*, the *Colour*, the *Idea* of it in the fancy: and when any thing is *heard*, wee reckon it not; but the *hearing*, or *sound* onely, which is our fancy or conception of it by the Eare: and such are names of fancies.

Fourthly, we bring into account, consider, and give names, to *Names* themselves, and to *Speeches*: For, *generall, universall, speciall, æquivocall*, are names of Names. And *Affirmation, Interrogation, Commandement, Narration, Syllogisme, Sermon, Oration*, and many other such, are names of Speeches. And this is all the variety of Names *Positive*; which are put to mark somewhat which is in Nature, or may be feigned by the mind of man, as Bodies that are, or may be conceived to be; or of bodies, the Properties that are, or may be feigned to be; or Words and Speech.

There be also other Names, called *Negative*; which are notes to signifie that a word is not the name of the thing in question; as these words *Nothing, no man, infinite, indocible, three want foure*, and the like; which are nevertheless of use in reckoning, or in correcting of reckoning; and call to mind our past cogitations, though they be not names of any thing; because they make us refuse to admit of Names not rightly used.

All other Names, are but insignificant sounds; and those of two sorts. One, when they are new, and yet their meaning not explained by Definition; whereof there have been aboundance coyned by Schoole-men, and pusled Philosophers.

Another, when men make a name of two Names, whose significations are contradictory and inconsistent; as this name, an *incorporeall body*, or (which is all one) an *incorporeall substance*, and a great number more. For whensoever any affirmation is false, the two names of which it is composed, put together and made one, signifie nothing at all. For example, if it be a false affirmation to say a *quadrangle is round*, the word *round quadrangle* signifies nothing; but is a meere sound. So likewise if it be false, to say that vertue can be powred, or blown up and down; the words *In-powred vertue, In-blown vertue*, are as absurd and insignificant, as a *round quadrangle*. And therefore you shall hardly meet with a senslesse and insignificant word, that is not made up of some Latin or Greek names. A Frenchman seldome hears our Saviour called by the name of *Parole*, but by the name of *Verbe* often; yet *Verbe* and *Parole* differ no more, but that one is Latin, the other French.

When a man upon the hearing of any Speech, hath those thoughts which the words of that Speech, and their connexion, were ordained and constituted to signifie; Then he is said to understand it: *Understanding* being nothing else, but conception caused by Speech. And therefore if Speech be peculiar to man (as for ought I know it is,) then is Understanding peculiar to him also. And therefore of absurd and false affirmations, in case they be universall, there can be no Understanding; though many think they understand, then, when they do but repeat the words softly, or con them in their mind.

What kinds of Speeches signifie the Appetites, Aversions, and Passions of mans mind; and of their use and abuse, I shall speak when I have spoken of the Passions.

The names of such things as affect us, that is, which please, and displease us, because all men be not alike affected with the same thing, nor the same man at all times, are in the common discourses of men, of *inconstant* signification. For seeing all names are imposed to signifie our conceptions; and all our affections are but conceptions; when we conceive the same things differently, we can hardly avoyd different naming of them. For though the nature of that we conceive, be the same; yet the diversity of our receptio ₁ of it, in respect of different constitutions of body, and prejudices of opinion, gives every thing a tincture of our different passions. And therefore in reasoning, a man must take heed of words; which besides the signification of what we imagine of their nature, have a signification also of the nature, disposition, and interest of the speaker; such as are the names of Vertues, and Vices; For one man calleth *Wisdome*, what another calleth *feare*; and one *cruelty*, what another *justice*; one *prodigality*, what another *magnanimity*; and one *gravity*, what another *stupidicy*, &c. And therefore such names can never be true grounds of any ratiocination. No more can Metaphors, and Tropes of speech: but these are less dangerous, because they profess their inconstancy; which the other do not.

## CHAP. V

### *Of* REASON, and SCIENCE

WHEN a man *Reasoneth*, hee does nothing else but conceive a summe totall, from *Addition* of parcels; or conceive a Remainder, from *Substraction* of one summe from another: which (if it be done by Words,) is conceiving of the consequence of the names of all the parts, to the name of the whole; or from the names of the whole and one part, to the name of the other part. And though in some things, (as in numbers,) besides *Adding* and *Substracting*, men name other operations, as *Multiplying* and *Dividing*; yet they are the same; for Multiplication, is but Adding together of things equall; and Division, but Substracting of one thing, as often as we can. These operations are not incident to Numbers onely, but to all manner of things that can be added together, and taken one out of another. For as Arithmeticians teach to adde and substract in *numbers*; so the Geometricians teach the same in *lines, figures* (solid and super-ficiall,) *angles, proportions, times,* degrees of *swiftnesse, force, power,* and the like; The Logicians teach the same in *Consequences of words*; adding together *two Names*, to make an *Affirmation*; and *two Affirmations*, to make a *Syllogisme*; and *many Syllogismes* to make a *Demonstration*; and from the *summe*, or *Conclusion* of a *Syllogisme*, they substract one *Proposition*, to finde the other. Writers of Poli-tiques, adde together *Pactions*, to find mens *duties*; and Lawyers, *Lawes*, and *facts*, to find what is *right* and *wrong* in the actions of private men. In summe, in what matter soever there is place for *addition* and *subtraction*, there is also place for *Reason*; and where these have no place, there *Reason* has nothing at all to do.

Out of all which we may define, (that is to say determine,) what that is, which is meant by this word *Reason*, when wee reckon it amongst the Faculties of the mind. For REASON, in this sense, is nothing but *Reckoning* (that is, Adding and Substracting) of the Consequences of generall names agreed upon, for the *marking* and *signifying* of our thoughts; I say *marking* them, when we reckon by our selves; and *signifying,* when we demonstrate, or approve our reckonings to other men.

And as in Arithmetique, unpractised men must, and Professors themselves may often erre, and cast up false; so also in any other subject of Reasoning, the ablest, most attentive, and most practised men, may deceive themselves, and inferre false Conclusions; Not but that Reason it selfe is alwayes Right Reason, as well as Arithmetique is a certain and infallible Art: But no one mans Reason, nor the Reason of any one number of men, makes the certaintie; no more than an account is therefore well cast up, because a great many men have unanimously approved it. And therfore, as when there is a controversy in an account, the parties must by their own accord, set up for right Reason, the Reason of some Arbitrator, or Judge, to whose sentence they will both stand, or their controversie must either come to blowes, or be undecided, for want of a right Reason constituted by Nature; so is it also in all debates of what kind soever: And when men that think themselves wiser than all others, clamor and demand right Reason for judge; yet seek no more, but that things should be determined, by no other mens reason but their own, it is as intolerable in the society of men, as it is in play after trump is turned, to use for trump on every occasion, that suite whereof they have most in their hand. For they do nothing els, that will have every of their passions, as it comes to bear sway in them, to be taken for right Reason, and that in their own controversies: bewraying their want of right Reason, by the claym they lay to it.

The Use and End of Reason, is not the finding of the summe, and truth of one, or a few consequences, remote from the first definitions, and settled significations of names; but to begin at these; and proceed from one consequence to another. For there can be no certainty of the last Conclusion, without a certainty of all those Affirmations and Negations, on which it was grounded, and inferred. As when a master of a family, in taking an account, casteth up the summs of all the bills of expence, into one sum; and not regarding how each bill is summed up, by those that give them in account; nor what it is he payes for; he advantages himself no more, than if he allowed the account in grosse, trusting to every of the accountants skill and honesty: so also in Reasoning of all other things, he that takes up conclusions on the trust of Authors, and doth not fetch them from the first Items in every Reckoning, (which are the significations of names settled by definitions), loses his labour; and does not know any thing; but onely beleeveth.

When a man reckons without the use of words, which may be done in particular things, (as when upon the sight of any one thing, wee conjecture what was likely to have preceded, or is likely to follow upon it;) if that which he thought likely to follow, followes not; or that which he thought likely to have preceded it, hath not preceded it, this is called ERROR; to which even the most prudent men are subject. But when we Reason in Words of generall signification, and fall upon a generall inference which is false; though it be commonly called *Error*, it is indeed an ABSURDITY, or senslesse Speech. For Error is but a deception, in presuming that somewhat is past, or to come; of which, though it were not past, or not to come; yet there was no impossibility discoverable. But when we make a generall assertion, unlesse it be a true one, the possibility of it is unconceivable. And words whereby we conceive nothing but the sound, are those we call *Absurd, Insignificant,* and *Non-sense.* And therefore if a man should talk to me of a *round Quadrangle*; or *accidents of Bread in Cheese*; or *Immateriall Substances*; or of *A free Subject*; *A free-Will*; or any *Free,* but free from being hindred by opposition, I should not say he were in an Errour; but that his words were without meaning; that is to say, Absurd.

I have said before, (in the second chapter,) that a Man did excell all other Animals in this faculty, that when he conceived any thing whatsoever, he was apt to enquire the consequences of it, and what effects he could do with it. And now I adde this other degree of the same excellence, that he can by words reduce the consequences he findes to generall Rules, called *Theoremes,* or *Aphorismes*; that is, he can Reason, or reckon, not onely in number; but in all other things, whereof one may be added unto, or substracted from another.

But this priviledge, is allayed by another; and that is, by the priviledge of Absurdity; to which no living creature is subject, but man onely. And of men, those are of all most subject to it, that professe Philosophy. For it is most true that *Cicero* sayth of them somewhere; that there can be nothing so absurd, but may be found in the books of Philosophers. And the reason is manifest. For there is not one of them that begins his ratiocination from the Definitions, or Explications of the names they are to use; which is a method that hath been used onely in Geometry; whose Conclusions have thereby been made indisputable.

The first cause of Absurd conclusions I ascribe to the want of Method; in that they begin not their Ratiocination from Definitions; that is, from settled significations of their words: as if they could cast account, without knowing the value of the numerall words, *one, two,* and *three.*

And whereas all bodies enter into account upon divers considerations, (which I have mentioned in the precedent chapter;) these considerations being diversly named, divers absurdities proceed from the confusion, and unfit connexion of their names into assertions. And therefore

The second cause of Absurd assertions, I ascribe to the giving of names of *bodies,* to *accidents*; or of *accidents* to *bodies*; As they do, that say, *Faith is infused,* or *inspired*; when nothing can be *powred,* or *breathed* into any thing, but body; and that, *extension* is *body*; that *phantasmes* are *spirits,* &c.

The third I ascribe to the giving of the names of the *accidents* of *bodies without us*, to the *accidents* of our *own bodies*; as they do that say, the *colour is in the body*; *the sound is in the ayre*, &c.

The fourth, to the giving of the names of *bodies*, to *names*, or *speeches*; as they do that say, that *there be things universall*; that *a living creature is Genus*, or *a generall thing*, &c.

The fifth, to the giving of the names of *accidents*, to *names* and *speeches*; as they do that say, *the nature of a thing is its definition*; *a mans command is his will*; and the like.

The sixth, to the use of Metaphors, Tropes, and other Rhetoricall figures, in stead of words proper. For though it be lawfull to say, (for example) in common speech, *the way goeth, or leadeth hither, or thither, The Proverb sayes this or that* (whereas wayes cannot go, nor Proverbs speak;) yet in reckoning, and seeking of truth, such speeches are not to be admitted.

The seventh, to names that signifie nothing; but are taken up, and learned by rote from the Schooles, as *hypostatical, transubstantiate, consubstantiate, eternal - Now*, and the like canting of Schoolemen.

To him that can avoyd these things, it is not easie to fall into any absurdity, unlesse it be by the length of an account; wherein he may perhaps forget what went before. For all men by nature reason alike, and well, when they have good principles. For who is so stupid, as both to mistake in Geometry, and also to persist in it, when another detects his error to him?

By this it appears that Reason is not as Sense, and Memory, borne with us; nor gotten by Experience onely, as Prudence is; but attayned by Industry; first in apt imposing of Names; and secondly by getting a good and orderly Method in proceeding from the Elements, which are Names, to Assertions made by Connexion of one of them to another; and so to Syllogismes, which are the Connexions of one Assertion to another, till we come to a knowledge of all the Consequences of names appertaining to the subject in hand; and that is it, men call SCIENCE. And whereas Sense and Memory are but knowledge of Fact, which is a thing past, and irrevocable; *Science* is the knowledge of Consequences, and dependance of one fact upon another: by which, out of that we can pres ntly do, we know how to do something else when we will, or the like, another time: Because when we see how any thing comes about, upon what causes, and by what manner; when the like causes come into our power, wee see how to make it produce the like effects.

Children therefore are not endued with Reason at all, till they have attained the use of Speech: but are called Reasonable Creatures, for the possibility apparent of having the use of Reason in time to come. And the most part of men, though they have the use of Reasoning a little way, as in numbring to some degree; yet it serves them to little use in common life; in which they govern themselves, some better, some worse, according to their differences of experience, quicknesse of memory, and inclinations to severall ends; but specially according to good or evill fortune, and the errors of one another. For as for *Science*, or certain rules of their actions, they are so farre from it, that they know not what it is. Geometry they have thought Conjuring: But for other Sciences, they who have not been taught the beginnings, and some progresse in them, that they may see how they be acquired and generated, are in this point like children, that having no thought of generation, are made believe by the women, that their brothers and sisters are not born, but found in the garden.

But yet they that have no *Science*, are in better, and nobler condition with their naturall Prudence; than men, that by mis-reasoning, or by trusting them that reason wrong, fall upon false and absurd generall rules. For ignorance of causes, and of rules, does not set men so farre out of their way, as relying on false rules, and taking for causes of what they aspire to, those that are not so, but rather causes of the contrary.

To conclude, The Light of humane minds is Perspicuous Words, but by exact definitions first snuffed, and purged from ambiguity; *Reason* is the *pace*; Encrease of *Science*, the *way*; and the Benefit of man-kind, the *end*. And on the contrary, *Metaphors*, and senselesse and ambiguous words, are like *ignes fatui*; and reasoning upon them, is wandering amongst innumerable absurdities; and their end, contention, and sedition, or contempt.

As, much Experience, is *Prudence*; so, is much Science, *Sapience*. For though wee usually have one name of Wisedome for them both; yet the Latines did alwayes distinguish between *Prudentia* and *Sapientia*; ascribing the former to Experience, the later to Science. But to make their difference appeare more cleerly, let us suppose one man endued with an excellent naturall use, and dexterity in handling his armes; and another to have added to that dexterity, an acquired Science, of where he can offend, or be offended by his adversarie, in every possible posture, or guard: The ability of the former, would be to the ability of the later, as Prudence to Sapience; both usefull; but the later infallible. But they that trusting onely to the authority of books, follow the blind blindly, are like him that trusting to the false rules of a master of Fence, ventures præsumptuously upon an adversary, that either kills, or disgraces him.

The signes of Science, are some, certain and infallible; some, uncertain. Certain, when he that pretendeth the Science of any thing, can teach the same; that is to say, demonstrate the truth thereof perspicuously to another: Uncertain, when onely some particular events answer to his pretence, and upon many occasions prove so as he sayes they must. Signes of prudence are all uncertain; because to observe by experience, and remember all circumstances that may alter the successe, is impossible. But in any businesse, whereof a man has not infallible Science to proceed by; to forsake his own naturall judgement, and be guided by generall sentences read in Authors, and subject to many exceptions, is a signe of folly, and generally scorned by the name of Pedantry. And even of those men themselves, that in Councells of the Commonwealth, love to shew their reading of Politiques and History, very few do it in their domestique affaires, where their particular interest is concerned; having Prudence enough for their private affaires: but in publique they study more the reputation of their owne wit, than the successe of anothers businesse.


## CHAP. VI

*Of the Interiour Beginnings of Voluntary Motions: commonly called the* PASSIONS. *And the Speeches by which they are expressed*

THERE be in Animals, two sorts of *Motions* peculiar to them: One called *Vitall*; begun in generation, and continued without interruption through their whole life; such as are the *course* of the *Bloud*, the *Pulse*, the *Breathing*, the *Concoction, Nutrition, Excretion*, &c; to which Motions there needs no help of Imagination: The other is *Animall motion*, otherwise called *Voluntary motion*; as to *go*, to *speak*, to *move* any of our limbes, in such manner as is first fancied in our minds. That Sense, is Motion in the organs and interiour parts of mans body, caused by the action of the things we See, Heare, &c; And that Fancy is but the Reliques of the same Motion, remaining after Sense, has been already sayd in the first and second Chapters. And because *going, speaking*, and the like Voluntary motions, depend alwayes upon a precedent thought of *whither, which way*, and *what*; it is evident, that the Imagination is the first internall beginning of all Voluntary Motion. And although unstudied men, doe not conceive any motion at all to be there, where the thing moved is invisible; or the space it is moved in, is (for the shortnesse of it) insensible; yet that doth not hinder, but that such Motions are. For let a space be never so little, that which is moved over a greater space, whereof that little one is part, must first be moved over that. These small beginnings of Motion, within the body of Man, before they appear in walking, speaking, striking, and other visible actions, are commonly called ENDEAVOUR.

This Endeavour, when it is toward something which causes it, is called APPETITE, or DESIRE; the later, being the generall name; and the other, often-times restrayned to signifie the Desire of Food, namely *Hunger* and *Thirst*. And when the Endeavour is fromward something, it is generally called AVERSION. These words *Appetite*, and *Aversion* we have from the *Latines*; and they both of them signifie the motions, one of approaching, the other of retiring. So also do the Greek words for the same, which are ὁρμὴ, and ἀφορμὴ. For Nature it selfe does often presse upon men those truths, which afterwards, when they look for somewhat beyond Nature, they stumble at. For the Schooles find in meere Appetite to go, or move, no actuall Motion at all: but because some Motion they must acknowledge, they call it Metaphoricall Motion; which is but an absurd speech: for though Words may be called metaphoricall; Bodies, and Motions çannot.

That which men Desire, they are also sayd to LOVE: and to HATE those things, for which they have Aversion. So that Desire, and Love, are the same thing; save that by Desire, we always signifie the Absence of the Object; by Love, most commonly the Presence of the same. So also by Aversion, we signifie the Absence; and by Hate, the Presence of the Object.

Of Appetites, and Aversions, some are born with men; as appetite of food, Appetite of excretion, and exoneration, (which may also and more properly be called Aversions, from somewhat they feele in their Bodies;) and some other Appetites, not many. The rest, which are Appetites of particular things, proceed from Experience, and triall of their effects upon themselves, or other men. For of things wee know not at all, or believe not to be, we can have no further Desire, than to tast and try. But Aversion wee have for things, not onely which we know have hurt us; but also that we do not know whether they will hurt us, or not.

Those things which we neither Desire, nor Hate, we are said to *Contemne*: CONTEMPT being nothing else but an immobility, or contumacy of the Heart, in resisting the action of certain things; and proceeding from that the Heart is already moved otherwise, by other more potent objects; or from want of experience of them.

And because the constitution of a mans Body, is in continuall Mutation; it is impossible that all the same things should alwayes cause in him the same Appetites, and Aversions: much lesse can all men consent, in the Desire of almost any one and the same Object.

But whatsoever is the object of any mans Appetite or Desire; that is it, which he for his part calleth *Good*: And the object of his Hate, and Aversion, *Evill*; And of his Contempt, *Vile* and *Inconsiderable*. For these words of Good, Evill, and Contemptible, are ever used with relation to the person that useth them: There being nothing simply and absolutely so; nor any common Rule of Good and Evill, to be taken from the nature of the objects themselves; but from the Person of the man (where there is no Common-wealth;) or, (in a Common-wealth,) from the Person that representeth it; or from an Arbitrator or Judge, whom men disagreeing shall by consent set up, and make his sentence the Rule thereof.

The Latine Tongue has two words, whose significations approach to those of Good and Evill; but are not precisely the same; And those are *Pulchrum* and *Turpe*. Whereof the former signifies that, which by some apparent signes promiseth Good; and the later, that, which promiseth Evil. But in our Tongue we have not so generall names to expresse them by. But for *Pulchrum*, we say in some things, *Fayre*: in others, *Beautifull*, or *Handsome*; or *Gallant*, or *Honourable*, or *Comely*, or *Amiable*; and for *Turpe*,

*Foule, Deformed, Ugly, Base, Nauseous,* and the like, as the subject shall require; All which words, in their proper places signifie nothing els, but the *Mine,* or Countenance, that promiseth Good and Evil. So that of Good there be three kinds; Good in the Promise, that is *Pulchrum;* Good in Effect, as the end desired, which is called *Jucundum, Delightfull;* and Good as the Means, which is called *Utile, Profitable;* and as many of Evil: For *Evill,* in Promise, is that they call *Turpe;* Evil in Effect, and End, is *Molestum, Unpleasant, Troublesome;* and Evill in the Means, *Inutile, Unprofitable, Hurtfull.*

As, in Sense, that which is really within us, is (as I have sayd before) onely Motion, caused by the action of externall objects, but in apparence; to the Sight, Light and Colour; to the Eare, Sound; to the Nostrill, Odour, &c: so, when the action of the same object is contued from the Eyes, Eares, and other organs to the Heart; the real effect there is nothing but Motion, or Endeavour; which consisteth in Appetite, or Aversion, to, or from the object moving. But the apparence, or sense of that motion, is that wee either call DELIGHT, or TROUBLE OF MIND.

This Motion, which is called Appetite, and for the apparence of it *Delight,* and *Pleasure,* seemeth to be, a corroboration of Vitall motion, and a help thereunto; and therefore such things as caused Delight, were not improperly called *Jacunda,* (*à Juvando*), from helping or fortifying; and the contrary, *Molesta, Offensive,* from hindering, and troubling the motion vitall.

*Pleasure* therefore, (or *Delight,*) is the apparence, or sense of Good; and *Molestation* or *Displeasure,* the apparence, or sense of Evill. And consequently All Appetite, Desire, and Love, is accompanied with some Delight more or lesse; and all Hatred, and Aversion, with more or lesse Displeasure and Offence.

Of Pleasures, or Delights, some arise from the sense of an object Present; And those may be called *Pleasures of Sense,* (The word *sensuall,* as it is used by those onely that condemn them, having no place till there be Lawes.) Of this kind are all Onerations and Exonerations of the body: as also all that is pleasant, in the *Sight, Hearing, Smell, Tast, or Touch;* Others arise from the Expectation, that proceeds from foresight of the End, or Consequence of things; whether those things in the Sense Please or Displease: And these are *Pleasures of the Mind* of him that draweth those consequences; and are generally called JOY. In the like manner, Displeasures, are some in the Sense, and called PAYNE; others, in the Expectation of consequences, and are called GRIEFE.

These simple Passions called *Appetite, Desire, Love, Aversion, Hate, Joy,* and *Griefe,* have their names for divers considerations diversified. As first, when they one succeed another, they are diversly called from the opinion men have of the likelihood of attaining what they desire. Secondly, from the object loved or hated. Thirdly, from the consideration of many of them together. Fourthly, from the Alteration or succession it selfe.

For *Appetite* with an opinion of attaining, is called HOPE.

The same, without such opinion, DESPAIRE.

*Aversion*, with opinion of *Hurt* from the object, FEARE.

The same, with hope of avoyding that Hurt by resistence, COURAGE.

Sudden *Courage*, ANGER.

Constant *Hope*, CONFIDENCE of our selves.

Constant *Despayre*, DIFFIDENCE of our selves.

*Anger* for great hurt done to another, when we conceive the same to be done by Injury, INDIGNATION.

*Desire* of good to another, BENEVOLENCE, GOOD WILL, CHARITY. If to man generally, GOOD NATURE.

*Desire* of Riches, COVETOUSNESSE: a name used alwayes in signification of blame; because men contending for them, are displeased with one anothers attaining them; though the desire in it selfe, be to be blamed, or allowed, according to the means by which those Riches are sought.

*Desire* of Office, or precedence, AMBITION: a name used also in the worse sense, for the reason before mentioned.

*Desire* of things that conduce but a little to our ends; And fear of things that are but of little hindrance, PUSILLANIMITY.

*Contempt* of little helps, and hindrances, MAGNANIMITY.

*Magnanimity*, in danger of Death, or Wounds, VALOUR, FORTITUDE.

*Magnanimity*, in the use of Riches, LIBERALITY.

*Pusillanimity*, in the same WRETCHEDNESSE, MISERABLENESSE; or PARSIMONY; as it is liked, or disliked.

*Love* of Persons for society, KINDNESSE.

*Love* of Persons for Pleasing the sense onely, NATURALL LUST.

*Love* of the same, acquired from Rumination, that is, Imagination of Pleasure past, LUXURY.

*Love* of one singularly, with desire to be singularly beloved, THE PASSION OF LOVE. The same, with fear that the love is not mutuall, JEALOUSIE.

*Desire*, by doing hurt to another, to make him condemn some fact of his own, REVENGEFULNESSE.

*Desire*, to know why, and how, CURIOSITY; such as is in no living creature but *Man*: so that Man is distinguished, not onely by his Reason; but also by this singular Passion from other *Animals*; in whom the appetite of food, and other pleasures of Sense, by prædominance, take away the care of knowing causes; which is a Lust of the mind, that by a perseverance of delight in the continuall and indefatigable generation of Knowledge, exceedeth the short vehemence of any carnall Pleasure.

*Feare* of power invisible, feigned by the mind, or imagined from tales publiquely allowed, RELIGION; not allowed, SUPERSTITION. And when the power imagined, is truly such as we imagine, TRUE RELIGION.

*Feare*, without the apprehension of why, or what, PANIQUE

TERROR; called so from the Fables, that make *Pan* the author of them; whereas in truth, there is alwayes in him that so feareth, first, some apprehension of the cause, though the rest run away by Example; every one supposing his fellow to know why. And therefore this Passion happens to none but in a throng, or multitude of people.

*Joy*, from apprehension of novelty, ADMIRATION; proper to Man, because it excites the appetite of knowing the cause.

*Joy*, arising from imagination of a mans own power and ability, is that exultation of the mind which is called GLORYING: which if grounded upon the experience of his own former actions, is the same with *Confidence*: but if grounded on the flattery of others; or onely supposed by himself, for delight in the consequences of it, is called VAINE-GLORY: which name is properly given; because a well grounded *Confidence* begetteth Attempt; whereas the supposing of power does not, and is therefore rightly called *Vaine*.

*Griefe*, from opinion of want of power, is called DEJECTION of mind.

The *vain-glory* which consisteth in the feigning or supposing of abilities in our selves, which we know are not, is most incident to young men, and nourished by the Histories, or Fictions of Gallant Persons; and is corrected oftentimes by Age, and Employment.

*Sudden Glory*, is the passion which maketh those *Grimaces* called LAUGHTER; and is caused either by some sudden act of their own, that pleaseth them; or by the apprehension of some deformed thing in another, by comparison whereof they suddenly applaud themselves. And it is incident most to them, that are conscious of the fewest abilities in themselves; who are forced to keep themselves in their own favour, by observing the imperfections of other men. And therefore much Laughter at the defects of others, is a signe of Pusillanimity. For of great minds, one of the proper workes is, to help and free others from scorn; and compare themselves onely with the most able.

On the contrary, *Sudden Dejection*, is the passion that causeth WEEPING; and is caused by such accidents, as suddenly take away some vehement hope, or some prop of their power: And they are most subject to it, that rely principally on helps externall, such as are Women and Children. Therefore some Weep for the losse of Friends; Others for their unkindnesse; others for the sudden stop made to their thoughts of revenge, by Reconciliation. But in all cases, both Laughter, and Weeping, are sudden motions; Custome taking them both away. For no man Laughs at old jests; or Weeps for an old calamity.

*Griefe*, for the discovery of some defect of ability, is SHAME, or the passion that discovereth it selfe in BLUSHING; and consisteth in the apprehension of some thing dishonourable; and in young men, is a signe of the love of good reputation; and commendable: In old men it is a signe of the same; but because it comes too late, not commendable.

The *Contempt* of good Reputation is called IMPUDENCE.

*Griefe,* for the Calamity of another, is PITTY; and ariseth from the imagination that the like calamity may befall himselfe; and therefore is called also COMPASSION, and in the phrase of this present time a FELLOW-FEELING: And therefore for Calamity arriving from great wickedness, the best men have the least Pitty; and for the same Calamity, those have least Pitty, that think themselves least obnoxious to the same.

*Contempt,* or little sense of the calamity of others, is that which men call CRUELTY; proceeding from Security of their own fortune. For, that any man should take pleasure in other mens great harmes, without other end of his own, I do not conceive it possible.

*Griefe,* for the successe of a Competitor in wealth, honour, or other good, if it be joyned with Endeavour to enforce our own abilities to equall or exceed him, is called EMULATION: But joyned with Endeavour to supplant, or hinder a Competitor, ENVIE.

When in the mind of man, Appetites, and Aversions, Hopes, and Feares, concerning one and the same thing, arise alternately; and divers good and evill consequences of the doing, or omitting the thing propounded, come successively into our thoughts; so that sometimes we have an Appetite to it; sometimes an Aversion from it; sometimes Hope to be able to do it; sometimes Despaire, or Feare to attempt it; the whole summe of Desires, Aversions, Hopes and Fears, continued till the thing be either done, or thought impossible, is that we call DELIBERATION.

Therefore of things past, there is no *Deliberation*; because manifestly impossible to be changed: nor of things known to be impossible, or thought so; because men know, or think such Deliberation vain. But of things impossible, which we think possible, we may Deliberate; not knowing it is in vain. And it is called *Deliberation*; because it is a putting an end to the *Liberty* we had of doing, or omitting, according to our own Appetite, or Aversion.

This alternate Succession of Appetites, Aversions, Hopes and Fears, is no lesse in other living Creatures then in Man: and therefore Beasts also Deliberate.

Every *Deliberation* is then sayd to *End,* when that whereof they Deliberate, is either done, or thought impossible; because till then wee retain the liberty of doing, or omitting, according to our Appetite or Aversion.

In *Deliberation,* the last Appetite, or Aversion, immediately adhæring to the action, or to the omission thereof, is that wee call the WILL; the Act, (not the faculty,) of *Willing.* And Beasts that have *Deliberation,* must necessarily also have *Will.* The Definition of the *Will,* given commonly by the Schooles, that it is a *Rationall Appetite,* is not good. For if it were, then could there be no Voluntary Act against Reason. For a *Voluntary Act* is that, which proceedeth from the *Will,* and no other. But if in stead of a Rationall Appetite, we shall say an Appetite resulting from a precedent Deliberation, then the Definition is the same that I have given here. *Will* therefore *is the last Appetite in Deliberating.* And though we say in common Discourse, a man had a Will once to do a thing, that neverthelesse he forbore to do; yet that is properly but an Inclination, which makes no Action Voluntary; because the action depends not of it, but of the last Inclination, or Appetite. For if the intervenient Appetites, make any action Voluntary; then by the same Reason all intervenient Aversions, should make the same action Involuntary; and so one and the same action, should be both Voluntary & Involuntary.

By this it is manifest, that not onely actions that have their beginning from Covetousnesse, Ambition, Lust, or other Appetites to the thing propounded; but also those that have their beginning from Aversion, or Feare of those consequences that follow the omission, are *voluntary actions.*

The formes of Speech by which the Passions are expressed, are partly the same, and partly different from those, by which wee expresse our Thoughts. And first, generally all Passions may be expressed *Indicatively*; as *I love, I feare, I joy, I deliberate, I will, I command*: but some of them have particular expressions by themselves, which neverthelesse are not affirmations, unlesse it be when they serve to make other inferences, besides that of the Passion they proceed from. Deliberation is expressed *Subjunctively*; which is a speech proper to signifie suppositions, with their consequences; as, *If this be done, then this will follow*; and differs not from the language of Reasoning, save that Reasoning is in generall words; but Deliberation for the most part is of Particulars. The language of Desire, and Aversion, is *Imperative*; as *Do this, forbeare that*; which when the party is obliged to do, or forbeare, is *Command*; otherwise *Prayer*; or els *Counsell*. The language of Vain-Glory, of Indignation, Pitty and Revengefulness, *Optative*: But of the Desire to know, there is a peculiar expression, called *Interrogative*; as, *What is it, when shall it, how is it done*, and *why so*? other language of the Passions I find none: For Cursing, Swearing, Reviling, and the like, do not signifie as Speech; but as the actions of a tongue accustomed.

These formes of Speech, I say, are expressions, or voluntary significations of our Passions: but certain signes they be not; because they may be used arbitrarily, whether they that use them, have such Passions or not. The best signes of Passions present, are either in the countenance, motions of the body, actions, and ends, or aimes, which we otherwise know the man to have.

And because in Deliberation, the Appetites, and Aversions are raised by foresight of the good and evill consequences, and sequels of the action whereof we Deliberate; the good or evill effect thereof dependeth on the foresight of a long chain of consequences, of which very seldome any man is able to see to the end. But for so farre as a man seeth, if the Good in those consequences, be greater than the Evill, the whole chaine is that which Writers call *Apparent*, or

*Seeming Good.* And contrarily, when the Evill exceedeth the Good, the whole is *Apparent* or *Seeming Evill*: so that he who hath by Experience, or Reason, the greatest and surest prospect of Consequences, Deliberates best himselfe; and is able when he will, to give the best counsell unto others.

*Continuall successe* in obtaining those things which a man from time to time desireth, that is to say, continuall prospering, is that men call FELICITY; I mean the Felicity of this life. For there is no such thing as perpetuall Tranquillity of mind, while we live here; because Life it selfe is but Motion, and can never be without Desire, nor without Feare, no more than without Sense. What kind of Felicity God hath ordained to them that devoutly honour him, a man shall no sooner know, than enjoy; being joyes, that now are as incomprehensible, as the word of Schoole-men *Beatificall Vision* is unintelligible.

The forme of Speech whereby men signifie their opinion of the Goodnesse of any thing, is PRAISE. That whereby they signifie the power and greatnesse of any thing, is MAGNIFYING. And that whereby they signifie the opinion they have of a mans Felicity, is by the Greeks called μακαρισμός, for which wee have no name in our tongue. And thus much is sufficient for the present purpose, to have been said of the PASSIONS.

## CHAP. VII

### *Of the* Ends, *or* Resolutions *of* DISCOURSE

OF all *Discourse*, governed by desire of Knowledge, there is at last an *End*, either by attaining, or by giving over. And in the chain of Discourse, wheresoever it be interrupted, there is an End for that time.

If the Discourse be meerly Mentall, it consisteth of thoughts that the thing will be, and will not be, or that it has been, and has not been, alternately. So that wheresoever you break off the chayn of a mans Discourse, you leave him in a Præsumption if *it will be,* or, *it will not be;* or *it has been,* or, *has not been.* All which is *Opinion.* And that which is alternate Appetite, in Deliberating concerning Good and Evil; the same is alternate Opinion, in the Enquiry of the truth of *Past,* and *Future.* And as the last Appetite in Deliberation, is called the *Will;* so the last Opinion in search of the truth of Past, and Future, is called the JUDGEMENT, or *Resolute* and *Finall Sentence* of him that *discourseth.* And as the whole chain of Appetites alternate, in the question of Good, or Bad, is called *Deliberation;* so the whole chain of Opinions alternate, in the question of True, or False, is called DOUBT.

No Discourse whatsoever, can End in absolute knowledge of Fact, past, or to come. For, as for the knowledge of Fact, it is originally, Sense; and ever after, Memory. And for the knowledge of Consequence, which I have said before is called Science, it is not Absolute, but Conditionall. No man can know by Discourse, that this, or that, is, has been, or will be; which is to know absolutely: but onely, that if This be, That is; if This has been, That has been; if This shall be, That shall be: which is to know conditionally; and that not the consequence of one thing to another; but of one name of a thing, to another name of the same thing.

And therefore, when the Discourse is put into Speech, and begins with the Definitions of Words, and proceeds by Connexion of the same into generall Affirmations, and of these again into Syllogismes; the End or last summe is called the Conclusion; and the thought of the mind by it signified, is that conditionall Knowledge, or Knowledge of the consequence of words, which is commonly called SCIENCE. But if the first ground of such Discourse, be not Definitions; or if the Definitions be not rightly joyned together into Syllogismes, then the End or Conclusion, is again OPINION, namely of the truth of somewhat said, though sometimes in absurd and senslesse words, without possibility of being understood. When two, or more men, know of one and the same fact, they are said to be CONSCIOUS of it one to another; which is as much as to know it together. And because such are fittest witnesses of the facts of one another, or of a third; it was, and ever will be reputed a very Evill act, for any man to speak against his *Conscience*; or to corrupt or force another so to do: Insomuch that the plea of Conscience, has been alwayes hearkened unto very diligently in all times. Afterwards, men made use of the same word metaphorically, for the knowledge of their own secret facts, and secret thoughts; and therefore it is Rhetorically said, that the Conscience is a thousand witnesses. And last of all, men, vehemently in love with their own new opinions, (though never so absurd,) and obstinately bent to maintain them, gave those their opinions also that reverenced name of Conscience, as if they would have it seem unlawfull, to change or speak against them; and so pretend to know they are true, when they know at most, but that they think so.

When a mans Discourse beginneth not at Definitions, it beginneth either at some other contemplation of his own, and then it is still called Opinion; Or it beginneth at some saying of another, of whose ability to know the truth, and of whose honesty in not deceiving, he doubteth not; and then the Discourse is not so much concerning the Thing, as the Person; And the Resolution is called BELEEFE, and FAITH: *Faith, in* the man; *Beleefe,* both *of* the man, and *of* the truth of what he sayes. So that in Beleefe are two opinions; one of the saying of the man; the other of his vertue. To *have faith in,* or *trust to,* or *beleeve a man,* signifie the same thing; namely, an opinion of the veracity of the man: But to *beleeve what is said,* signifieth onely an opinion of the truth of the saying. But wee are to observe that this Phrase, *I beleeve in*; as also the Latine, *Credo in*; and the Greek, πιστέυω έις, are never used but in the writings of Divines. In stead of them, in other writings are put, *I beleeve him*; *I trust him*; *I have faith in him*; *I rely on him*; and in Latin, *Credo illi*; *fido illi*: and in Greek, πιστεύω αὐτῷ: and that this singularity of the Ecclesiastique use of the word hath raised many disputes about the right object of the Christian Faith.

But by *Beleeving in*, as it is in the Creed, is meant, not trust in the Person; but Confession and acknowledgement of the Doctrine. For not onely Christians, but all manner of men do so believe in God, as to hold all for truth they heare him say, whether they understand it, or not; which is all the Faith and trust can possibly be had in any person whatsoever: But they do not all believe the Doctrine of the Creed.

From whence we may inferre, that when wee believe any saying whatsoever it be, to be true, from arguments taken, not from the thing it selfe, or from the principles of naturall Reason, but from the Authority, and good opinion wee have, of him that hath sayd it; then is the speaker, or person we believe in, or trust in, and whose word we take, the object of our Faith; and the Honour done in Believing, is done to him onely. And consequently, when wee Believe that the Scriptures are the word of God, having no immediate revelation from God himselfe, our Beleefe, Faith, and Trust is in the Church; whose word we take, and acquiesce therein. And they that believe that which a Prophet relates unto them in the name of God, take the word of the Prophet, do honour to him, and in him trust, and believe, touching the truth of what he relateth, whether he be a true, or a false Prophet. And so it is also with all other History. For if I should not believe all that is written by Historians, of the glorious acts of *Alexander*, or *Cæsar*; I do not think the Ghost of *Alexander*, or *Cæsar*, had any just cause to be offended; or any body else, but the Historian. If *Livy* say the Gods made once a Cow speak, and we believe it not; wee distrust not God therein, but *Livy*. So that it is evident, that whatsoever we believe, upon no other reason, then what is drawn from authority of men onely, and their writings; whether they be sent from God or not, is Faith in men onely.

## CHAP. VIII

*Of the* VERTUES *commonly called* INTELLECTUALL; *and their contrary* DEFECTS

VERTUE generally, in all sorts of subjects, is somewhat that is valued for eminence; and consisteth in comparison. For if all things were equally in all men, nothing would be prized. And by *Vertues* INTELLECTUALL, are always understood such abilityes of the mind, as men praise, value, and desire should be in themselves; and go commonly under the name of a *good wit*; though the same word WIT, be used also, to distinguish one certain ability from the rest.

These *Vertues* are of two sorts; *Naturall,* and *Acquired.* By Naturall, I mean not, that which a man hath from his Birth: for that is nothing else but Sense; wherein men differ so little one from another, and from brute Beasts, as it is not to be reckoned amongst Vertues. But I mean, that *Wit,* which is gotten by Use onely, and Experience; without Method, Culture, or Instruction. This NATURALL WIT, consisteth principally in two things; *Celerity of Imagining,* (that is, swift succession of one thought to another;) and *steddy direction* to some approved end. On the Contrary a slow Imagination, maketh that Defect, or fault of the mind, which is commonly called DULNESSE, *Stupidity,* and sometimes by other names that signifie slownesse of motion, or difficulty to be moved.

And this difference of quicknesse, is caused by the difference of mens passions; that love and dislike, some one thing, some another: and therefore some mens thoughts run one way, some another; and are held to, and observe differently the things that passe through their imagination. And whereas in this succession of mens thoughts, there is nothing to observe in the things they think on, but either in what they be *like one another,* or in what they be *unlike,* or *what they serve for,* or *how they serve to such a purpose;* Those that observe their similitudes, in case they be such as are but rarely observed by others, are sayd to have a *Good Wit;* by which, in this occasion, is meant a *Good Fancy.* But they that observe their differences, and dissimilitudes; which is called *Distinguishing,* and *Discerning,* and *Judging* between thing and thing; in case, such discerning be not easie, are said to have a *good Judgement*: and particularly in matter of conversation and businesse; wherein, times, places, and persons are to be discerned, this Vertue is called DISCRETION. The former, that is, Fancy, without the help of Judgement, is not commended as a Vertue: but the later which is Judgement, and Discretion, is commended for it selfe, without the help of Fancy. Besides the Discretion of times, places, and persons, necessary to a good Fancy, there is required also an often application of his thoughts to their End; that is to say, to some use to be made of them. This done; he that hath this Vertue, will be easily fitted with similitudes, that will please, not onely by illustration of his discourse, and adorning it with new and apt metaphors; but also, by the rarity of their invention. But without Steddinesse, and Direction to some End, a great Fancy is one kind of Madnesse; such as they have, that entring into any discourse, are snatched from their purpose, by every thing that comes in their thought, into so many, and so long digressions, and Parentheses, that they utterly lose themselves: Which kind of folly, I know no particular name for: but the cause of it is, sometimes want of experience; whereby that seemeth to a man new and rare, which doth not so to others: sometimes Pusillanimity; by which that seems great to him, which other men think a trifle: and whatsoever is new, or great, and therefore thought fit to be told, withdrawes a man by degrees from the intended way of his discourse.

In a good Poem, whether it be *Epique* or *Dramatique*; as also in *Sonnets*, *Epigrams*, and other Pieces, both Judgement and Fancy are required: But the Fancy must be more eminent; because they please for the Extravagancy; but ought not to displease by Indiscretion.

In a good History, the Judgement must be eminent; because the goodnesse consisteth, in the Method, in the Truth, and in the Choyse of the actions that are most profitable to be known. Fancy has no place, but onely in adorning the stile.

In Orations of Prayse, and in Invectives, the Fancy is prædominant; because the designe is not truth, but to Honour or Dishonour; which is done by noble, or by vile comparisons. The Judgement does but suggest what circumstances make an action laudable, or culpable.

In Hortatives, and Pleadings, as Truth, or Disguise serveth best to the Designe in hand; so is the Judgement, or the Fancy most required.

In Demonstration, in Councell, and all rigorous search of Truth, Judgement does all; except sometimes the understanding have need to be opened by some apt similitude; and then there is so much use of Fancy. But for Metaphors, they are in, this case utterly excluded. For seeing they openly professe deceipt; to admit them into Councell, or Reasoning, were manifest folly.

And in any Discourse whatsoever, if the defect of Discretion be apparent, how extravagant soever the Fancy be, the whole discourse will be taken for a signe of want of wit; and so will it never when the Discretion is manifest, though the Fancy be never so ordinary.

The secret thoughts of a man run over all things, holy, prophane, clean, obscene, grave, and light, without shame, or blame; which verball discourse cannot do, farther than the Judgement shall approve of the Time, Place, and Persons. An Anatomist, or a Physitian may speak, or write his judgement of unclean things; because it is not to please, but profit: but for another man to write his extravagant, and pleasant fancies of the same, is as if a man, from being tumbled into the dirt, should come and present himselfe before good company. And 'tis the want of Discretion that makes the difference. Again, in profest remissnesse of mind, and familiar company, a man may play with the sounds, and æquivocall significations of words; and that many times with encounters of extraordinary Fancy: but in a Sermon, or in publique, or before persons unknown, or whom we ought to reverence, there is no Gingling of words that will not be accounted folly: and the difference is onely in the want of Discretion. So that where Wit is wanting, it is not Fancy that is wanting, but Discretion. Judgement therefore without Fancy is Wit, but Fancy without Judgement not.

When the thoughts of a man, that has a designe in hand, running over a multitude of things, observes how they conduce to that designe; or what designe they may conduce unto; if his observations be such as are not easie, or usuall, This wit of his is called PRUDENCE: and dependeth on much Experience, and Memory of the like things, and their consequences heretofore. In which there is not so much difference of Men, as there is in their Fancies and Judgements; Because the Experience of men equall in age, is not much unequall, as to the quantity; but lyes in different occasions; every one having his private designes. To govern well a family, and a kingdome, are not different degrees of Prudence; but different sorts of businesse; no more then to draw a picture in little, or as great, or greater then the life, are different degrees of Art. A plain husband-man is more Prudent in affaires of his own house, then a Privy Counseller in the affaires of another man.

To Prudence, if you adde the use of unjust, or dishonest means, such as usually are prompted to men by Feare, or Want; you have that Crooked Wisdome, which is called CRAFT; which is a signe of Pusillanimity. For Magnanimity is contempt of unjust, or dishonest helps. And that which the Latines call *Versutia*, (translated into English, *Shifting*,) and is a putting off of a present danger or incommodity, by engaging into a greater, as when a man robbs one to pay another, is but a shorter sighted Craft, called *Versutia*, from *Versura*, which signifies taking mony at usurie, for the present payment of interest.

As for *acquired Wit*, (I mean acquired by method and instruction,) there is none but Reason; which is grounded on the right use of Speech; and produceth the Sciences. But of Reason and Science, I have already spoken in the fifth and sixth Chapters.

The causes of this difference of Witts, are in the Passions: and the difference of Passions, proceedeth partly from the different Constitution of the body, and partly from different Education. For if the difference proceeded from the temper of the brain, and the organs of Sense, either exterior or interior, there would be no lesse difference of men in their Sight, Hearing, or other Senses, than in their Fancies, and Discretions. It proceeds therefore from the Passions; which are different, not onely from the difference of mens complexions; but also from their difference of customes, and education.

The Passions that most of all cause the differences of Wit, are principally, the more or lesse Desire of Power, of Riches, of Knowledge, and of Honour. All which may be reduced to the first, that is Desire of Power. For Riches, Knowledge and Honour are but severall sorts of Power.

And therefore, a man who has no great Passion for any of these things; but is as men terme it indifferent; though he may be so farre a good man, as to be free from giving offence; yet he cannot possibly have either a great Fancy, or much Judgement. For the Thoughts, are to the Desires, as Scouts, and Spies, to range abroad, and find the way to the things Desired: All Stedinesse of the minds motion, and all quicknesse of the same, proceeding from thence. For as to have no Desire, is to be Dead: so to have weak Passions, is Dulnesse; and to have Passions indifferently for every thing, GIDDINESSE, and *Distraction*; and to have stronger, and more vehement Passions for any thing, than is ordinarily seen in others, is that which men call MADNESSE.

Whereof there be almost as many kinds, as of the Passions themselves. Sometimes the extraordinary and extravagant Passion, proceedeth from the evill constitution of the organs of the Body, or harme done them; and sometimes the hurt, and indisposition of the Organs, is caused by the vehemence, or long continuance of the Passion. But in both cases the Madnesse is of one and the same nature.

The Passion, whose violence, or continuance maketh Madnesse, is either great *vaine-Glory*; which is commonly called *Pride*, and *selfe-conceipt*; or great *Dejection* of mind.

Pride, subjecteth a man to Anger, the excesse whereof, is the Madnesse called RAGE, and FURY. And thus it comes to passe that excessive desire of Revenge, when it becomes habituall, hurteth the organs, and becomes Rage; That excessive love, with jealousie, becomes also Rage: Excessive opinion of a mans own selfe, for divine inspiration, for wisdome, learning, forme, and the like, becomes Distraction, and Giddinesse: The same, joyned with Envy, Rage: Vehement opinion of the truth of any thing, contradicted by others, Rage.

Dejection, subjects a man to causelesse fears; which is a Madnesse commonly called MELANCHOLY, apparent also in divers manners; as in haunting of solitudes, and graves; in superstitious behaviour; and in fearing some one, some another particular thing. In summe, all Passions that produce strange and unusuall behaviour, are called by the generall name of Madnesse. But of the severall kinds of Madnesse, he that would take the paines, might enrowle a legion. And if the Excesses be madnesse, there is no doubt but the Passions themselves, when they tend to Evill, are degrees of the same.

(For example,) Though the effect of folly, in them that are possessed of an opinion of being inspired, be not visible alwayes in one man, by any very extravagant action, that proceedeth from such Passion; yet when many of them conspire together, the Rage of the whole multitude is visible enough. For what argument of Madnesse can there be greater, than to clamour, strike, and throw stones at our best friends? Yet this is somewhat lesse than such a multitude will do. For they will clamour, fight against, and destroy those, by whom all their life-time before, they have been protected, and secured from injury. And if this be Madnesse in the multitude, it is the same in every particular man. For as in the middest of the sea, though a man perceive no sound of that part of the water next him; yet he is well assured, that part contributes as much, to the Roaring of the Sea, as any other part, of the same quantity: so also, though wee perceive no great unquiet-nesse, in one, or two men; yet we may be well assured, that their singular Passions, are parts of the Seditious roaring of a troubled Nation. And if there were nothing else that bewrayed their madnesse; yet that very arrogating such inspiration to themselves, is argument enough. If some man in Bedlam should entertaine you with sober discourse; and you desire in taking leave, to know what he were, that you might another time requite his civility; and he should tell you, he were God the Father; I think you need expect no extravagant action for argument of his Madnesse.

This opinion of Inspiration, called commonly, Private Spirit, begins very often, from some lucky finding of an Errour generally held by others; and not knowing, or not remembring, by what conduct of reason, they came to so singular a truth, (as they think it, though it be many times an untruth they light on,) they presently admire themselves; as being in the speciall grace of God Almighty, who hath revealed the same to them supernaturally, by his Spirit.

Again, that Madnesse is nothing else, but too much appearing Passion, may be gathered out of the effects of Wine, which are the same with those of the evill disposition of the organs. For the variety of behaviour in men that have drunk too much, is the same with that of Mad-men: some of them Raging, others Loving, others Laughing, all extravagantly, but according to their severall domineering Passions: For the effect of the wine, does but remove Dissimulation; and take from them the sight of the deformity of their Passions. For, (I believe) the most sober men, when they walk alone without care and employment of the mind, would be unwilling the vanity and Extravagance of their thoughts at that time should be publiquely seen: which is a confession, that Passions unguided, are for the most part meere Madnesse.

The opinions of the world, both in antient and later ages, concerning the cause of madnesse, have been two. Some, deriving them from the Passions; some, from Dæmons, or Spirits, either good, or bad, which they thought might enter into a man, possesse him, and move his organs in such strange, and uncouth manner, as madmen use to do. The former sort therefore, called such men, Mad-men: but the Later, called them sometimes *Dæmoniaks*, (that is, possessed with spirits;) sometimes *Energumeni*, (that is, agitated, or moved with spirits;) and now in *Italy* they are called not onely *Pazzi*, Mad-men; but also *Spiritati*, men possess.

There was once a great conflux of people in *Abdera*, a City of the Greeks, at the acting of the Tragedy of *Andromeda*, upon an extream hot day: whereupon, a great many of the spectators falling into Fevers, had this accident from the heat, and from the Tragedy together, that they did nothing but pronounce Iambiques, with the names of *Perseus* and *Andromeda*; which together with the Fever, was cured, by the comming on of Winter: And this madnesse was thought to proceed from the Passion imprinted by the Tragedy. Likewise there raigned a fit of madnesse in another Græcian City, which seized onely the young Maidens; and caused many of them to hang themselves. This was by most then thought an act of the Divel. But one that suspected, that contempt of life in them, might proceed from some Passion of the mind, and supposing they did not contemne also their honour, gave counsell to the Magistrates, to strip such as so hang'd themselves, and let them hang out naked. This the story sayes cured that madnesse. But on the other side, the same Græcians, did often ascribe madnesse, to the operation of the Eumenides, or Furyes; and sometimes of *Ceres*, *Phœbus*, and other Gods: so much did men attribute to Phantasmes, as to think them aëreal living bodies; and generally to call them Spirits. And as the Romans in this, held the same opinion with the Greeks: so also did the Jewes; For they called mad-men Prophets, or (according as they thought the spirits good or bad) Dæmoniacks; and some of them called both Prophets, and Dæmoniacks, mad-men; and some called the same man both Dæmoniack, and mad-man. But for the Gentiles, 'tis no wonder; because Diseases, and Health; Vices, and Vertues; and many naturall accidents, were with them termed, and worshipped as Dæmons. So that a man was to understand by Dæmon, as well (sometimes) an Ague, as a Divell. But for the Jewes to have such opinion, is somewhat strange. For neither *Moses*, nor *Abraham* pretended to Prophecy by possession of a Spirit; but from the voyce of God; or by a Vision or Dream: Nor is there any thing in his Law, Morall, or Ceremoniall, by which they were taught, there was any such Enthusiasme; or any Possession. When God is sayd, *Numb.* 11. 25. to take from the Spirit that was in *Moses*, and give to the 70. Elders, the Spirit of God (taking it for the substance of God) is not divided. The Scriptures by the Spirit of God in man, mean a mans spirit, enclined to Godlinesse. And where it is said *Exod.* 28. 3. *Whom I have filled with the spirit of wisdome to make garments for Aaron*, is not meant a spirit put into them, that can make garments; but the wisdome of their own spirits in that kind of work. In the like sense, the spirit of man, when it produceth unclean actions, is ordinarily called an unclean spirit; and so other spirits, though not alwayes, yet as often as the vertue or vice so stiled, is extraordinary, and Eminent. Neither did the other Prophets of the old Testament pretend Enthusiasme; or, that God spake in them; but to them by Voyce, Vision, or Dream; and the *Burthen of the Lord* was not Possession, but Command. How then could the Jewes fall into this opinion of possession? I can imagine no reason, but that which is common to all men; namely, the want of curiosity to search naturall causes; and their placing Felicity, in the acquisition of the grosse pleasures of the Senses, and the things that most immediately conduce thereto. For they that see any strange, and unusuall ability, or defect in a mans mind; unlesse they see withall, from what cause it may probably proceed, can hardly think it naturall; and if not naturall, they must needs thinke it supernaturall; and then what can it be, but that either

God, or the Divell is in him? And hence it came to passe, when our Saviour (*Mark* 3. 21.) was compassed about with the multitude, those of the house doubted he was mad, and went out to hold him: but the Scribes said he had *Belzebub*, and that was it, by which he cast out divels; as if the greater mad-man had awed the lesser. And that (*John* 10. 20.) some said, *He hath a Divell, and is mad*; whereas others holding him for a Prophet, sayd. *These are not the words of one that hath a Divell*. So in the old Testament he that came to anoynt *Jehu*, 2 *Kings* 9. 11. was a Prophet; but some of the company asked *Jehu, What came that mad-man for?* So that in summe, it is manifest, that whosoever behaved himselfe in extraordinory manner, was thought by the Jewes to be possessed either with a good, or evill spirit; except by the Sadduces, who erred so farre on the other hand, as not to believe there were at all any spirits, (which is very neere to direct Atheisme;) and thereby perhaps the more provoked others, to terme such men Dæmoniacks, rather than mad-men.

But why then does our Saviour proceed in the curing of them, as if they were possest; and not as if they were mad? To which I can give no other kind of answer, but that which is given to those that urge the Scripture in like manner against the opinion of the motion of the Earth. The Scripture was written to shew unto men the kingdome of God, and to prepare their mindes to become his obedient subjects; leaving the world, and the Philosophy thereof, to the disputation of men, for the exercising of their naturall Reason. Whether the Earths, or Suns motion make the day, and night; or whether the Exorbitant actions of men, proceed from Passion, or from the Divell, (so we worship him not) it is all one, as to our obedience, and subjection to God Almighty; which is the thing for which the Scripture was written. As for that our Saviour speaketh to the disease, as to a person; it is the usuall phrase of all that cure by words onely, as Christ did, (and Inchanters pretend to do, whether they speak to a Divel or not.) For is not Christ also said (*Math*. 8. 26.) to have rebuked the winds? Is not he said also (*Luk*. 4. 39.) to rebuke a Fever? Yet this does not argue that a Fever is a Divel. And whereas many of those Divels are said to confesse Christ; it is not necessary to interpret those places otherwise, than that those mad-men confessed him. And whereas our Saviour (*Math*. 12. 43.) speaketh of an unclean Spirit, that having gone out of a man, wandreth through dry places, seeking rest, and finding none; and returning into the same man, with seven other spirits worse than himselfe; It is manifestly a Parable, alluding to a man, that after a little endeavour to quit his lusts, is vanquished by the strength of them; and becomes seven times worse than he was. So that I see nothing at all in the Scripture, that requireth a beliefe, that Dæmoniacks were any other thing but Mad-men.

There is yet another fault in the Discourses of some men; which may also be numbred amongst the sorts of Madnesse; namely, that abuse of words, whereof I have spoken before in the fifth chapter, by the Name of Absurdity. And that is, when men speak such words, as put together, have in them no signification at all; but are fallen upon by some, through misunderstanding of the words they have received, and repeat by rote; by others, from intention to deceive by obscurity. And this is incident to none but those, that converse in questions of matters incomprehensible, as the Schoolemen; or in questions of abstruse Philosophy. The common sort of men seldome speak Insignificantly, and are therefore, by those other Egregious persons counted Idiots. But to be assured their words are without any thing correspondent to them in the mind, there would need some Examples; which if any man require, let him take a Schoole-man into his hands, and see if he can translate any one chapter concerning any difficult point; as the Trinity; the Deity; the nature of Christ; Transubstantiation; Free-will, &c. into any of the moderne tongues, so as to make the same intelligible; or into any tolerable Latine, such as they were acquainted withall, that lived when the Latine tongue was Vulgar. What is the meaning of these words. *The first cause does not necessarily inflow any thing into the second, by force of the Essentiall subordination of the second causes, by Which it may help it to worke?* They are the Translation of the Title of the sixth chapter of *Suarez* first Booke, *Of the Concourse, Motion, and Help of God.* When men write whole volumes of such stuffe, are they not Mad, or intend to make others so? And particularly, in the question of Transubstantiation; where after certain words spoken, they that say, the White*nesse*, Round*nesse*, Magni*tude*, Quali*ty*, Corruptibili*ty*, all which are incorporeall, &c. go out of the Wafer, into the Body of our blessed Saviour, do they not make those *Nesses, Tudes,* and *Ties,* to be so many spirits possessing his body? For by Spirits, they mean alwayes things, that being incorporeall, are neverthelesse moveable from one place to another. So that this kind of Absurdity, may rightly be numbred amongst the many sorts of Madnesse; and all the time that guided by clear Thoughts of their worldly lust, they forbear disputing, or writing thus, but Lucide Intervals. And thus much of the Vertues and Defects Intellectuall.

# Thomas Hobbes

## CHAP. IX

*Of the Severall* SUBJECTS *of* KNOWLEDGE

THERE are of KNOWLEDGE two kinds; whereof one is *Knowledge of Fact* : the other *Knowledge of the Consequence of one Affirmation to another.* The former is nothing else, but Sense and Memory, and is *Absolute Knowledge*; as when we see a Fact doing, or remember it done: And this is the Knowledge required in a Witnesse. The later is called *Science*; and is *Conditionall*; as when we know, that, *If the figure showne be a Circle, then any straight line through the Center shall divide it into two equall parts.* And this is the Knowledge required in a Philosopher; that is to say, of him that pretends to Reasoning.

The Register of *Knowledge of Fact* is called *History.* Whereof there be two sorts: one called *Naturall History*; which is the History of such Facts, or Effects of Nature, as have no Dependance on Mans *Will*; Such as are the Histories of *Metalls, Plants, Animals, Regions,* and the like. The other, is *Civill History*; which is the History of the Voluntary Actions of men in Common-wealths.

The Registers of Science, are such *Books* as contain the *Demonstrations* of Consequences of one Affirmation, to another; and are commonly called *Books of Philosophy*; whereof the sorts are many, according to the diversity of the Matter; And may be divided in such manner as I have divided them in the following Table.

**SCIENCE, that is, Knowledge of Consequences; which is called also PHILOSOPHY.**

- **Consequences from the Accidents of Bodies Naturall; which is called NATURALL PHILOSOPHY.**
  - Consequences from all Accidents common to all Bodies Naturall; which are *Quantity*, and *Motion*.
    - Consequences from *Quantity*, and *Motion indeterminate*; which being the Principles, or first foundations of Philosophy, is called *Philosophia Prima.* — PHILOSOPHIA PRIMA.
    - Consequences from *Motion*, and *Quantity determined.*
      - Consequences from Quantity, and Motion determined.
        - By Figure, . . . — GEOMETRY.
        - By Number, . . . — ARITHMETIQUE.
        
        *(Mathematiques)*
      - Consequences from the Motion, and Quantity of Bodies in *speciall.*
        - Consequences from the Motion, and Quantity of the great parts of the World, as the *Earth* and *Starres* *(Cosmography)* —
          - ASTRONOMY.
          - GEOGRAPHY.
        - Consequences from the Motion of special kinds, and Figures of Body *(Mechaniques, Doctrine of Weight)* —
          - Science of Engineers.
          - ARCHITECTURE.
          - NAVIGATION.
  - **PHYSIQUES, or Consequences from Qualities.**
    - Consequences from the Qualities of Bodyes *Transient*, such as sometimes appear, sometimes vanish. — METEOROLOGY.
    - Consequences from the Qualities of Bodies *Permanent.*
      - Consequences from the Qualities of the *Starres*,
        - Consequences from the *Light* of the Starres. Out of this, and the Motion of the Sunne, is made the Science of . . . — SCIOGRAPHY.
        - Consequences from the *Influence* of the Starres . . . — ASTROLOGY.
      - Consequences from the Qualities of Bodies *Terrestriall.*
        - Consequences from the parts of the Earth, that are without *Sense*,
          - Consequences of the Qualities from *Liquid* Bodies that fill the space between the Starres; such as are the *Ayre*, or substance aetheriall.
          - Consequences from the Qualities of *Minerals*, as *Stones, Metalls,* &c.
          - Consequences from the Qualities of *Vegetables.*
        - Consequences from the Qualities of *Animals,*
          - Consequences from the Qualities of *Animals in generall*
            - Consequences from *Vision*, — OPTIQUES.
            - Consequences from *Sounds*, — MUSIQUE.
            - Consequences from the rest of the *Senses.*
          - Consequences from the Qualities of *Men in speciall*
            - Consequences from the *Passions of Men* — ETHIQUES.
            - Consequences from *Speech*,
              - In *Magnifying, Vilifying*, &c. — POETRY.
              - In *Perswading*, — RHETORIQUE.
              - In *Reasoning*, — LOGIQUE.
              - In *Contracting*, — The *Science of Just and Unjust.*

- **Consequences from the Accidents of *Politique* Bodies; which is called POLITIQUES, and CIVILL PHILOSOPHY.**
  1. Of Consequences from the *Institution* of COMMON-WEALTHS, to the *Rights*, and *Duties* of the *Body Politique*, or *Soveraign.*
  2. Of Consequences from the same, to the *Duty* and *Right* of the *Subjects.*

## CHAP. X

*Of* POWER, WORTH, DIGNITY, HONOUR, *and* WORTHINESSE

THE POWER *of a Man*, (to take it Universally,) is his present means, to obtain some future apparent Good. And is either *Originall*, or *Instrumentall*.

*Naturall Power*, is the eminence of the Faculties of Body, or Mind: as extraordinary Strength, Forme, Prudence, Arts, Eloquence, Liberality, Nobility. *Instrumentall* are those Powers, which acquired by these, or by fortune, are means and Instruments to acquire more: as Riches, Reputation, Friends, and the secret working of ·God, which men call Good Luck. For the nature of Power, is in this point, like to Fame, increasing as it proceeds; or like the motion of heavy bodies, which the further they go, make still the more hast.

The Greatest of humane Powers, is that which is compounded of the Powers of most men, united by consent, in one person, Naturall, or Civill, that has the use of all their Powers depending on his will; such as is the Power of a Common-wealth: Or depending on the wills of each particular; such as is the Power of a Faction, or of divers factions leagued. Therefore to have servants, is Power; To have friends, is Power: for they are strengths united.

Also Riches joyned with liberality, is Power; because it procureth friends, and servants: Without liberality, not so; because in this case they defend not; but expose men to Envy, as a Prey.

Reputation of power, is Power; because it draweth with it the adhærence of those that need protection.

So is Reputation of love of a mans Country, (called Popularity,) for the same Reason.

Also, what quality soever maketh a man beloved, or feared of many; or the reputation of such quality, is Power; because it is a means to have the assistance, and service of many.

Good successe is Power; because it maketh reputation of Wisdome, or good fortune; which makes men either feare him, or rely on him.

Affability of men already in power, is encrease of Power; because it gaineth love.

Reputation of Prudence in the conduct of Peace or War, is Power; because to prudent men, we commit the government of our selves, more willingly than to others.

Nobility is Power, not in all places, but onely in those Commonwealths, where it has Priviledges: for in such priviledges consisteth their Power.

Eloquence is power; because it is seeming Prudence.

Forme is Power; because being a promise of Good, it recommendeth men to the favour of women and strangers.

The Sciences, are small Power; because not eminent; and there-fore, not acknowledged in any ,man; nor are at all, but in a few; and in them, but of a few things. For Science is of that nature, as none can understand it to be, but such as in a good measure have attayned it.

Arts of publique use, as Fortification, making of Engines, and other Instruments of War; because they conferre to Defence, and Victory, are Power: And though the true Mother of them, be Science, namely the Mathematiques; yet, because they are brought into the Light, by the hand of the Artificer, they be esteemed (the Midwife passing with the vulgar for the Mother,) as his issue.

The *Value*, or WORTH of a man, is as of all other things, his Price; that is to say, so much as would be given for the use of his Power: and therefore is not absolute; but a thing dependant on the need and judgement of another. An able conductor of Souldiers, is of great Price in time of War present, or imminent; but in Peace n·t so. A learned and uncorrupt Judge, is much Worth in time of Peace; but not so much in War. And as in other things, so in men, not the seller, but the buyer determines the Price. For let a man (as most men do,) rate themselves at the highest Value they can; yet their true Value is no more than it is esteemed by others.

The manifestation of the Value we set on one another, is that which is commonly called Honouring, and Dishonouring. To Value a man at a high rate, is to *Honour* him; at a low rate, is to *Dis-honour* him. But high, and low, in this case, is to be understood by comparison to the rate that each man setteth on himselfe.

The publique worth of a man, which is·the Value set on him by the Common-wealth, is that which men commonly call DIGNITY. And this Value of him by the Common-wealth, is understood, by offices of Command, Judicature, publike Employment; or by Names and Titles, introduced for distinction of such Value.

To pray to another, for ayde of any kind, is *to* HONOUR; because a signe we have an opinion he has power to help; and the more difficult the ayde is, the more is the Honour.

To obey, is to Honour; because no man obeyes them, whom they think have no power to help, or hurt them. And consequently to disobey, is to *Dishonour*.

To give great gifts to a man, is to Honour him; because 'tis buying of Protection, and acknowledging of Power. To give little gifts, is to Dishonour; because it is but Almes, and signifies an opinion of the need of small helps.

To be sedulous in promoting anothers good; also to flatter, is to Honour; as a signe we seek his protection or ayde. To neglect, is to Dishonour.

To give way, or place to another, in any Commodity, is to Honour; being a confession of greater power. To arrogate, is to Dishonour.

To shew any signe of love, or feare of another, is to Honour; for both to love, and to feare, is to value. To contemne, or lesse to love or feare, then he expects, is to Dishonour; for 'tis under-valuing.

To praise, magnifie, or call happy, is to Honour; because nothing but goodnesse, power, and felicity is valued. To revile, mock, or pitty, is to Dishonour.

To speak to another with consideration, to appear before him with decency, and humility, is to Honour him; as signes of fear to offend. To speak to him rashly, to do any thing before him obscenely, slovenly, impudently, is to Dishonour.

To believe, to trust, to rely on another, is to Honour him; signe of opinion of his vertue and power. To distrust, or not believe, is to Dishonour.

To hearken to a mans counsell, or discourse of what kind soever, is to Honour; as a signe we think him wise, or eloquent, or witty. To sleep, or go forth, or talk the while, is to Dishonour.

To do those things to another, which he takes for signes of Honour, or which the Law or Custome makes so, is to Honour; because in approving the Honour done by others, he acknowledgeth the power which others acknowledge. To refuse to do them, is to Dishonour.

To agree with in opinion, is to Honour; as being a signe of approving his judgement, and wisdome. To dissent, is Dishonour; and an upbraiding of errour; and (if the dissent be in many things) of folly.

To imitate, is to Honour; for it is vehemently to approve. To imitate ones Enemy, is to Dishonour.

To honour those another honours, is to Honour him; as a signe of approbation of his judgement. To honour his Enemies, is to Dishonour him.

To employ in counsell, or in actions of difficulty, is to Honour; as a signe of opinion of his wisdome, or other power. To deny employment in the same cases, to those that seek it, is to Dishonour.

All these wayes of Honouring, are naturall; and as well within, as without Common-wealths. But in Common-wealths, where he, or they that have the supreme Authority, can make whatsoever they please, to stand for signes of Honour, there be other Honours.

A Soveraigne doth Honour a Subject, with whatsoever Title, or Office, or Employment, or Action, that he himselfe will have taken for a signe of his will to Honour him.

The King of *Persia*, Honoured *Mordecay*, when he appointed he should be conducted through the streets in the Kings Garment, upon one of the Kings Horses, with a Crown on his head, and a Prince before him, proclayming, *Thus shall it be done to him that the King will honour.* And yet another King of *Persia*, or the same another time, to one that demanded for some great service, to weare one of the Kings robes, gave him leave so to do; but with this addition, that he should weare it as the Kings foole; and then it was Dishonour. So that of Civill Honour, the Fountain is in the person of the Common-wealth, and dependeth on the Will of the Soveraigne; and is therefore temporary, and called *Civill Honour*; such as are Magistracy, Offices, Titles; and in some places Coats, and Scutchions painted: and men Honour such as have them, as having so many signes of favour in the Common-wealth; which favour is Power.

*Honourable* is whatsoever possession, action, or quality, is an argument and signe of Power.

And therefore To be Honoured, loved, or feared of many, is Honourable; as arguments of Power. To be Honoured of few or none, *Dishonourable*.

Dominion, and Victory is Honourable; because acquired by Power; and Servitude, for need, or feare, is Dishonourable.

Good fortune (if lasting,) Honourable; as a signe of the favour of God. Ill fortune, and losses, Dishonourable. Riches, are Honourable; for they are Power. Poverty, Dishonourable. Magnanimity, Liberality, Hope, Courage, Confidence, are Honourable; for they proceed from the conscience of Power. Pusillanimity, Parsimony, Fear, Diffidence, are Dishonourable.

Timely Resolution, or determination of what a man is to do, is Honourable; as being the contempt of small difficulties, and dangers. And Irresolution, Dishonourable; as a signe of too much valuing of little impediments, and little advantages: For when a man has weighed things as long as the time permits, and resolves not, the difference of weight is but little; and therefore if he resolve not, he overvalues little things, which is Pusillanimity.

All Actions, and Speeches, that proceed, or seem to proceed from much Experience, Science, Discretion, or Wit, are Honourable; For all these are Powers. Actions, or Words that proceed from Errour, Ignorance, or Folly, Dishonourable.

Gravity, as farre forth as it seems to proceed from a mind employed on some thing else, is Honourable; because employment is a signe of Power. But if it seem to proceed from a purpose to appear grave, it is Dishonourable. For the gravity of the former, is like the steddinesse of a Ship laden with Merchandise; but of the later, like the steddinesse of a Ship ballasted with Sand, and other trash.

To be Conspicuous, that is to say, to be known, for Wealth, Office, great Actions, or any eminent Good, is Honourable; as a signe of the power for which he is conspicuous. On the contrary, Obscurity, is Dishonourable.

To be descended from conspicuous Parents, is Honourable; because they the more easily attain the aydes, and friends of their Ancestors. On the contrary, to be descended from obscure Parentage, is Dishonourable.

Actions proceeding from Equity, joyned with losse, are Honourable; as signes of Magnanimity: for Magnanimity is a signe of Power. On the contrary, Craft, Shifting, neglect of Equity, is Dishonourable.

Covetousnesse of great Riches, and ambition of great Honours, are

Honourable; as signes of power to obtain them. Covetousnesse, and ambition, of little gaines, or preferments, is Dishonourable.

Nor does it alter the case of Honour, whether an action (so it be great and difficult, and consequently a signe of much power,) be just or unjust: for Honour consisteth onely in the opinion of Power. Therefore the ancient Heathen did not thinke they Dishonoured, but greatly Honoured the Gods, when they introduced them in their Poems, committing Rapes, Thefts, and other great, but unjust, or unclean acts: In so much as nothing is so much celebrated in *Jupiter*, as his Adulteries; nor in *Mercury*, as his Frauds, and Thefts: of whose praises, in a hymne of *Homer*, the greatest is this, that being born in the morning, he had invented Musique at noon, and before night, stolne away the Cattell of *Apollo*, from his Herdsmen.

Also amongst men, till there were constituted great Commonwealths, it was thought no dishonour to be a Pyrate, or a High-way Theefe; but rather a lawfull Trade, not onely amongst the Greeks, but also amongst all other Nations; as is manifest by the Histories of antient time. And at this day, in this part of the world, private Duels are, and alwayes will be Honourable, though unlawfull, till such time as there shall be Honour ordained for them that refuse, and Ignominy for them that make the Challenge. For Duels also are many times effects of Courage; and the ground of Courage is alwayes Strength or Skill, which are Power; though for the most part they be effects of rash speaking, and of the fear of Dishonour, in one, or both the Combatants; who engaged by rashnesse, are driven into the Lists to avoyd disgrace.

Scutchions, and Coats of Armes hæreditary, where they have any eminent Priviledges, are Honourable; otherwise not: for their Power consisteth either in such Priviledges, or in Riches, or some such thing as is equally honoured in other men. This kind of Honour, commonly called Gentry, has been derived from the Antient Germans. For there never was any such thing known, where the German Customes were unknown. Nor is it now any where in use, where the Germans have not inhabited. The antient Greek Commanders, when they went to war, had their Shields painted with such Devises as they pleased; insomuch as an unpainted Buckler was a signe of Poverty, and of a common Souldier: but they transmitted not the Inheritance of them. The Romans transmitted the Marks of their Families: but they were the Images, not the Devises of their Ancestors. Amongst the people of *Asia, Afrique,* and *America,* there is not, nor was ever, any such thing. The Germans onely had that custome; from whom it has been derived into *England, France, Spain,* and *Italy,* when in great numbers they either ayded the Romans, or made their own Conquests in these Westerne parts of the world.

For *Germany,* being antiently, as all other Countries, in their beginnings, divided amongst an infinite number of little Lords, or Masters of Families, that continually had wars one with another;

those Masters, or Lords, principally to the end they might, when they were Covered with Arms, be known by their followers; and partly for ornament, both painted their Armor, or their Scutchion, or Coat, with the picture of some Beast, or other thing; and also put some eminent and visible mark upon the Crest of their Helmets. And this ornament both of the Armes, and Crest, descended by inheritance to their Children; to the eldest pure, and to the rest with some note of diversity, such as the Old master, that is to say in Dutch, the *Here-alt* thought fit.   But when many such Families, joyned together, made a greater Monarchy, this duty of the Herealt, to distinguish Scutchions, was made a private Office a part.   And the issue of these Lords, is the great and antient Gentry; which for the most part bear living creatures, noted for courage, and rapine; or Castles, Battlements, Belts, Weapons, Bars, Palisadoes, and other notes of War; nothing being then in honour, but vertue military.   Afterwards, not onely Kings, but popular Common-wealths, gave divers manners of Scutchions, to such as went forth to the War, or returned from it, for encouragement, or recompence to their service.   All which, by an observing Reader, may be found in such antient Histories, Greek and Latine, as make mention of the German Nation, and Manners, in their times.

Titles of *Honour*, such as are Duke, Count, Marquis, and Baron, are Honourable; as signifying the value set upon them by the Soveraigne Power of the Commonwealth: Which Titles, were in old time titles of Office, and Command, derived some from the Romans, some from the Germans, and French.   Dukes, in Latine *Duces*, being Generalls in War: Counts, *Comites*, such as bare the Generall company out of friendship; and were left to govern and defend places conquered, and pacified: Marquises, *Marchiones*, were Counts that governed the Marches, or bounds of the Empire. Which titles of Duke, Count, and Marquis, came into the Empire, about the time of *Constantine* the Great, from the customes of the German *Militia*.   But Baron, seems to have been a Title of the Gaules, and signifies a Great man; such as were the Kings, or Princes men, whom they employed in war about their persons; and seems to be derived from *Vir*, to *Ber*, and *Bar*, that signified the same in the Language of the Gaules, that *Vir* in Latine; and thence to *Bero*, and *Baro*: so that such men were called *Berones*, and after *Barones*; and (in Spanish) *Varones*.   But he that would know more particularly the originall of Titles of Honour, may find it, as I have done this, in Mr. *Seldens* most excellent Treatise of that subject.   In processe of time these offices of Honour, by occasion of trouble, and for reasons of good and peaceable government, were turned into meer Titles; serving for the most part, to distinguish the precedence, place, and order of subjects in the Common-wealth: and men were made Dukes, Counts, Marquises, and Barons of Places, wherein they had neither possession, nor command: and other Titles also, were devised to the same end.

WORTHINESSE, is a thing different from the worth, or value of a man; and also from his merit, or desert; and consisteth in a particular power, or ability for that, whereof he is said to be worthy: which particular ability, is usually named FITNESSE, or *Aptitude.* For he is Worthiest to be a Commander, to be a Judge, or to have any other charge, that is best fitted, with the qualities required to the well discharging of it; and Worthiest of Riches, that has the qualities most requisite for the well using of them: any of which qualities being absent, one may neverthelesse be a Worthy man, and valuable for some thing else. Again, a man may be Worthy of Riches, Office, and Employment, that neverthelesse, can plead no right to have it before another; and therefore cannot be said to merit or deserve it. For Merit, præsupposeth a right, and that the thing deserved is due by promise: Of which I shall say more hereafter, when I shall speak of Contracts.

## CHAP. XI

### *Of the difference of* MANNERS

BY MANNERS, I mean not here, Decency of behaviour; as how one man should salute another, or how a man should wash his mouth, or pick his teeth before company, and such other points of the *Small Moralls*; But those qualities of man-kind, that concern their living together in Peace, and Unity. To which end we are to consider, that the Felicity of this life, consisteth not in the repose of a mind satisfied. For there is no such *Finis ultimus,* (utmost ayme,) nor *Summum Bonum,* (greatest Good,) as is spoken of in the Books of the old Morall Philosophers. Nor can a man any more live, whose Desires are at an end, than he, whose Senses and Imaginations are at a stand. Felicity is a continuall progresse of the desire, from one object to another; the attaining of the former, being still but the way to the later. The cause whereof is, That the object of mans desire, is not to enjoy once onely, and for one instant of time; but to assure for ever, the way of his future desire. And therefore the voluntary actions, and inclinations of all men, tend, not onely to the procuring, but also to the assuring of a contented life; and differ onely in the way; which ariseth partly from the diversity of passions, in divers men; and partly from the difference of the knowledge, or opinion each one has of the causes, which produce the effect desired.

So that in the first place, I put for a generall inclination of all mankind, a perpetuall and restlesse desire of Power after power, that ceaseth onely in Death. And the cause of this, is not alwayes that a man hopes for a more intensive delight, than he has already attained to; or that he cannot be content with a moderate power: but because he cannot assure the power and means to live well, which he hath present, without the acquisition of more. And from hence it is, that Kings, whose power is greatest, turn their endeavours to the assuring it at home by Lawes, or abroad by Wars: and when that is done, there succeedeth a new desire; in some, of Fame from new Conquest; in others, of ease and sensuall pleasure; in others, of admiration, or being flattered for excellence in some art, or other ability of the mind.

Competition of Riches, Honour, Command, or other power, enclineth to Contention, Enmity, and War: Because the way of one Competitor, to the attaining of his desire, is to kill, subdue, supplant, or repell the other. Particularly, competition of praise, enclineth to a reverence of Antiquity. For men contend with the living, not with the dead; to these ascribing more than due, that they may obscure the glory of the other.

Desire of Ease, and sensuall Delight, disposeth men to obey a common Power: Because by such Desires, a man doth abandon the protection might be hoped for from his own Industry, and labour. Fear of Death, and Wounds, disposeth to the same; and for the same reason. On the contrary, needy men, and hardy, not contented with their present condition: as also, all men that are ambitious of Military command, are enclined to continue the causes of warre; and to stirre up trouble and sedition: for there is no honour Military but by warre; nor any such hope to mend an ill game, as by causing a new shuffle.

Desire of Knowledge, and Arts of Peace, enclineth men to obey a common Power: For such Desire, containeth a desire of leasure; and consequently protection from some other Power than their own.

Desire of Praise, disposeth to laudable actions, such as please them whose judgement they value; for of those men whom we contemn, we contemn also the Praises. Desire of Fame after death does the same. And though after death, there be no sense of the praise given us on Earth, as being joyes, that are either swallowed up in the unspeakable joyes of Heaven, or extinguished in the extreme torments of Hell: yet is not such Fame vain; because men have a present delight therein, from the foresight of it, and of the benefit that may redound thereby to their posterity: which though they now see not, yet they imagine; and any thing that is pleasure in the sense, the same also is pleasure in the imagination.

To have received from one, to whom we think our selves equall, greater benefits than there is hope to Requite, disposeth to counterfeit love; but really secret hatred; and puts a man into the estate of a desperate debtor, than in declining the sight of his creditor, tacitely wishes him there, where he might never see him more. For benefits oblige; and obligation is thraldome; and unrequitable obligation, perpetuall thraldome; which is to ones equall, hatefull. But to have received benefits from one, whom we acknowledge for superiour, enclines to love; because the obligation is no new depression: and cheerful acceptation, (which men call *Gratitude*,) is such an honour done to the obliger, as is taken generally for retribution.   Also to receive benefits, though from an equall, or inferiour, as long as there is hope of requitall, disposeth to love: for in the intention of the receiver, the obligation is of ayd, and service mutuall; from whence proceedeth an Emulation of who shall exceed in benefiting; the most noble and profitable contention possible; wherein the victor is pleased with his victory, and the other revenged by confessing it.

To have done more hurt to a man, than he can, or is willing to expiate, enclineth the doer to hate the sufferer.   For he must expect revenge, or forgivenesse; both which are hatefull.

Feare of oppression, disposeth a man to anticipate, or to seek ayd by society: for there is no other way by which a man can secure his life and liberty.

Men that distrust their own subtilty, are in tumult, and sedition, better disposed for victory, than they that suppose themselves wise, or crafty.   For these love to consult, the other (fearing to be circumvented,) to strike first.   And in sedition, men being alwayes in the procincts of battell, to hold together, and use all advantages of force, is a better stratagem, than any that can proceed from subtilty of Wit.

Vain-glorious men, such as without being conscious to themselves of great sufficiency, delight in supposing themselves gallant men, are enclined onely to ostentation; but not to attempt: Because when danger or difficulty appears, they look for nothing but to have their insufficiency discovered.

Vain-glorious men, such as estimate their sufficiency by the flattery of other men, or the fortune of some precedent action, without assured ground of hope from the true knowledge of themselves, are enclined to rash engaging; and in the approach of danger, or difficulty, to retire if they can: because not seeing the way of safety, they will rather hazard their honour, which may be salved with an excuse; than their lives, for which no salve is sufficient.

Men that have a strong opinion of their own wisdome in matter of government, are disposed to Ambition.   Because without publique Employment in counsell or magistracy, the honour of their wisdome is lost.   And therefore Eloquent speakers are enclined to Ambition; for Eloquence seemeth wisedome, both to themselves and others.

Pusillanimity disposeth men to Irresolution, and consequently to lose the occasions, and fittest opportunities of action.   For after men have been in deliberation till the time of action approach, if it be not then manifest what is best to be done, 'tis a signe, the difference of Motives, the one way and the other, are not great: Therefore not to resolve then, is to lose the occasion by weighing of trifles; which is Pusillanimity.

Frugality, (though in poor men a Vertue,) maketh a man unapt to atchieve such actions, as require the strength of many men at once: For it weakeneth their Endeavour, which is to be nourished and kept in vigor by Reward.

Eloquence, with flattery, disposeth men to confide in them that have it; because the former is seeming Wisdome, the later seeming Kindnesse. Adde to them Military reputation, and it disposeth men to adhære, and subject themselves to those men that have them. The two former, having given them caution against danger from him; the later given them caution against danger from others.

Want of Science, that is, Ignorance of causes, disposeth, or rather constraineth a man to rely on the advise, and authority of others. For all men whom the truth concernes, if they rely not on their own, must rely on the opinion of some other, whom they think wiser than themselves, and see not why he should deceive them.

Ignorance of the signification of words; which is, want of understanding, disposeth men to take on trust, not onely the truth they know not; but also the errors; and which is more, the non-sense of them they trust: For neither Error, nor non-sense, can without a perfect understanding of words, be detected.

From the same it proceedeth, that men give different names, to one and the same thing, from the difference of their own passions: As they that approve a private opinion, call it Opinion; but they that mislike it, Hæresie: and yet hæresie signifies no more than private opinion; but has onely a greater tincture of choler.

From the same also it proceedeth, that men cannot distinguish, without study and great understanding, between one action of many men, and many actions of one multitude; as for example, between the one action of all the Senators of *Rome* in killing *Catiline*, and the many actions of a number of Senators in killing *Cæsar*; and therefore are disposed to take for the action of the people, that which is a multitude of actions done by a multitude of men, led perhaps by the perswasion of one.

Ignorance of the causes, and originall constitution of Right, Equity, Law, and Justice, disposeth a man to make Custome and Example the rule of his actions; in such manner, as to think that Unjust which it hath been the custome to punish; and that Just, of the impunity and approbation whereof they can produce an Example, or (as the Lawyers which onely use this false measure of Justice barbarously call it) a Precedent; like little children, that have no other rule of good and evill manners, but the correction they receive from their Parents, and Masters; save that children are constant to their rule, whereas men are not so; because grown strong, and stubborn, they appeale from custome to reason, and from reason to custome, as it serves their turn; receding from custome when their interest requires it, and setting themselves against reason, as oft as reason is against them: Which is the cause, that the doctrine of Right and Wrong, is perpetually disputed, both by the Pen and the Sword: Whereas the doctrine of Lines, and Figures, is not so; because men care not, in that subject what be truth, as a thing that crosses no mans ambition, profit, or lust. For I doubt not, but if it had been a thing contrary to any mans right of dominion, or to the interest of men that have dominion, *That the three Angles of a Triangle, should be equall to two Angles of a Square*; that doctrine should have been, if not disputed, yet by the burning of all books of Geometry, suppressed, as farre as he whom it concerned was able.

Ignorance of remote causes, disposeth men to attribute all events, to the causes immediate, and Instrumentall; For these are all the causes they perceive. And hence it comes to passe, that in all places, men that are grieved with payments to the Publique, discharge their anger upon the Publicans, that is to say, Farmers, Collectors, and other Officers of the publique Revenue; and adhære to such as find fault with the publike Government; and thereby, when they have engaged themselves beyond hope of justification, fall also upon the Supreme Authority, for feare of punishment, or shame of receiving pardon.

Ignorance of naturall causes disposeth a man to Credulity, so as to believe many times impossibilities: For such know nothing to the contrary, but that they may be true; being unable to detect the Impossibility. And Credulity, because men love to be hearkened unto in company, disposeth them to lying: so that Ignorance it selfe without Malice, is able to make a man both to believe lyes, and tell them; and sometimes also to invent them.

Anxiety for the future time, disposeth men to enquire into the causes of things: because the knowledge of them, maketh men the better able to order the present to their best advantage.

Curiosity, or love of the knowledge of causes, draws a man from consideration of the effect, to seek the cause; and again, the cause of that cause; till of necessity he must come to this thought at last, that there is some cause, whereof there is no former cause, but is eternall; which is it men call God. So that it is impossible to make any profound enquiry into naturall causes, without being enclined thereby to believe there is one God Eternall; though they cannot have any Idea of him in their mind, answerable to his nature. For as a man that is born blind, hearing men talk of warming themselves by the fire, and being brought to warm himself by the same, may easily conceive, and assure himselfe, there is somewhat there, which men call *Fire*, and is the cause of the heat he feeles; but cannot imagine what it is like; nor have an Idea of it in his mind, such as they have that see it: so also, by the visible things of this world, and their admirable order, a man may conceive there is a cause of them, which men call God; and yet not have an Idea, or Image of him in his mind.

And they that make little, or no enquiry into the naturall causes of things, yet from the feare that proceeds from the ignorance it selfe, of what it is that hath the power to do them much good or harm, are enclined to suppose, and feign unto themselves, severall kinds of Powers Invisible; and to stand in awe of their own imaginations; and in time of distresse to invoke them; as also in the time of an expected good successe, to give them thanks; making the creatures of their own fancy, their Gods. By which means it hath come to passe, that from the innumerable variety of Fancy, men have created in the world innumerable sorts of Gods. And this Feare of things invisible, is the naturall Seed of that, which every one in himself calleth Religion; and in them that worship, or feare that Power otherwise than they do, Superstition.

And this seed of Religion, having been observed by many; some of those that have observed it, have been enclined thereby to nourish, dresse, and forme it into Lawes; and to adde to it of their own invention, any opinion of the causes of future events, by which they thought they should best be able to govern others, and make unto themselves the greatest use of their Powers.

## CHAP. XII

### Of Religion

SEEING there are no signes, nor fruit of *Religion*, but in Man onely; there is no cause to doubt, but that the seed of *Religion*, is also onely in Man; and consisteth in some peculiar quality, or at least in some eminent degree thereof, not to be found in other Living creatures.

And first, it is peculiar to the nature of Man, to be inquisitive into the Causes of the Events they see, some more, some lesse; but all men so much, as to be curious in the search of the causes of their own good and evill fortune.

Secondly, upon the sight of any thing that hath a Beginning, to think also it had a cause, which determined the same to begin, then when it did, rather than sooner or later.

Thirdly, whereas there is no other Felicity of Beasts, but the enjoying of their quotidian Food, Ease, and Lusts; as having little, or no foresight of the time to come, for want of observation, and memory of the order, consequence, and dependence of the things they see; Man observeth how one Event hath been produced by another; and remembreth in them Antecedence and Consequence; And when he cannot assure himselfe of the true causes of things, (for the causes of good and evill fortune for the most part are invisible,) he supposes causes of them, either such as his own fancy suggesteth; or trusteth to the Authority of other men, such as he thinks to be his friends, and wiser than himselfe.

The two first, make Anxiety. For being assured that there be causes of all things that have arrived hitherto, or shall arrive hereafter; it is impossible for a man, who continually endeavoureth to secure himselfe against the evill he feares, and procure the good he desireth, not to be in a perpetuall solicitude of the time to come; So that every man, especially those that are over provident, are in an estate like to that of *Prometheus*. For as *Prometheus*, (which interpreted, is, *The prudent man*,) was bound to the hill *Caucasus*, a place of large prospect, where, an Eagle feeding on his liver, devoured in the day, as much as was repayred in the night: So that man, which looks too far before him, in the care of future time, hath his heart all the day long, gnawed on by feare of death, poverty, or other calamity; and has no repose, nor pause of his anxiety, but in sleep.

This perpetuall feare, alwayes accompanying mankind in the ignorance of causes, as it were in the Dark, must needs have for object something. And therefore when there is nothing to be seen, there is nothing to accuse, either of their good, or evill fortune, but some *Power*, or Agent *Invisible*: In which sense perhaps it was, that some of the old Poets said, that the Gods were at first created by humane Feare: which spoken of the Gods, (that is to say, of the many Gods of the Gentiles) is very true. But the acknowledging of one God Eternall, Infinite, and Omnipotent, may more easily be derived, from the desire men have to know the causes of naturall bodies, and their severall vertues, and operations; than from the feare of what was to befall them in time to come. For he that from any effect hee seeth come to passe, should reason to the next and immediate cause thereof, and from thence to the cause of that cause, and plonge himselfe profoundly in the pursuit of causes; shall at last come to this, that there must be (as even the Heathen Philosophers confessed) one First Mover; that is, a First, and an Eternall cause of all things; which is that which men mean by the name of God: And all this without thought of their fortune; the solicitude whereof, both enclines to fear, and hinders them from the search of the causes of other things; and thereby gives occasion of feigning of as many Gods, as there be men that feigne them.

And for the matter, or substance of the Invisible Agents, so fancyed; they could not by naturall cogitation, fall upon any other conceipt, but that it was the same with that of the Soule of man; and that the Soule of man, was of the same substance, with that which appeareth in a Dream, to one that sleepeth; or in a Looking-glasse, to one that is awake; which, men not knowing that such apparitions are nothing else but creatures of the Fancy, think to be reall, and externall Substances; and therefore call them Ghosts; as the Latines called them *Imagines*, and *Umbræ*; and thought them Spirits, that is, thin aëreall bodies; and those Invisible Agents, which they feared, to bee like them; save that they appear, and vanish when they please. But the opinion that such Spirits were Incorporeall, or Immateriall, could never enter into the mind of any man by nature; because, though men may put together words of contradictory signification, as *Spirit*, and *Incorporeall*; yet they can never have the imagination of any thing answering to them: And therefore, men that by their own meditation, arrive to the acknowledgement of one Infinite, Omnipotent, and Eternall God, choose rather to confesse he is Incomprehensible, and above their understanding; than to define his Nature by *Spirit Incorporeall*, and then confesse their definition to be unintelligible: or if they give him such a title, it is not *Dogmatically*, with intention to make the Divine Nature understood; but *Piously*, to honour him with attributes, of significations, as remote as they can from the grossenesse of Bodies Visible.

Then, for the way by which they think these Invisible Agents wrought their effects; that is to say, what immediate causes they used, in bringing things to passe, men that know not what it is that we call *causing*, (that is, almost all men) have no other rule to guesse by, but by observing, and remembring what they have seen to precede the like effect at some other time, or times before, without seeing between the antecedent and subsequent Event, any dependance or connexion at all: And therefore from the like things past, they expect the like things to come; and hope for good or evill luck, superstitiously, from things that have no part at all in the causing of it: As the Athenians did for their war at *Lepanto*, demand another *Phormio*; The Pompeian faction for their warre in *Afrique*, another *Scipio*; and others have done in divers other occasions since. In like manner they attribute their fortune to a stander by, to a lucky or unlucky place, to words spoken, especially if the name of God be amongst them; as Charming, and Conjuring (the Leiturgy of Witches;) insomuch as to believe, they have power to turn a stone into bread, bread into a man, or any thing, into any thing.

Thirdly, for the worship which naturally men exhibite to Powers invisible, it can be no other, but such expressions of their reverence, as they would use towards men; Gifts, Petitions, Thanks, Submission of Body, Considerate Addresses, sober Behaviour, premeditated Words, Swearing (that is, assuring one another of their promises,) by invoking them. Beyond that reason suggesteth nothing; but leaves them either to rest there; or for further ceremonies, to rely on those they believe to be wiser than themselves.

Lastly, concerning how these Invisible Powers declare to men the things which shall hereafter come to passe, especially concerning their good or evill fortune in generall, or good or ill successe in any particular undertaking, men are naturally at a stand; save that using to conjecture of the time to come, by the time past, they are very apt, not onely to take casuall things, after one or two encounters, for Prognostiques of the like encounter ever after, but also to believe the like Prognostiques from other men, of whom they have once conceived a good opinion.

And in these foure things, Opinion of Ghosts, Ignorance of second causes, Devotion towards what men fear, and Taking of things Casuall for Prognostiques, consisteth the Naturall seed of *Religion*; which by reason of the different Fancies, Judgements, and Passions of severall men, hath grown up into ceremonies so different, that those which are used by one man, are for the most part ridiculous to another.

For these seeds have received culture from two sorts of men.

One sort have been they, that have nourished, and ordered them, according to their own invention. The other, have done it, by Gods commandement, and direction: but both sorts have done it, with a purpose to make those men that relyed on them, the more apt to Obedience, Lawes, Peace, Charity, and civill Society. So that the Religion of the former sort, is a part of humane Politiques; and teacheth part of the duty which Earthly Kings require of their Subjects. And the Religion of the later sort is Divine Politiques; and containeth Precepts to those that have yeelded themselves subjects in the Kingdome of God. Of the former sort, were all the founders of Common-wealths, and the Law-givers of the Gentiles: Of the later sort, were *Abraham, Moses,* and our *Blessed Saviour*; by whom have been derived unto us the Lawes of the Kingdome of God.

And for that part of Religion, which consisteth in opinions concerning the nature of Powers Invisible, there is almost nothing that has a name, that has not been esteemed amongst the Gentiles, in one place or another, a God, or Divell; or by their Poets feigned to be inanimated, inhabited, or possessed by some Spirit or other.

The unformed matter of the World, was a God, by the name of *Chaos.*

The Heaven, the Ocean, the Planets, the Fire, the Earth, the Winds, were so many Gods.

Men, Women, a Bird, a Crocodile, a Calf, a Dogge, a Snake, an Onion, a Leeke, Deified. Besides that, they filled almost all places, with spirits called *Dœmons*: the plains, with *Pan,* and *Panises,* or Satyres; the Woods, with Fawnes, and Nymphs; the Sea, with Tritons, and other Nymphs; every River, and Fountayn, with a Ghost of his name, and with Nymphs; every house, with its *Lares,* or Familiars; every man, with his *Genius*; Hell, with Ghosts, and spirituall Officers, as *Charon, Cerberus,* and the *Furies*; and in the night time, all places with *Larvœ, Lemures,* Ghosts of men deceased, and a whole kingdome of Fayries, and Bugbears. They have also ascribed Divinity, and built Temples to meer Accidents, and Qualities; such as are Time, Night, Day, Peace, Concord, Love, Contention, Vertue, Honour, Health, Rust, Fever, and the like; which when they prayed for, or against, they prayed to, as if there were Ghosts of those names hanging over their heads, and letting fall, or withholding that Good, or Evill, for, or against which they prayed. They invoked also their own Wit, by the name of *Muses*; their own Ignorance, by the name of *Fortune*; their own Lust, by the name of *Cupid*; their own Rage, by the name *Furies*; their own privy members by the name of *Priapus*; and attributed their pollutions, to *Incubi,* and *Succubœ*: insomuch as there was nothing, which a Poet could introduce as a person in his Poem, which they did not make either a *God,* or a *Divel.*

The same authors of the Religion of the Gentiles, observing the second ground for Religion, which is mens Ignorance of causes; and thereby their aptnesse to attribute their fortune to causes, on which there was no dependence at all apparent, took occasion to obtrude on their ignorance, in stead of second causes, a kind of second and ministeriall Gods; ascribing the cause of Fœcundity, to *Venus*; the cause of Arts, to *Apollo*; of Subtilty and Craft, to *Mercury*; of Tempests and stormes, to *Æolus*; and of other effects, to other Gods: insomuch as there was amongst the Heathen almost as great variety of Gods, as of businesse.

And to the Worship, which naturally men conceived fit to bee used towards their Gods, namely Oblations, Prayers, Thanks, and the rest formerly named; the same Legislators of the Gentiles have added their Images, both in Picture, and Sculpture; that the more ignorant sort, (that is to say, the most part, or generality of the people,) thinking the Gods for whose representation they were made, were really included, and as it were housed within them, might so much the more stand in feare of them: And endowed them with lands, and houses, and officers, and revenues, set apart from all other humane uses; that is, consecrated, and made holy to those their idols; as Caverns, Groves, Woods, Mountains, and whole Ilands; and have attributed to them, not onely the shapes, some of Men, some of Beasts, some of Monsters; but also the Faculties, and Passions of men and beasts; as Sense, Speech, Sex, Lust, Generation, (and this not onely by mixing one with another, to propagate the kind of Gods; but also by mixing with men, and women, to beget mongrill Gods, and but inmates of Heaven, as *Bacchus, Hercules*, and others;) besides, Anger, Revenge, and other passions of living creatures, and the actions proceeding from them, as Fraud, Theft, Adultery, Sodomie, and any vice that may be taken for an effect of Power, or a cause of Pleasure; and all such Vices, as amongst men are taken to be against Law, rather than against Honour.

Lastly, to the Prognostiques of time to come; which are naturally, but Conjectures upon the Experience of time past; and supernaturally, divine Revelation; the same authors of the Religion of the Gentiles, partly upon pretended Experience, partly upon pretended Revelation, have added innumerable other superstitious wayes of Divination; and made men believe they should find their fortunes, sometimes in the ambiguous or senslesse answers of the Priests at *Delphi, Delos, Ammon*, and other famous Oracles; which answers, were made ambiguous by designe, to own the event both wayes; or absurd, by the intoxicating vapour of the place, which is very frequent in sulphurous Cavernes: Sometimes in the leaves of the Sibills; of whose Prophecyes (like those perhaps of *Nostradamus*; for the fragments now extant seem to be the invention of later times) there were some books in reputation in the time of the Roman Republique: Sometimes in the insignificant Speeches of Mad-men, supposed to be possessed with a divine Spirit; which Possession they called Enthusiasme; and these kinds of foretelling events, were accounted Theomancy, or Prophecy: Sometimes in the aspect of the Starres at their Nativity; which was called Horoscopy, and esteemed a part of judiciary Astrology: Sometimes in their own hopes and feares, called Thumomancy, or Presage: Sometimes in the Prediction of Witches, that pretended conference with the dead; which is called Necromancy, Conjuring, and Witchcraft; and is but juggling and confederate knavery: Sometimes in the Casuall flight, or feeding of birds; called Augury: Sometimes in the Entrayles of a sacrificed beast; which was *Aruspicina*: Sometimes in Dreams: Sometimes in Croaking of Ravens, or chattering of Birds: Sometimes in the Lineaments of the face; which was called Metoposcopy; or by Palmistry in the lines of the hand; in casuall words, called *Omina*: Sometimes in Monsters, or unusuall accidents; as Ecclipses, Comets, rare Meteors, Earthquakes, Inundations, uncouth Births, and the like, which they called *Portenta*, and *Ostenta*, because they thought them to portend, or foreshew some great Calamity to come: Sometimes, in meer Lottery, as Crosse and Pile; counting holes in a sive; dipping of Verses in *Homer*, and *Virgil*; and innumerable other such vaine conceipts. So easie are men to be drawn to believe any thing, from such men as have gotten credit with them; and can with gentlenesse, and dexterity, take hold of their fear, and ignorance.

And therefore the first Founders, and Legislators of Commonwealths amongst the Gentiles, whose ends were only to keep the people in obedience, and peace, have in all places taken care; First, to imprint in their minds a beliefe, that those precepts which they gave concerning Religion, might not be thought to proceed from their own device, but from the dictates of some God, or other Spirit; or else that they themselves were of a higher nature than mere mortalls, that their Lawes might the more easily be received: So *Numa Pompilius* pretended to receive the Ceremonies he instituted amongst the Romans, from the Nymph *Egeria*: and the first King and founder of the Kingdome of *Peru*, pretended himselfe and his wife to be the children of the Sunne: and *Mahomet*, to set up his new Religion, pretended to have conferences with the Holy Ghost, in forme of a Dove. Secondly, they have had a care, to make it believed, that the same things were displeasing to the Gods, which were forbidden by the Lawes. Thirdly, to prescribe Ceremonies, Supplications, Sacrifices, and Festivalls, by which they were to believe, the anger of the Gods might be appeased; and that ill success in War, great contagions of Sicknesse, Earthquakes, and each mans private Misery, came from the Anger of the Gods; and their Anger from the Neglect of their Worship, or the forgetting, or mistaking some point of the Ceremonies required. And though amongst the antient Romans, men were not forbidden to deny, that which in the Poets is written of the paines, and pleasures after this life; which divers of great authority, and gravity in that state have in their *Harangues* openly derided; yet that beliefe was alwaies more cherished, than the contrary.

And by these, and such other Institutions, they obtayned in order to their end, (which was the peace of the Commonwealth,)

that the common people in their misfortunes, laying the fault on
neglect, or errour in their Ceremonies, or on their own disobedience
to the lawes, were the lesse apt to mutiny against their Governors.
And being entertained with the pomp, and pastime of Festivalls,
and publike Games, made in honour of the Gods, needed nothing
else but bread, to keep them from discontent, murmuring, and
commotion against the State.    And therefore the Romans, that had
conquered the greatest part of the then known World, made no
scruple of tollerating any Religion whatsoever in the City of *Rome*
it selfe; unlesse it had something in it, that could not consist with
their Civill Government; nor do we read, that any Religion was
there forbidden, but that of the Jewes; who (being the peculiar
Kingdome of God) thought it unlawfull to acknowledge subjection
to any mortall King or State whatsoever.    And thus you see how
the Religion of the Gentiles was a part of their Policy.

But where God himselfe, by supernaturall Revelation, planted
Religion; there he also made to himselfe a peculiar Kingdome;
and gave Lawes, not only of behaviour towards himselfe; but also
towards one another; and thereby in the Kingdome of God, the
Policy, and lawes Civill, are a part of Religion; and therefore the
distinction of Temporall, and Spirituall Domination, hath there
no place.    It is true, that God is King of all the Earth: Yet may he
be King of a peculiar, and chosen Nation.    For there is no more
incongruity there in, than that he that hath the generall command
of the whole Army, should have withall a peculiar Regiment, or
Company of his own.    God is King of all the Earth by his Power:
but of his chosen people, he is King by Covenant.    But to speake
more largly of the Kingdome of God, both by Nature, and Covenant,
I have in the following discourse assigned an other place.

From the propagation of Religion, it is not hard to understand the causes of the resolution of the same into its first seeds,
or principles; which are only an opinion of a Deity, and Powers
invisible, and supernaturall; that can never be so abolished out of
humane nature, but that new Religions may againe be made to
spring out of them, by the culture of such men, as for such purpose
are in reputation.

For seeing all formed Religion, is founded at first, upon the
faith which a multitude hath in some one person, whom they
believe not only to be a wise man, and to labour to procure their
happiness, but also to be a holy man, to whom God himselfe vouch-
safeth to declare his will supernaturally; It followeth necessarily,
when they that have the Government of Religion, shall come to
have either the wisedome of those men, their sincerity, or their
love suspected; or that they shall be unable to shew any probable
token of Divine Revelation; that the Religion which they desire
to uphold, must be suspected likewise; and (without the fear of
the Civill Sword) contradicted and rejected.

That which taketh away the reputation of Wisedome, in him
that formeth a Religion, or addeth to it when it is allready formed,

is the enjoyning of a beliefe of contradictories: For both parts of a contradiction cannot possibly be true: and therefore to enjoyne the beliefe of them, is an argument of ignorance; which detects the Author in that; and discredits him in all things else he shall propound as from revelation supernaturall: which revelation a man may indeed have of many things above, but of nothing against naturall reason.

That which taketh away the reputation of Sincerity, is the doing, or saying of such things, as appeare to be signes, that what they require other men to believe, is not believed by themselves; all which doings, or sayings are therefore called Scandalous, because they be stumbling blocks, that make men to fall in the way of Religion: as Injustice, Cruelty, Prophanesse, Avarice, and Luxury. For who can believe, that he that doth ordinarily such actions, as proceed from any of these rootes, believeth there is any such Invisible Power to be feared, as he affrighteth other men withall, for lesser faults?

That which taketh away the reputation of Love, is the being detected of private ends: as when the beliefe they require of others, conduceth or seemeth to conduce to the acquiring of Dominion, Riches, Dignity, or secure Pleasure, to themselves onely, or specially. For that which men reap benefit by to themselves, they are thought to do for their own sakes, and not for love of others.

Lastly, the testimony that men can render of divine Calling, can be no other, than the operation of Miracles; or true Prophecy, (which also is a Miracle;) or extraordinary Felicity. And therefore, to those points of Religion, which have been received from them that did such Miracles; those that are added by such, as approve not their Calling by some Miracle, obtain no greater beliefe, than what the Custome, and Lawes of the places, in which they be educated, have wrought into them. For as in naturall things, men of judgement require naturall signes, and arguments; so in supernaturall things, they require signes supernaturall, (which are Miracles,) before they consent inwardly, and from their hearts.

All which causes of the weakening of mens faith, do manifestly appear in the Examples following. First, we have the Example of the children of Israel; who when *Moses*, that had approved his Calling to them by Miracles, and by the happy conduct of them out of *Egypt*, was absent but 40 dayes, revolted from the worship of the true God, recommended to them by him; and setting up [1] a Golden Calfe for their God, relapsed into the Idolatry of the Egyptians; from whom they had been so lately delivered. And again, after *Moses, Aaron, Joshua,* and that generation which had seen the great works of God in Israel,[2] were dead; another generation arose and served *Baal.* So that Miracles fayling, Faith also failed.

Again, when the sons of *Samuel,*[3] being constituted by their father Judges in *Bersabee,* received bribes, and judged unjustly,

---

[1] *Exod.* 32. 1, 2.    [2] *Judges* 2. 11.    [3] 1 *Sam.* 8. 3.

the people of Israel refused any more to have God to be their King, in other manner than he was King of other people; and therefore cryed out to *Samuel*, to choose them a King after the manner of the Nations. So that Justice fayling, Faith also fayled: Insomuch, as they deposed their God, from reigning over them.

And whereas in the planting of Christian Religion, the Oracles ceased in all parts of the Roman Empire, and the number of Christians encreased wonderfully every day, and in every place, by the preaching of the Apostles, and Evangelists; a great part of that successe, may reasonably be attributed, to the contempt, into which the Priests of the Gentiles of that time, had brought themselves, by their uncleannesse, avarice, and jugling between Princes. Also the Religion of the Church of *Rome*, was partly, for the same cause abolished in *England*, and many other parts of Christendome; insomuch, as the fayling of Vertue in the Pastors, maketh faith faile in the People: and partly from bringing of the Philosophy, and doctrine of *Aristotle* into Religion, by the Schoole-men; from whence there arose so many contradictions, and absurdities, as brought the Clergy into a reputation both of Ignorance, and of Fraudulent intention; and enclined people to revolt from them, either against the will of their own Princes, as in *France*, and *Holland*: or with their will, as in *England*.

Lastly, amongst the points by the Church of *Rome* declared necessary for Salvation, there be so many, manifestly to the advantage of the Pope, and of his spirituall subjects, residing in the territories of other Christian Princes, that were it not for the mutuall emulation of those Princes, they might without warre, or trouble, exclude all forraign Authority, as easily as it has been excluded in *England*. For who is there that does not see, to whose benefit it conduceth, to have it believed, that a King hath not his Authority from Christ, unlesse a Bishop crown him? That a King, if he be a Priest, cannot Marry? That whether a Prince be born in lawfull Marriage, or not, must be judged by Authority from *Rome*? That Subjects may be freed from their Alleageance, if by the Court of *Rome*, the King be judged an Heretique? That a King (as *Chilperique* of *France*) may be deposed by a Pope (as Pope *Zachary*,) for no cause; and his Kingdome given to one of his Subjects? That the Clergy, and Regulars, in what Country soever, shall be exempt from the Jurisdiction of their King, in cases criminall? Or who does not see, to whose profit redound the Fees of private Masses, and Vales of Purgatory; with other signes of private interest, enough to mortifie the most lively Faith, if (as I sayd) the civill Magistrate, and Custome did not more sustain it, than any opinion they have of the Sanctity, Wisdome, or Probity of their Teachers? So that I may attribute all the changes of Religion in the world, to one and the same cause; and that is, unpleasing Priests; and those not onely amongst Catholiques, but even in that Church that hath presumed most of Reformation.

## CHAP. XIII

*Of the* NATURALL CONDITION *of Mankind, as concerning their Felicity, and Misery*

NATURE hath made men so equall, in the faculties of body, and mind; as that though there bee found one man sometimes manifestly stronger in body, or of quicker mind then another; yet when all is reckoned together, the difference between man, and man, is not so considerable, as that one man can thereupon claim to himselfe any benefit, to which another may not pretend, as well as he. For as to the strength of body, the weakest has strength enough to kill the strongest, either by secret machination, or by confederacy with others, that are in the same danger with himselfe.

And as to the faculties of the mind, (setting aside the arts grounded upon words, and especially that skill of proceeding upon generall, and infallible rules, called Science; which very few have, and but in few things; as being not a native faculty, born with us; nor attained, (as Prudence,) while we look after somewhat els,) I find yet a greater equality amongst men, than that of strength. For Prudence, is but Experience; which equall time, equally bestowes on all men, in those things they equally apply themselves unto. That which may perhaps make such equality incredible, is but a vain conceipt of ones owne wisdome, which almost all men think they have in a greater degree, than the Vulgar; that is, than all men but themselves, and a few others, whom by Fame, or for concurring with themselves, they approve. For such is the nature of men, that howsoever they may acknowledge many others to be more witty, or more eloquent, or more learned; Yet they will hardly believe there be many so wise as themselves: For they see their own wit at hand, and other mens at a distance. But this proveth rather that men are in that point equall, than unequall. For there is not ordinarily a greater signe of the equall distribution of any thing, than that every man is contented with his share.

From this equality of ability, ariseth equality of hope in the attaining of our Ends. And therefore if any two men desire the same thing, which neverthelesse they cannot both enjoy, they become enemies; and in the way to their End, (which is principally their owne conservation, and sometimes their delectation only,) endeavour to destroy, or subdue one an other. And from hence it comes to passe, that where an Invader hath no more to feare, than an other mans single power; if one plant, sow, build, or possesse a convenient Seat, others may probably be expected to come prepared with forces united, to dispossesse, and deprive him, not only of the fruit of his labour, but also of his life, or liberty. And the Invader again is in the like danger of another.

And from this diffidence of one another, there is no way for any man to secure himselfe, so reasonable, as Anticipation; that is, by force, or wiles, to master the persons of all men he can, so long, till he see no other power great enough to endanger him: And this is no more than his own conservation requireth, and is generally allowed. Also because there be some, that taking pleasure in contemplating their own power in the acts of conquest, which they pursue farther than their security requires; if others, that otherwise would be glad to be at ease within modest bounds, should not by invasion increase their power, they would not be able, long time, by standing only on their defence, to subsist. And by consequence, such augmentation of dominion over men, being necessary to a mans conservation, it ought to be allowed him.

Againe, men have no pleasure, (but on the contrary a great deale of griefe) in keeping company, where there is no power able to over-awe them all. For every man looketh that his companion should value him, at the same rate he sets upon himselfe: And upon all signes of contempt, or undervaluing, naturally endeavours, as far as he dares (which amongst them that have no common power to keep them in quiet, is far enough to make them destroy each other,) to extort a greater value from his contemners, by dommage; and from others, by the example.

So that in the nature of man, we find three principall causes of quarrell. First, Competition; Secondly, Diffidence; Thirdly, Glory.

The first, maketh men invade for Gain; the second, for Safety; and the third, for Reputation. The first use Violence, to make themselves Masters of other mens persons, wives, children, and cattell; the second, to defend them; the third, for trifles, as a word, a smile, a different opinion, and any other signe of undervalue, either direct in their Persons, or by reflexion in their Kindred, their Friends, their Nation, their Profession, or their Name.

Hereby it is manifest, that during the time men live without a common Power to keep them all in awe, they are in that condition which is called Warre; and such a warre, as is of every man against every man. For WARRE, consisteth not in Battell onely, or the act of fighting; but in a tract of time, wherein the Will to contend by Battell is sufficiently known: and therefore the notion of *Time*, is to be considered in the nature of Warre; as it is in the nature of Weather. For as the nature of Foule weather, lyeth not in a showre or two of rain; but in an inclination thereto of many dayes together; So the nature of War, consisteth not in actuall fighting; but in the known disposition thereto, during all the time there is no assurance to the contrary. All other time is PEACE.

Whatsoever therefore is consequent to a time of Warre, where every man is Enemy to every man; the same is consequent to the time, wherein men live without other security, than what their own strength, and their own invention shall furnish them withall. In such condition, there is no place for Industry; because the fruit thereof is uncertain: and consequently no Culture of the Earth, no Navigation, nor use of the commodities that may be imported by Sea; no commodious Building; no Instruments of moving, and removing such things as require much force; no Knowledge of the face of the Earth; no account of Time; no Arts; no Letters; no Society; and which is worst of all, continuall feare, and danger of violent death; And the life of man, solitary, poore, nasty, brutish, and short.

It may seem strange to some man, that has not well weighed these things; that Nature should thus dissociate, and render men apt to invade, and destroy one another: and he may therefore, not trusting to this Inference, made from the Passions, desire perhaps to have the same confirmed by Experience. Let him therefore consider with himselfe, when taking a journey, he armes himselfe, and seeks to go well accompanied; when going to sleep, he locks his dores; when even in his house he locks his chests; and this when he knowes there bee Lawes, and publike Officers, armed, to revenge all injuries shall bee done him; what opinion he has of his fellow subjects, when he rides armed; of his fellow Citizens, when he locks his dores; and of his children, and servants, when he locks his chests. Does he not there as much accuse mankind by his actions, as I do by my words? But neither of us accuse mans nature in it. The Desires, and other Passions of man, are in themselves no Sin. No more are the Actions, that proceed from those Passions, till they know a Law that forbids them: which till Lawes be made they cannot know: nor can any Law be made, till they have agreed upon the Person that shall make it.

It may peradventure be thought, there was never such a time, nor condition of warre as this; and I believe it was never generally so, over all the world: but there are many places, where they live so now. For the savage people in many places of *America*, except the government of small Families, the concord whereof dependeth on naturall lust, have no government at all; and live at this day in that brutish manner, as I said before. Howsoever, it may be perceived what manner of life there would be, where there were no common Power to feare; by the manner of life, which men that have formerly lived under a peacefull government, use to degenerate into, in a civill Warre.

But though there had never been any time, wherein particular men were in a condition of warre one against another; yet in all times, Kings, and Persons of Soveraigne authority, because of their Independency, are in continuall jealousies, and in the state and posture of Gladiators; having their weapons pointing, and their eyes fixed on one another; that is, their Forts, Garrisons, and Guns, upon the Frontiers of their Kingdomes; and continuall Spyes upon their neighbours; which is a posture of War. But because they uphold thereby, the Industry of their Subjects; there does not follow from it, that misery, which accompanies the Liberty of particular men.

To this warre of every man against every man, this also is consequent; that nothing can be Unjust. The notions of Right and Wrong, Justice and Injustice have there no place. Where there is no common Power, there is no Law: where no Law, no Injustice. Force, and Fraud, are in warre the two Cardinall vertues. Justice, and Injustice are none of the Faculties neither of the Body, nor Mind. If they were, they might be in a man that were alone in the world, as well as his Senses, and Passions. They are Qualities, that relate to men in Society, not in Solitude. It is consequent also to the same condition, that there be no Propriety, no Dominion, no *Mine* and *Thine* distinct; but onely that to be every mans, that he can get; and for so long, as he can keep it. And thus much for the ill condition, which man by meer Nature is actually placed in; though with a possibility to come out of it, consisting partly in the Passions, partly in his Reason.

The Passions that encline men to Peace, are Feare of Death; Desire of such things as are necessary to commodious living; and a Hope by their Industry to obtain them. And Reason suggesteth convenient Articles of Peace, upon which men may be drawn to agreement. These Articles, are they, which otherwise are called the Lawes of Nature: whereof I shall speak more particularly, in the two following Chapters.

## CHAP. XIV

### *Of the first and second* NATURALL LAWES, *and of* CONTRACTS

THE RIGHT OF NATURE, which Writers commonly call *Jus Naturale*, is the Liberty each man hath, to use his own power, as he will himselfe, for the preservation of his own Nature; that is to say, of his own Life; and consequently, of doing any thing, which in his own Judgement, and Reason, hee shall conceive to be the aptest means thereunto.

By LIBERTY, is understood, according to the proper signification of the word, the absence of externall Impediments: which Impediments, may oft take away part of a mans power to do what hee would; but cannot hinder him from using the power left him, according as his judgement, and reason shall dictate to him.

A LAW OF NATURE, (*Lex Naturalis*,) is a Precept, or generall Rule, found out by Reason, by which a man is forbidden to do, that, which is destructive of his life, or taketh away the means of preserving the same; and to omit, that, by which he thinketh it may be best preserved. For though they that speak of this subject, use to confound *Jus*, and *Lex*, *Right* and *Law*; yet they ought to be distinguished; because RIGHT, consisteth in liberty to do, or to forbeare; Whereas LAW, determineth, and bindeth to one of them:

so that Law, and Right, differ as much, as Obligation, and Liberty; which in one and the same matter are inconsistent.

And because the condition of Man, (as hath been declared in the precedent Chapter) is a condition of Warre of every one against every one; in which case every one is governed by his own Reason; and there is nothing he can make use of, that may not be a help unto him, in preserving his life against his enemyes; It followeth, that in such a condition, every man has a Right to every thing; even to one anothers body. And therefore, as long as this naturall Right of every man to every thing endureth, there can be no security to any man, (how strong or wise soever he be,) of living out the time, which Nature ordinarily alloweth men to live. And consequently it is a precept, or generall rule of Reason, *That every man, ought to endeavour Peace, as farre as he has hope of obtaining it ; and when he cannot obtain it, that he may seek, and use, all helps, and advantages of Warre.* The first branch of which Rule, containeth the first, and Fundamentall Law of Nature; which is, *to seek Peace, and follow it.* The Second, the summe of the Right of Nature; which is, *By all means we can, to defend our selves.*

From this Fundamentall Law of Nature, by which men are commanded to endeavour Peace, is derived this second Law; *That a man be willing, when others are so too, as farre-forth, as for Peace, and defence of himselfe he shall think it necessary, to lay down this right to all things ; and be contented with so much liberty against other men, as he would allow other men against himselfe.* For as long as every man holdeth this Right, of doing any thing he liketh; so long are all men in the condition of Warre. But if other men will not lay down their Right, as well as he; then there is no Reason for any one, to devest himselfe of his: For that were to expose himselfe to Prey, (which no man is bound to) rather than to dispose himselfe to Peace. This is that Law of the Gospell; *Whatsoever you require that others should do to you, that do ye to them.* And that Law of all men, *Quod tibi fieri non vis, alteri ne feceris.*

To *lay downe* a mans *Right* to any thing, is to *devest* himselfe of the *Liberty*, of hindring another of the benefit of his own Right to the same. For he that renounceth, or passeth away his Right, giveth not to any other man a Right which he had not before; because there is nothing to which every man had not Right by Nature: but onely standeth out of his way, that he may enjoy his own originall Right, without hindrance from him; not without hindrance from another. So that the effect which redoundeth to one man, by another mans defect of Right, is but so much diminution of impediments to the use of his own Right originall.

Right is layd aside, either by simply Renouncing it; or by Transferring it to another. By *Simply* RENOUNCING; when he cares not to whom the benefit thereof redoundeth. By TRANSFERRING; when he intendeth the benefit thereof to some certain person, or persons. And when a man hath in either manner abandoned, or granted away his Right; then is he said to be

OBLIGED, or BOUND, not to hinder those, to whom such Right is
granted, or abandoned, from the benefit of it: and that he *Ought*,
and it is his DUTY, not to make voyd that voluntary act of his own:
and that such hindrance is INJUSTICE, and INJURY, as being *Sine
Jure*; the Right being before renounced, or transferred. So that
*Injury*, or *Injustice*, in the controversies of the world, is somewhat
like to that, which in the disputations of Scholers is called *Absurdity*.
For as it is there called an Absurdity, to contradict what one maintained in the Beginning: so in the world, it is called Injustice, and
Injury, voluntarily to undo that, which from the beginning he
had voluntarily done. The way by which a man either simply
Renounceth, or Transferreth his Right, is a Declaration, or Signification, by some voluntary and sufficient signe, or signes, that he doth
so Renounce, or Transferre; or hath so Renounced, or Transferred
the same, to him that accepteth it. And these Signes are either
Words onely, or Actions onely; or (as it happeneth most often)
both Words, and Actions. And the same are the BONDS, by which
men are bound, and obliged: Bonds, that have their strength, not
from their own Nature, (for nothing is more easily broken then a
mans word,) but from Feare of some evill consequence upon the
rupture.

Whensoever a man Transferreth his Right, or Renounceth it;
it is either in consideration of some Right reciprocally transferred
to himselfe; or for some other good he hopeth for thereby. For
it is a voluntary act: and of the voluntary acts of every man, the
object is some *Good to himselfe*. And therefore there be some
Rights, which no man can be understood by any words, or other
signes, to have abandoned, or transferred. As first a man cannot
lay down the right of resisting them, that assault him by force, to
take away his life; because he cannot be understood to ayme
thereby, at any Good to himselfe. The same may be sayd of
Wounds, and Chayns, and Imprisonment; both because there is
no benefit consequent to such patience; as there is to the patience
of suffering another to be wounded, or imprisoned: as also because
a man cannot tell, when he seeth men proceed against him by
violence, whether they intend his death or not. And lastly the
motive, and end for which this renouncing, and transferring of
Right is introduced, is nothing else but the security of a mans
person, in his life, and in the means of so preserving life, as not to
be weary of it. And therefore if a man by words, or other signes,
seem to despoyle himselfe of the End, for which those signes were
intended; he is not to be understood as if he meant it, or that it
was his will; but that he was ignorant of how such words and actions
were to be interpreted.

The mutuall transferring of Right, is that which men call
CONTRACT.

There is difference, between transferring of Right to the Thing;
and transferring, or tradition, that is, delivery of the Thing it selfe.
For the Thing may be delivered together with the Translation of

the Right; as in buying and selling with ready mony; or exchange of goods, or lands: and it may be delivered some time after.

Again, one of the Contractors, may deliver the Thing contracted for on his part, and leave the other to perform his part at some determinate time after, and in the mean time be trusted; and then the Contract on his part, is called PACT, or COVENANT: Or both parts may contract now, to performe hereafter: in which cases, he that is to performe in time to come, being trusted, his performance is called *Keeping of Promise*, or Faith; and the fayling of performance (if it be voluntary) *Violation of Faith.*

When the transferring of Right, is not mutuall; but one of the parties transferreth, in hope 'to gain thereby friendship, or service from another, or from his friends; or in hope to gain the reputation of Charity, or Magnanimity; or to deliver his mind from the pain of compassion; or in hope of reward in heaven; This is not Contract, but GIFT, FREE-GIFT, GRACE: which words signifie one and the same thing.

Signes of Contract, are either *Expresse*, or *by Inference.* Expresse, are words spoken with understanding of what they signifie: And such words are either of the time *Present*, or *Past*; as, *I Give, I Grant, I have Given, I have Granted, I will that this be yours :* Or of the future; as, *I will Give, I will Grant :* which words of the future, are called PROMISE.

Signes by Inference, are sometimes the consequence of Words; sometimes the consequence of Silence; sometimes the consequence of Actions; sometimes the consequence of Forbearing an Action: and generally a signe by Inference, of any Contract, is whatsoever sufficiently argues the will of the Contractor.

Words alone, if they be of the time to come, and contain a bare promise, are an insufficient signe of a Free-gift and therefore not obligatory. For if they be of the time to Come, as, *To morrow I will Give*, they are a signe I have not given yet, and consequently that my right is not transferred, but remaineth till I transferre it by some other Act. But if the words be .of the time Present, or Past, as, *I have given, or do give to be delivered to morrow*, then is my to morrows Right given away to day; and that by the vertue of the words, though there were no other argument of my will. And there is a great difference in the signification of these words, *Volo hoc tuum esse cras*, and *Cras dabo*; that is, between *I will that this be thine to morrow*, and, *I will give it thee to morrow :* For the word *I will*, in the former manner of speech, signifies an act of the will Present; but in the later, it signifies a promise of an act of the will to Come: and therefore the former words, being of the Present, transferre a future right; the later, that be of the Future, transferre nothing. But if there be other signes of the Will to transferre a Right, besides Words; then, though the gift be Free, yet may the Right be understood to passe by words of the future: as if a man propound a Prize to him that comes first to the end of a race, The gift is Free; and though the words be of the Future, yet the Right passeth: for if he would not have his words so be understood, he should not have let them runne.

In Contracts, the right passeth, not onely where the words are of the time Present, or Past; but also where they are of the Future: because all Contract is mutuall translation, or change of Right; and therefore he that promiseth onely, because he hath already received the benefit for which he promiseth, is to be understood as if he intended the Right should passe: for unlesse he had been content to have his words so understood, the other would not have performed his part first. And for that cause, in buying, and selling, and other acts of Contract, a Promise is equivalent to a Covenant; and therefore obligatory.

He that performeth first in the case of a Contract, is said to MERIT that which he is to receive by the performance of the other; and he hath it as *Due*. Also when a Prize is propounded to many, which is to be given to him onely that winneth; or mony is thrown amongst many, to be enjoyed by them that catch it; though this be a Free gift; yet so to Win, or so to Catch, is to *Merit*, and to have it as DUE. For the Right is transferred in the Propounding of the Prize, and in throwing down the mony; though it be not deter-mined to whom, but by the Event of the contention. But there is between these two sorts of Merit, this difference, that In Contract, I Merit by vertue of my own power, and the Contractors need; but in this case of Free gift, I am enabled to Merit onely by the benignity of the Giver: In Contract, I merit at the Contractors hand that he should depart with his right; In this case of Gift, I Merit not that the giver should part with his right; but that when he has parted with it, it should be mine, rather than anothers. And this I think to be the meaning of that distinction of the Schooles, between *Meritum congrui*, and *Meritum condigni*. For God Almignty, having promised Paradise to those men (hoodwinkt with carnall desires,) that can walk through this world according to the Precepts, and Limits prescribed by him; they say, he that shall so walk, shall Merit Paradise *Ex congruo*. But because no man can demand a right to it, by his own Righteousnesse, or any other power in himselfe, but by the Free Grace of God onely; they say, no man can Merit Paradise *ex condigno*. This I say, I think is the meaning of that distinction; but because Disputers do not agree upon the signification of their own termes of Art, longer than it serves their turn; I will not affirme any thing of their meaning: onely this I say; when a gift is given indefinitely, as a prize to be contended for, he that winneth Meriteth, and may claime the Prize as Due.

If a Covenant be made, wherein neither of the parties performe presently, but trust one another; in the condition of meer Nature, (which is a condition of Warre of every man against every man,) upon any reasonable suspition, it is Voyd: But if there be a common Power set over them both, with right and force sufficient to compell performance; it is not Voyd. For he that performeth first, has no assurance the other will performe after; because the bonds of words are too weak to bridle mens ambition, avarice, anger, and other Passions, without the feare of some coerceive Power; which in the condition of meer Nature, where all men are equall, and judges of the justnesse of their own fears, cannot possibly be supposed. And therefore he which performeth first, does but betray himselfe to his enemy; contrary to the Right (he can never abandon) of defending his life, and means of living.

But in a civill estate, where there is a Power set up to constrain those that would otherwise violate their faith, that feare is no more reasonable; and for that cause, he which by the Covenant is to perform first, is obliged so to do.

The cause of feare, which maketh such a Covenant invalid, must be always something arising after the Covenant made; as some new fact, or other signe of the Will not to performe: else it cannot make the Covenant voyd. For that which could not hinder a man from promising, ought not to be admitted as a hindrance of performing.

He that transferreth any Right, transferreth the Means of enjoying it, as farre as lyeth in his power. As he that selleth Land, is understood to transferre the Herbage, and whatsoever growes upon it; Nor can he that sells a Mill turn away the Stream that drives it. And they that give to a man the Right of government in Soveraignty, are understood to give him the right of levying mony to maintain Souldiers; and of appointing Magistrates for the administration of Justice.

To make Covenants with bruit Beasts, is impossible; because not understanding our speech, they understand not, nor accept of any translation of Right; nor can translate any Right to another: and without mutuall acceptation, there is no Covenant.

To make Covenant with God, is impossible, but by Mediation of such as God speaketh to, either by Revelation supernaturall, or by his Lieutenants that govern under him, and in his Name: For otherwise we know not whether our Covenants be accepted, or not. And therefore they that Vow any thing contrary to any law of Nature, Vow in vain; as being a thing unjust to pay such Vow. And if it be a thing commanded by the Law of Nature, it is not the Vow, but the Law that binds them.

The matter, or subject of a Covenant, is always something that falleth under deliberation; (For to Covenant, is an act of the Will; that is to say an act, and the last act, of deliberation;) and is therefore always understood to be something to come; and which is judged Possible for him that Covenanteth, to performe.

And therefore, to promise that which is known to be Impossible, is no Covenant. But if that prove impossible afterwards, which before was thought possible, the Covenant is valid, and bindeth, (though not to the thing it selfe,) yet to the value; or, if that also be impossible, to the unfeigned endeavour of performing as much as is possible: for to more no man can be obliged.

Men are freed of their Covenants two wayes; by Performing; or by being Forgiven. For Performance, is the naturall end of obligation; and Forgivenesse, the restitution of liberty; as being a re-transferring of that Right, in which the obligation consisted.

Covenants entred into by fear, in the condition of meer Nature, are obligatory. For example, if I Covenant to pay a ransome, or service for my life, to an enemy; I am bound by it. For it is a Contract, wherein one receiveth the benefit of life; the other is to receive mony, or service for it; and consequently, where no other Law (as in the condition, of meer nature) forbiddeth the performance, the Covenant is valid. Therefore Prisoners of warre, if trusted with the payment of their Ransome, are obliged to pay it: And if a weaker Prince, make a disadvantageous peace with a stronger, for feare; he is bound to keep it; unlesse (as hath been sayd before) there ariseth some new, and just cause to feare, to renew the war. And even in Common-wealths, if I be forced to redeem my selfe from a Theefe by promising him mony, I am bound to pay it, till the Civill Law discharge me. For whatsoever I may lawfully do without Obligation, the same I may lawfully Covenant to do through feare: and what I lawfully Covenant, I cannot lawfully break.

A former Covenant makes voyd a later. For a man that hath passed away his Right to one man to day, hath it not to passe to morrow to another: and therefore the later promise passeth no Right, but is null.

A Covenant not to defend my selfe from force, by force, is alwayes voyd. For (as I have shewed before) no man can transferre, or lay down his Right to save himselfe from Death, Wounds, and Imprisonment, (the avoyding whereof is the onely End of laying down any Right, and therefore the promise of not resisting force, in no Covenant transferreth any right; nor is obliging. For though a man may Covenant thus, *Unlesse I do so, or so, kill me*; he cannot Covenant thus, *Unlesse I do so, or so, I will not resist you, when you come to kill me*. For man by nature chooseth the lesser evill, which is danger of death in resisting; rather than the greater, which is certain and present death in not resisting. And this is granted to be true by all men, in that they lead Criminals to Execution, and Prison, with armed men, notwithstanding that such Criminals have consented to the Law, by which they are condemned.

A Covenant to accuse ones selfe, without assurance of pardon, is likewise invalid. For in the condition of Nature, where every man is Judge, there is no place for Accusation: and in the Civill State, the Accusation is followed with Punishment; which being Force, a man is not obliged not to resist. The same is also true, of the Accusation of those, by whose Condemnation a man falls into misery; as of a Father, Wife, or Benefactor.

For the Testimony of such an Accuser, if it be not willingly given, is præsumed to be corrupted by Nature; and therefore not to be received: and where a mans Testimony is not to be credited, he is not bound to give it. Also Accusations upon Torture, are not to be reputed as Testimonies. For Torture is to be used but as means of conjecture, and light, in the further examination, and search of truth: and what is in that case confessed, tendeth to the ease of him that is Tortured; not to the informing of the Torturers: and therefore ought not to have the credit of a sufficient Testimony: for whether he deliver himselfe by true, or false Accusation, he does it by the Right of preserving his own life.

The force of Words, being (as I have formerly noted) too weak to hold men to the performance of their Covenants; there are in mans nature, but two imaginable helps to strengthen it. And those are either a Feare of the consequence of breaking their word; or a Glory, or Pride in appearing not to need to breake it. This later is a Generosity too rarely found to be presumed on, especially in the pursuers of Wealth, Command, or sensuall Pleasure; which are the greatest part of Mankind. The Passion to be reckoned upon, is Fear; whereof there be two very generall Objects: one, The Power of Spirits Invisible; the other, The Power of those men they shall therein Offend. Of these two, though the former be the greater Power, yet the feare of the later is commonly the greater Feare. The Feare of the former is in every man, his own Religion, which hath place in the nature of man before Civill Society. The later hath not so; at least not place enough, to keep men to their promises; because in the condition of meer Nature, the inequality of Power is not discerned, but by the event of Battell. So that before the time of Civill Society, or in the interruption thereof by Warre, there is nothing can strengthen a Covenant of Peace agreed on, against the temptations of Avarice, Ambition, Lust, or other strong desire, but the feare of that Invisible Power, which they every one Worship as God; and Feare as a Revenger of their perfidy. All therefore that can be done between two men not subject to Civill Power, is to put one another to swear by the God he feareth: Which *Swearing*, or OATH, is a *Forme of Speech, added to a Promise; by which he that promiseth, signifieth, that unlesse he performe, he renounceth the mercy of his God, or calleth to him for vengeance on himselfe.* Such was the Heathen Forme, *Let* Jupiter *kill me else, as I kill this Beast.* So is our Forme, *I shall do thus, and thus, so help me God.* And this, with the Rites and Ceremonies, which every one useth in his own Religion, that the feare of breaking faith might be the greater.

By this it appears, that an Oath taken according to any other Forme, or Rite, then his, that sweareth, is in vain; and no Oath: And that there is no Swearing by any thing which the Swearer thinks not God. For though men have sometimes used to swear by their Kings, for feare, or flattery; yet they would have it thereby understood, they attributed to them Divine honour. And that Swearing unnecessarily by God, is but prophaning of his name: and Swearing by other things, as men do in common discourse, is not Swearing, but an impious Custome, gotten by too much vehemence of talking.

It appears also, that the Oath addes nothing to the Obligation. For a Covenant, if lawfull, binds in the sight of God, without the Oath, as much as with it: if unlawfull, bindeth not at all; though it be confirmed with an Oath.

## CHAP. XV

### Of other Lawes of Nature

FROM that law of Nature, by which we are obliged to transferre to another, such Rights, as being retained, hinder the peace of Mankind, there followeth a Third; which is this, *That men performe their Covenants made :* without which, Covenants are in vain, and but Empty words; and the Right of all men to all things remaining, wee are still in the condition of Warre.

And in this law of Nature, consisteth the Fountain and Originall of JUSTICE. For where no Covenant hath preceded, there hath no Right been transferred, and every man has right to every thing; and consequently, no action can be Unjust. But when a Covenant is made, then to break it is *Unjust*: And the definition of INIUSTICE, is no other than *the not Performance of Covenant*. And whatsoever is not Unjust, is *Just*.

But because Covenants of mutuall trust, where there is a feare of not performance on either part, (as hath been said in the former Chapter,) are invalid; though the Originall of Justice be the making of Covenants; yet Injustice actually there can be none, till the cause of such feare be taken away; which while men are in the naturall condition of Warre, cannot be done. Therefore before the names of Just, and Unjust can have place, there must be some coërcive Power, to compell men equally to the performance of their Covenants, by the terrour of some punishment, greater than the benefit they expect by the breach of their Covenant; and to make good that Propriety, which by mutuall Contract men acquire, in recompence of the universall Right they abandon: and such power there is none before the erection of a Common-wealth. And this is also to be gathered out of the ordinary definition of Justice in the Schooles: For they say, that *Justice is the constant Will of giving to every men his own.* And therefore where there is no *Own*, that is, no Propriety, there is no Injustice; and where there is no coërceive Power erected, that is, where there is no Common-wealth, there is no Propriety; all men having Right to all things: Therefore where there is no Common-wealth, there nothing is Unjust. So that the nature of Justice, consisteth in keeping of valid Covenants: but the Validity of Covenants begins not but with the Constitution of a Civill Power, sufficient to compell men to keep them: And then it is also that Propriety begins.

The Foole hath sayd in his heart, there is no such thing as Justice;

and sometimes also with his tongue; seriously alleaging, that every mans conservation, and contentment, being committed to his own care, there could be no reason, why every man might not do what he thought conduced thereunto: and therefore also to make, or not make: keep, or not keep Covenants, was not against Reason, when it conduced to ones benefit.  He does not therein deny, that there be Covenants; and that they are sometimes broken, sometimes kept; and 'that such breach of them may be called Injustice, and the observance of them Justice: but he questioneth, whether Injustice, taking away the feare of God, (for the same Foole hath said in his heart there is no God,) may not sometimes stand with that Reason, which dictateth to every man his own good; and particularly then, when it conduceth to such a benefit, as shall put a man in a condition, to neglect not onely the dispraise, and revilings, but also the power of other men.  The Kingdome of God is gotten by violence: but what if it could be gotten by unjust violence? were it against Reason so to get it, when it is impossible to receive hurt by it? and if it be not against Reason, it is not against Justice: or else Justice is not to be approved for good.  From such reasoning as this, Successfull wickednesse hath obtained the name of Vertue: and some that in all other things have disallowed the violation of Faith; yet have allowed it, when it is for the getting of a Kingdome. And the Heathen that believed, that *Saturn* was deposed by his son *Jupiter*, believed nevertheless the same *Jupiter* to be the avenger of Injustice: Somewhat like to a piece of Law in *Cokes* Commentaries on *Litleton*; where he sayes, If the right Heire of the Crown be attainted of Treason; yet the Crown shall descend to him, and *eo instante* the Atteynder be voyd: From which instances a man will be very prone to inferre; that when the Heire apparent of a Kingdome, shall kill him that is in possession, though his father; you may call it Injustice, or by what other name you will: yet it can never be against Reason, seeing all the voluntary actions of men tend to the benefit of themselves; and those actions are most Reasonable, that conduce most to their ends.  This specious reasoning is nevertheless false.

For the question is not of promises mutuall, where there is no security of performance on either side; as when there is no Civill Power erected over the parties promising; for such promises are no Covenants: But either where one of the parties has performed already; or where there is a Power to make him performe; there is the question whether it be against reason, that is, against the benefit of the other to performe, or not.  And I say it is not against reason.  For the manifestation whereof, we are of consider; First, that when a man doth a thing, which notwithstanding any thing can be foreseen, and reckoned on, tendeth to his own destruction, howsoever some accident which he could not expect, arriving may turne it to his benefit; yet such events do not make it reasonably or wisely done.  Secondly, that in a condition of Warre, wherein every man to every man, for want to a common Power to keep them all in awe, is an Enemy, there is no man can hope by his own strength, or wit, to defend himselfe from destruction, without the help of Confederates; where every one expects the same defence by the Confederation, that any one else does: and therefore he which declares he thinks it reason to deceive those that help him, can in reason expect no other means of safety, than what can be had from his own single Power. He therefore that breaketh his Covenant, and consequently declareth that he thinks he may with reason do so, cannot be received into any Society, that unite themselves for Peace and Defence, but by the errour of them that receive him; nor when he is received, be retayned in it, without seeing the danger of their errour; which errours a man cannot reasonably reckon upon as the means of his security: and therefore if he be left, or cast out of Society, he perisheth; and if he live in Society, it is by the errours of other men, which he could not foresee, nor reckon upon; and consequently against the reason of his preservation; and so, as all men that contribute not to his destruction, forbear him onely out of ignorance of what is good for themselves.

As for the Instance of gaining the secure and perpetual felicity of Heaven, by any way; it is frivolous: there being but one way imaginable; and that is not breaking, but keeping of Covenant.

And for the other Instance of attaining Soveraignty by Rebellion; it is manifest, that though the event follow, yet because it cannot reasonably be expected, but rather the contrary; and because by gaining it so, others are taught to gain the same in like manner, the attempt thereof is against reason. Justice therefore, that is to say, Keeping of Covenant, is a Rule of Reason, by which we are forbidden to do any thing destructive to our life; and consequently a Law of Nature.

There be some that proceed further; and will not have the Law of Nature, to be those Rules which conduce to the preservation of mans life on earth; but to the attaining of an eternall felicity after death; to which they think the breach of Covenant may conduce; and consequently be just and reasonable; (such are they that think it a work of merit to kill, or depose, or rebell against, the Soveraigne Power constituted over them by their own consent.) But because there is no naturall knowledge of mans estate after death; much lesse of the reward that is then to be given to breach of Faith; but onely a beliefe grounded upon other mens saying, that they know it supernaturally, or that they know those, that knew them, that knew others, that knew it supernaturally; Breach of Faith cannot be called a Precept of Reason, or Nature.

Others, that allow for a Law of Nature, the keeping of Faith, do neverthelesse make exception of certain persons; as Heretiques, and such as use not to performe their Covenant to others: And this also is against reason. For if any fault of a man, be sufficient to discharge our Covenant made; the same ought in reason to have been sufficient to have hindred the making of it.

The names of Just, and Injust, when they are attributed to Men, signifie one thing; and when they are attributed to Actions, another. When they are attributed to Men, they signifie Conformity, or Inconformity of Manners, to Reason. But when they are attributed to Actions, they signifie the Conformity or Inconformity to Reason, not of Manners, or manner of life, but of particular Actions. A Just man therefore, is he that taketh all the care he can, that his Actions may be all Just: and an Unjust man, is he that neglecteth it. And such men are more often in our Language stiled by the names of Righteous, and Unrighteous; then Just, and Unjust; though the meaning be the same. Therefore a Righteous man, does not lose that Title, by one, or a few unjust Actions, that proceed from sudden Passion, or mistake of Things, or Persons: nor does an Unrighteous man, lose his character, for such Actions, as he does, or forbeares to do, for feare: because his Will is not framed by the Justice, but by the apparent benefit of what he is to do. That which gives to humane Actions the relish of Justice, is a certain Noblenesse or Gallantnesse of courage, (rarely found,) by which a man scorns to be beholding for the contentment of his life, to fraud, or breach of promise. This Justice of the Manners, is that which is meant, where Justice is called a Vertue; and Injustice a Vice.

But the Justice of Actions denominates men, not Just, *Guiltlesse*: and the Injustice of the same, (which is also called Injury,) gives them but the name of *Guilty*.

Again, the Injustice of Manners, is the disposition, or aptitude to do Injurie; and is Injustice before it proceed to Act; and without supposing any individuall person injured. But the Injustice of an Action, (that is to say Injury,) supposeth an individuall person Injured; namely him, to whom the Covenant was made: And therefore many times the injury is received by one man, when the dammage redoundeth to another. As when the Master commandeth his servant to give mony to a stranger; if it be not done, the Injury is done to the Master, whom he had before Covenanted to obey; but the dammage redoundeth to the stranger, to whom he had no Obligation; and therefore could not Injure him. And so also in Common-wealths, private men may remit to one another their debts; but not robberies or other violences, whereby they are endammaged; because the detaining of Debt, is an Injury to themselves; but Robbery and Violence, are Injuries to the Person of the Common-wealth.

Whatsoever is done to a man, conformable to his own Will signified to the doer, is no Injury to him. For if he that doeth it, hath not passed away his originall right to do what he please, by some Antecedent Covenant, there is no breach of Covenant; and therefore no Injury done him. And if he have; then his Will to have it done being signified, is a release of that Covenant: and so again there is no Injury done him.

Justice of Actions, is by Writers divided into *Commutative*, and *Distributive* : and the former they say consisteth in proportion

Arithmeticall; the later in proportion Geometricall. Commutative therefore, they place in the equality of value of the things contracted for; And Distributive, in the distribution of equall benefit, to men of equall merit. As if it were Injustice to sell dearer than we buy; or to give more to a man than he merits. The value of all things contracted for, is measured by the Appetite of the Contractors: and therefore the just value, is that which they be contented to give. And Merit (besides that which is by Covenant, where the performance on one part, meriteth the performance of the other part, and falls under Justice Commutative, not Distributive,) is not due by Justice; but is rewarded of Grace onely. And therefore this distinction, in the sense wherein it useth to be expounded, is not right. To speak properly, Commutative Justice, is the Justice of a Contractor; that is, a Performance of Covenant, in Buying, and Selling; Hiring, and Letting to Hire; Lending, and Borrowing; Exchanging, Bartering, and other acts of Contract.

And Distributive Justice, the Justice of an Arbitrator; that is to say, the act of defining what is Just. Wherein, (being trusted by them that make him Arbitrator,) if he performe his Trust, he is said to distribute to every man his own: and this is indeed Just Distribution, and may be called (though improperly) Distributive Justice; but more properly Equity; which also is a Law of Nature, as shall be shewn in due place.

As Justice dependeth on Antecedent Covenant; so does GRATITUDE depend on Antecedent Grace; that is to say, Antecedent-Free-Gift: and is the fourth Law of Nature; which may be conceived in this Forme, *That a man which receiveth Benefit from another of meer Grace, Endeavour that he which giveth it, have no reasonable cause to repent him of his good will.* For no man giveth, but with intention of Good to himselfe; because Gift is Voluntary; and of all Voluntary Acts, the Object is to every man his own Good; of which if men see they shall be frustrated, there will be no beginning of benevolence, or trust; nor consequently of mutuall help; nor of reconciliation of one man to another; and therefore they are to remain still in the condition of *War*; which is contrary to the first and Fundamentall Law of Nature, which commandeth men to *Seek Peace*. The breach of this Law, is called *Ingratitude*; and hath the same relation to Grace, that Injustice hath to Obligation by Covenant.

A fifth Law of Nature, is COMPLEASANCE; that is to say, *That every man strive to accommodate himselfe to the rest.* For the understanding whereof, we may consider, that there is in mens aptnesse to Society, a diversity of Nature, rising from their diversity of Affections; not unlike to that we see in stones brought together for building of an Ædifice. For as that stone which by the asperity, and irregularity of Figure, takes more room from others, than it selfe fills; and for the hardnesse, cannot be easily made plain, and thereby hindereth the building, is by the builders cast away as unprofitable, and troublesome: so also, a man that by asperity of

Nature, will strive to retain those things which to himselfe are superfluous, and to others necessary; and for the stubbornness of his Passions, cannot be corrected, is to be left, or cast out of Society, as combersome thereunto. For seeing every man, not onely by Right, but also by necessity of Nature, is supposed to endeavour all he can, to obtain that which is necessary for his conservation; He that shall oppose himselfe against it, for things superfluous, is guilty of the warre that thereupon is to follow; and therefore doth that, which is contrary to the fundamentall Law of Nature, which commandeth *to seek Peace.* The observers of this Law, may be called SOCIABLE, (the Latines call them *Commodi;*) The contrary, *Stubborn, Insociable, Froward, Intractable.*

A sixth Law of Nature, is this, *That upon caution of the Future time, a man ought to pardon the offences past of them that repenting, desire it.* For PARDON, is nothing but granting of Peace; which though granted to them that persevere in their hostility, be not Peace, but Feare; yet not granted to them that give caution of the Future time, is signe of an aversion to Peace; and therefore contrary to the Law of Nature.

A seventh is, *That in Revenges,* (that is, retribution of Evil for Evil,) *Men look not at the greatnesse of the evill past, but the greatnesse of the good to follow.* Whereby we are forbidden to inflict punishment with any other designe, than for correction of the offender, or direction of others. For this Law is consequent to the next before it, that commandeth Pardon, upon security of the Future time. Besides, Revenge without respect to the Example, and profit to come, is a triumph, or glorying in the hurt of another, tending to no end; (for the End is alwayes somewhat to Come;) and glorying to no end, is vain-glory, and contrary to reason; and to hurt without reason, tendeth to the introduction of Warre; which is against the Law of Nature; and is commonly stiled by the name of *Cruelty.*

And because all signes of hatred, or contempt, provoke to fight; insomuch as most men choose rather to hazard their life, than not to be revenged; we may in the eighth place, for a Law of Nature, set down this Precept, *That no man by deed, word, countenance, or gesture, declare Hatred, or Contempt of another.* The breach of which Law, is commonly called *Contumely.*

The question who is the better man, has no place in the condition of meer Nature; where, (as has been shewn before,) all men are equall. The inequallity that now is, has bin introduced by the Lawes civill. I know that *Aristotle* in the first booke of his Politiques, for a foundation of his doctrine, maketh men by Nature, some more worthy to Command, meaning the wiser sort (such as he thought himselfe to be for his Philosophy;) others to Serve, (meaning those that had strong bodies, but were not Philosophers as he;) as if Master and Servant were not introduced by consent of men, but by difference of Wit: which is not only against reason; but also against experience. For there are very few so foolish, that had not rather governe themselves, than be governed by others: Nor when the wise in their own conceit, contend by force, with them who distrust their owne wisdome, do they alwaies, or often, or almost at any time, get the Victory. If Nature therefore have made men equall, that equalitie is to be acknowledged: or if Nature have made men unequall; yet because men that think themselves equall, will not enter into conditions of Peace, but upon Equall termes, such equalitie must be admitted. And therefore for the ninth law of Nature, I put this, *That every man acknowledge other for his Equall by Nature.* The breach of this Precept is *Pride.*

On this law, dependeth another, *That at the entrance into conditions of Peace, no man require to reserve to himselfe any Right, which he is not content should be reserved to every one of the rest.* As it is necessary for all men that seek peace, to lay down certaine Rights of Nature; that is to say, not to have libertie to do all they list: so is it necessarie for mans life, to retaine some; as right to governe their owne bodies; enjoy aire, water, motion, waies to go from place to place; and all things else without which a man cannot live, or not live well. If in this case, at the making of Peace, men require for themselves, that which they would not have to be granted to others, they do contrary to the precedent law, that commandeth the acknowledgment of naturall equalitie, and therefore also against the law of Nature. The observers of this law, are those we call *Modest,* and the breakers *Arrogant* men. The Greeks call the violation of this law πλεονεξία; that is, a desire of more than their share.

Also if *a man be trusted to judge between man and man,* it is a precept of the Law of Nature, *that he deale Equally between them.* For without that, the Controversies of men cannot be determined but by Warre. He therefore that is partiall in judgment, doth what in him lies, to deterre men from the use of Judges, and Arbitrators; and consequently, (against the fundamentall Lawe of Nature) is the cause of Warre.

The observance of this law, from the equall distribution to each man, of that which in reason belongeth to him, is called EQUITY, and (as I have sayd before) distributive Justice: the violation, *Acception of persons,* προσωποληψία.

And from this followeth another law, *That such things as cannot be divided, be enjoyed in Common, if it can be ; and if the quantity of the thing permit, without Stint ; otherwise Proportionably to the number of them that have Right.* For otherwise the distribution is Unequall, and contrary to Equitie.

But some things there be, that can neither be divided, nor enjoyed in common. Then, The Law of Nature, which prescribeth Equity, requireth, *That the Entire Right ; or else, (making the use alternate,) the First Possession, be determined by Lot.* For equall distribution, is of the Law of Nature; and other means of equall distribution cannot be imagined.

Of *Lots* there be two sorts, *Arbitrary,* and *Naturall.* Arbitrary, is that which is agreed on by the Competitors: Naturall, is either

*Primogeniture*, (which the Greek calls Κληρονομία, which signifies, *Given by Lot*;) or *First Seisure*.

And therefore those things which cannot be enjoyed in common, nor divided, ought to be adjudged to the First Possessor; and in some cases to the First-Borne, as acquired by Lot.

It is also a Law of Nature, *That all men that mediate Peace, be allowed safe Conduct.* For the Law that commandeth Peace, as the *End*, commandeth Intercession, as the *Means*; and to Intercession the Means is safe Conduct.

And because, though men be never so willing to observe these Lawes, there may neverthelesse arise questions concerning a mans action; First, whether it were done, or not done; Secondly (if done) whether against the Law, or not against the Law; the former whereof, is called a question *Of Fact*; the later a question *Of Right*; therefore unlesse the parties to the question, Covenant mutually to stand to the sentence of another, they are as farre from Peace as ever. This other, to whose Sentence they submit, is called an ARBITRATOR. And therefore it is of the Law of Nature, *That they that are at controversie, submit their Right to the judgement of an Arbitrator.*

And seeing every man is presumed to do all things in order to his own benefit, no man is a fit Arbitrator in his own cause: and if he were never so fit; yet Equity allowing to each party equall benefit, if one be admitted to be Judge, the other is to be admitted also; and so the controversie, that is, the cause of War, remains, against the Law of Nature.

For the same reason no man in any Cause ought to be received for Arbitrator, to whom greater profit, or honour, or pleasure apparently ariseth out of the victory of one party, than of the other; for hee hath taken (though an unavoydable bribe, yet) a bribe; and no man can be obliged to trust him. And thus also the controversie, and the condition of War remaineth, contrary to the Law of Nature.

And in a controversie of *Fact*, the Judge being to give no more credit to one, than to the other, (if there be no other Arguments) must give credit to a third; or to a third and fourth; or more: For else the question is undecided, and left to force, contrary to the Law of Nature.

These are the Lawes of Nature, dictating Peace, for a means of the conservation of men in multitudes; and which onely concern the doctrine of Civill Society. There be other things tending to the destruction of particular men; as Drunkenness, and all other parts of Intemperance; which may therefore also be reckoned amongst those things which the Law of Nature hath forbidden; but are not necessary to be mentioned, nor are pertinent enough to this place.

And though this may seem too subtile a deduction of the Lawes of Nature, to be taken notice of by all men; whereof the most part are too busie in getting food, and the rest too negligent to understand; yet to leave all men unexcusable, they have been contracted into one easie sum, intelligible, even to the meanest capacity; and that is, *Do not that to another, which thou wouldest not have done to thy selfe*; which sheweth him, that he has no more to do in learning the Lawes of Nature, but, when weighing the actions of other men with his own, they seem too heavy, to put them into the other part of the ballance, and his own into their place, that his own passions, and selfe-love, may adde nothing to the weight; and then there is none of these Lawes of Nature that will not appear unto him very reasonable.

The Lawes of Nature oblige *in foro interno*; that is to say, they bind to a desire they should take place: but *in foro externo*; that is, to the putting them in act, not alwayes. For he that should be modest, and tractable, and performe all he promises, in such time, and place, where no man els should do so, should but make himselfe a prey to others, and procure his own certain ruine, contrary to the ground of all Lawes of Nature, which tend to Natures preservation. And again, he that having sufficient Security, that others shall observe the same Lawes towards him, observes them not himselfe, seeketh not Peace, but War; & consequently the destruction of his Nature by Violence.

And whatsoever Lawes bind *in foro interno*, may be broken, not onely by a fact contrary to the Law, but also by a fact according to it, in case a man think it contrary. For though his Action in this case, be according to the Law; yet his Purpose was against the Law; which where the Obligation is *in foro interno*, is a breach.

The Lawes of Nature are Immutable and Eternall; For Injustice, Ingratitude, Arrogance, Pride, Iniquity, Acception of persons, and the rest, can never be made lawfull. For it can never be that Warre shall preserve life, and Peace destroy it.

The [same] Lawes, because they oblige onely to a desire, and endeavour, I mean an unfeigned and constant endeavour, are easie to be observed. For in that they require nothing but endeavour; he that endeavoureth their performance, fulfilleth them; and he that fulfilleth the Law, is Just.

And the Science of them, is the true and onely Moral Philosophy. For Morall Philosophy is nothing else but the Science of what is *Good*, and *Evill*, in the conversation, and Society of man-kind. *Good*, and *Evill*, are names that signifie our Appetites, and Aversions; which in different tempers, customes, and doctrines of men, are different: And divers men, differ not onely in their Judgement, on the senses of what is pleasant, and unpleasant to the tast, smell, hearing, touch, and sight; but also of what is conformable, or disagreeable to Reason, in the actions of common life. Nay, the same man, in divers times, differs from himselfe; and one time praiseth, that is, calleth Good, what another time he dispraiseth, and calleth Evil: From whence arise Disputes, Controversies, and at last War. And therefore so long a man is in the condition of meer Nature, (which is a condition of War,) as private Appetite is the measure of Good, and Evill: And consequently all men agree on this, that Peace is Good, and therefore also the way, or means of Peace, which (as I have shewed before) are *Justice, Gratitude, Modesty, Equity, Mercy,* & the rest of the Laws of Nature, are good; that is to say, *Morall Vertues*; and their contrarie *Vices, Evill.* Now the science of Vertue and Vice, is Morall Philosophie; and therfore the true Doctrine of the Lawes of Nature, is the true Morall Philosophie. But the Writers of Morall Philosophie, though they acknowledge the same Vertues and Vices; Yet not seeing wherein consisted their Goodnesse; not that they come to be praised, as the meanes of peaceable, sociable, and comfortable living; place them in a mediocrity of passions: as if not the Cause, but the Degree of daring, made Fortitude; or not the Cause, but the Quantity of a gift, made Liberality.

These dictates of Reason, men use to call by the name of Lawes; but improperly: for they are but Conclusions, or Theoremes concerning what conduceth to the conservation and defence of themselves; whereas Law, properly is the word of him, that by right hath command over others. But yet if we consider the same Theoremes, as delivered in the word of God, that by right commandeth all things; then are they properly called Lawes.

## CHAP. XVI

### *Of* PERSONS, AUTHORS, *and things Personated*

A PERSON, is he, *whose words or actions are considered, either as his own, or as representing the words or actions of an other man, or of any other thing to whom they are attributed, whether Truly or by Fiction.*

When they are considered as his owne, then is he called a *Naturall Person*: And when they are considered as representing the words and actions of an other, then is he a *Feigned* or *Artificiall person.*

The word Person is latine: insteed whereof the Greeks have πρόσωπον, which signifies the *Face*, as *Persona* in latine signifies the *disguise*, or *outward appearance* of a man, counterfeited on the Stage; and sometimes more particularly that part of it, which disguiseth the face, as a Mask or Visard: And from the Stage, hath been translated to any Representer of speech and action, as well in Tribunalls, as Theaters. So that a *Person*, is the same that an *Actor* is, both on the Stage and in common Conversation; and to *Personate*, is to *Act*, or *Represent* himselfe, or an other; and he that acteth another, is said to beare his Person, or act in his name; (in which sence *Cicero* useth it where he saies, *Unus sustineo tres Personas ; Mei, Adversarii, & Judicis*, I beare three Persons; my own, my Adversaries, and the Judges;) and is called in diverse occasions, diversly; as a *Representer*, or *Representative*, a *Lieutenant*, a *Vicar*, an *Attorney*, a *Deputy*, a *Procurator*, an *Actor*, and the like.

Of Persons Artificiall, some have their words and actions *Owned* by those whom they represent. And then the Person is the *Actor*; and he that owneth his words and actions, is the AUTHOR: In which case the Actor acteth by Authority. For that which in speaking of goods and possessions, is called an *Owner*, and in latine *Dominus*, in Greeke κύριος; speaking of Actions, is called Author. And as the Right of possession, is called Dominion; so the Right of doing any Action, is called AUTHORITY. So that by Authority, is alwayes understood a Right of doing any act: and *done by Authority*, done by Commission, or Licence from him whose right it is.

From hence it followeth, that when the Actor maketh a Covenant by Authority, he bindeth thereby the Author, no lesse than if he had made it himselfe; and no lesse subjecteth him to all the consequences of the same. And therfore all that hath been said formerly, (*Chap.* 14.) of the nature of Covenants between man and man in their naturall capacity, is true also when they are made by their Actors, Representers, or Procurators, that have authority from them so far-forth as is in their Commission, but no farther.

And therefore he that maketh a Covenant with the Actor, or Representer, not knowing the Authority he hath, doth it at his own perill. For no man is obliged by a Covenant, whereof he is not Author; nor consequently by a Covenant made against, or beside the Authority he gave.

When the Actor doth any thing against the Law of Nature by command of the Author, if he be obliged by former Covenant to obey him, not he, but the Author breaketh the Law of Nature: for though the Action be against the Law of Nature; yet it is not his: but contrarily, to refuse to do it, is against the Law of Nature, that forbiddeth breach of Covenant.

And he that maketh a Covenant with the Author, by mediation of the Actor, not knowing what Authority he hath, but onely takes his word; in case such Authority be not made manifest unto him upon demand, is no longer obliged: For the Covenant made with the Author, is not valid, without his Counter-assurance. But if he that so Covenanteth, knew before hand he was to expect no other assurance, than the Actors word; then is the Covenant valid; because the Actor in this case maketh himselfe the Author. And therefore, as when the Authority is evident, the Covenant obligeth the Author, not the Actor; so when the Authority is feigned, it obligeth the Actor onely; there being no Author but himselfe.

There are few things, that are uncapable of being represented by Fiction. Inanimate things, as a Church, an Hospital, a Bridge, may be personated by a Rector, Master, or Overseer. But things Inanimate, cannot be Authors, nor therefore give Authority to their Actors: Yet the Actors may have Authority to procure their maintenance, given them by those that are Owners, or Governours of those things. And therefore, such things cannot be Personated, before there be some state of Civill Government.

Likewise Children, Fooles, and Mad-men that have no use of Reason, may be Personated by Guardians, or Curators; but can be no Authors (during that time) of any action done by them, longer then (when they shall recover the use of Reason) they shall judge the same reasonable. Yet during the Folly, he that hath right of governing them, may give Authority to the Guardian. But this again has no place but in a State Civill, because before such estate, there is no Dominion of Persons.

An Idol, or meer Figment of the brain, may be Personated; as were the Gods of the Heathen; which by such Officers as the State appointed, were Personated, and held Possessions, and other Goods, and Rights, which men from time to time dedicated, and consecrated unto them. But Idols cannot be Authors: for an Idol is nothing. The Authority proceeded from the State: and therefore before introduction of Civill Government, the Gods of the Heathen could not be Personated.

The true God may be Personated. As he was; first, by *Moses*; who governed the Israelites, (that were not his, but Gods people,) not in his own name, with *Hoc dicit Moses*; but in Gods Name, with *Hoc dicit Dominus*. Secondly, by the Son of man, his own Son, our Blessed Saviour *Jesus Christ*, that came to reduce the Jewes, and induce all Nations into the Kingdome of his Father; not as of himselfe, but as sent from his Father. And thirdly, by the Holy Ghost, or Comforter, speaking, and working in the Apostles: which Holy Ghost, was a Comforter that came not of himselfe; but was sent, and proceeded from them both.

A Multitude of men, are made *One* Person, when they are by one man, or one Person, Represented; so that it be done with the consent of every one of that Multitude in particular. For it is the *Unity* of the Representer, not the *Unity* of the Represented, that maketh the Person *One*. And it is the Representer that beareth the Person, and but one Person: And *Unity*, cannot otherwise be understood in Multitude.

And because the Multitude naturally is not *One*, but *Many*; they cannot be understood for one; but many Authors, of every thing their Representative saith, or doth in their name; Every man giving their common Representer, Authority from himselfe in particular; and owning all the actions the Representer doth, in case they give him Authority without stint: Otherwise, when they limit him in what, and how farre he shall represent them, none of them owneth more, than they gave him commission to Act.

And if the Representative consist of many men, the voyce of the greater number, must be considered as the voyce of them all. For if the lesser number pronounce (for example) in the Affirmative, and the greater in the Negative, there will be Negatives more than enough to destroy the Affirmatives; and thereby the excesse of

Negatives, standing uncontradicted, are the onely voyce the Representative hath.

And a Representative of even number, especially when the number is not great, whereby the contradictory voyces are oftentimes equall, is therefore oftentimes mute, and uncapable of Action. Yet in some cases contradictory voyces equall in number, may determine a question; as in condemning, or absolving, equality of votes, even in that they condemne not, do absolve; but not on the contrary condemne, in that they absolve not. For when a Cause is heard; not to condemne, is to absolve: but on the contrary, to say that not absolving, is condemning, is not true. The like it is in a deliberation of executing presently, or deferring till another time: For when the voyces are equall, the not decreeing Execution, is a decree of Dilation.

Or if the number be odde, as three, or more, (men, or assemblies;) whereof every one has by a Negative Voice, authority to take away the effect of all the Affirmative Voices of the rest, This number is no Representative; because by the diversity of Opinions, and Interests of men, it becomes oftentimes, and in cases of the greatest consequence, a mute Person, and unapt, as for many things else, so for the government of a Multitude, especially in time of Warre.

Of Authors there be two sorts. The first simply so called; which I have before defined to be him, that owneth the Action of another simply. The second is he, that owneth an Action, or Covenant of another conditionally; that is to say, he undertaketh to do it, if the other doth it not, at, or before a certain time. And these Authors conditionall, are generally called SURETYES, in Latine *Fidejussores*, and *Sponsores*; and particularly for Debt, *Prædes*; and for Appearance before Judge, or Magistrate, *Vades*.

# PART II.—OF COMMON-WEALTH

## CHAP. XVII

*Of the Causes, Generation, and Definition of a* COMMON-WEALTH

THE finall Cause, End, or Designe of men, (who naturally love Liberty, and Dominion over others,) in the introduction of that restraint upon themselves, (in which wee see them live in Common-wealths,) is the foresight of their own preservation, and of a more contented live thereby; that is to say, of getting themselves out from that miserable condition of Warre, which is necessarily consequent (as hath been shewn) to the naturall Passions of men, when there is no visible Power to keep them in awe, and tye them by feare of punishment to the performance of their Covenants, and observation of those Lawes of Nature set down in the fourteenth and fifteenth Chapters.

For the Lawes of Nature (as *Justice, Equity, Modesty, Mercy,* and (in summe) *doing to others, as wee would be done to,*) of themselves, without the terrour of some Power, to cause them to be observed, are contrary to our naturall Passions, that carry us to Partiality, Pride, Revenge, and the like. And Covenants, without the Sword, are but Words, and of no strength to secure a man at all. Therefore notwithstanding the Lawes of Nature, (which every one hath then kept, when he has the will to keep them, when he can do it safely,) if there be no Power erected, or not great enough for our security; every man will, and may lawfully rely on his own strength and art, for caution against all other men. And in all places, where men have lived by small Families, to robbe and spoyle one another, has been a Trade, and so farre from being reputed against the Law of Nature, that the greater spoyles they gained, the greater was their honour; and men observed no other Lawes therein, but the Lawes of Honour; that is, to abstain from cruelty, leaving to men their lives, and instruments of husbandry. And as small Familyes did then; so now do Cities and Kingdomes, which are but greater Families (for their own security) enlarge their Dominions, upon all pretences of danger, and fear of Invasion, or assistance that may be given to Invaders, endeavour as much as they can, to subdue, or weaken their neighbours, by open force, and secret arts, for want of other Caution, justly; and are remembered for it in after ages with honour.

Nor is it the joyning together of a small number of men, that gives them this security; because in small numbers, small additions on the one side or the other, make the advantage of strength so great, as is sufficient to carry the Victory; and therefore gives encouragement to an Invasion. The Multitude sufficient to confide in for our Security, is not determined by any certain number, but by comparison with the Enemy we feare; and is then sufficient, when the odds of the Enemy is not of so visible and conspicuous moment, to determine the event of warre, as to move him to attempt.

And be there never so great a Multitude; yet if their actions be directed according to their particular judgements, and particular appetites, they can expect thereby no defence, nor protection, neither against a common enemy, nor against the injuries of one another. For being distracted in opinions concerning the best use and application of their strength, they do not help, but hinder one another; and reduce their strength by mutuall opposition to nothing: whereby they are easily, not onely subdued by a very few that agree together; but also when there is no common enemy, they make warre upon each other, for their particular interests. For if we could suppose a great Multitude of men to consent in the observation of Justice, and other Lawes of Nature, without a common Power to keep them all in awe; we might as well suppose all Man-kind to do the same; and then there neither would be, nor need to be any Civill Government, or Common-wealth at all; because there would be Peace without subjection.

Nor is it enough for the security, which men desire should last all the time of their life, that they be governed, and directed by one judgement, for a limited time; as in one Battel, or one Warre. For though they obtain a Victory by their unanimous endeavour against a forraign enemy; yet afterwards, when either they have no common enemy, or he that by one part is held for an enemy, is by another part held for a friend, they must needs by the difference of their interests dissolve, and fall again into a Warre amongst themselves.

It is true, that certain living creatures, as Bees, and Ants, live sociably one with another, (which are therefore by *Aristotle* numbred amongst Politicall creatures;) and yet have no other direction, than their particular judgements and appetites; nor speech, whereby one of them can signifie to another, what he thinks expedient for the common benefit: and therefore some man may perhaps desire to know, why Man-kind cannot do the same. To which I answer,

First, that men are continually in competition for Honour and Dignity, which these creatures are not; and consequently amongst men there ariseth on that ground, Envy and Hatred, and finally Warre; but amongst these not so.

Secondly, that amongst these creatures, the Common good differeth not from the Private; and being by nature enclined to their private, they procure thereby the common benefit. But man, whose Joy consisteth in comparing himselfe with other men, can relish nothing but what is eminent.

Thirdly, that these creatures, having not (as man) the use of reason, do not see, nor think they see any fault, in the administration of their common businesse: whereas amongst men, there are very many, that thinke themselves wiser, and abler to govern the Publique, better than the rest; and these strive to reforme and innovate, one this way, another that way; and thereby bring it into Distraction and Civill warre.

Fourthly, that these creatures, though they have some use of voice, in making knowne to one another their desires, and other affections; yet they want that art of words, by which some men can represent to others, that which is Good, in the likenesse of Evill; and Evill, in the likenesse of Good; and augment, or diminish the apparent greatnesse of Good and Evill; discontenting men, and troubling their Peace at their pleasure.

Fiftly, irrationall creatures cannot distinguish betweene *Injury*, and *Dammage*; and therefore as long as they be at ease, they are not offended with their fellowes: whereas Man is then most trouble-some, when he is most at ease: for then it is that he loves to shew his Wisdome, and controule the Actions of them that governe the Common-wealth.

Lastly, the agreement of these creatures is Naturall; that of men, is by Covenant only, which is Artificiall: and therefore it is no wonder if there be somewhat else required (besides Covenant) to make their Agreement constant and lasting; which is a Common Power, to keep them in awe, and to direct their actions to the Common Benefit.

The only way to erect such a Common Power, as may be able to defend them from the invasion of Forraigners, and the injuries of one another, and thereby to secure them in such sort, as that by their owne industrie, and by the fruites of the Earth, they may nourish themselves and live contentedly; is, to conferre all their power and strength upon one Man, or upon one Assembly of men, that may reduce all their Wills, by plurality of voices, unto one Will: which is as much as to say, to appoint one Man, or Assembly of men, to beare their Person; and every one to owne, and acknow-ledge himselfe to be Author of whatsoever he that so beareth their Person, shall Act, or cause to be Acted, in those things which concerne the Common Peace and Safetie; and therein to submit their Wills, every one to his Will, and their Judgements, to his Judgement. This is more than Consent, or Concord; it is a reall Unitie of them all, in one and the same Person, made by Covenant of every man with every man, in such manner, as if every man should say to every man, *I Authorise and give up my Right of Govern-ing my selfe, to this Man, or to this Assembly of men, on this condition, that thou give up thy Right to him, and Authorise all his Actions in like manner.* This done, the Multitude so united in one Person, is called a COMMON-WEALTH, in latine CIVITAS. This is the Generation of that great LEVIATHAN, or rather (to speake more reverently) of that *Mortall God*, to which wee owe under the *Immortall God*, our peace and defence. For by this Authoritie, given him by every particular man in the Common-Wealth, he hath the use of so much Power and Strength conferred on him, that by terror thereof, he is

inabled to forme the wills of them all, to Peace at home, and mutuall
ayd against their enemies abroad. And in him consisteth the
Essence of the Common-wealth; which (to define it,) is *One Person,
of whose Acts a great Multitude, by mutuall Covenants one with another,
have made themselves every one the Author, to the end he may use the
strength and means of them all, as he shall think expedient, for their
Peace and Common Defence.*

And he that carryeth this Person, is called SOVERAIGNE, and said
to have *Soveraigne Power*; and every one besides, his SUBJECT.

The attaining to this Soveraigne Power, is by two wayes. One,
by Naturall force; as when a man maketh his children, to submit
themselves, and their children to his government, as being able to
destroy them if they refuse; or by Warre subdueth his enemies
to his will, giving them their lives on that condition. The other,
is when men agree amongst themselves, to submit to some Man,
or Assembly of men, voluntarily, on confidence to be protected by
him against all others. This later, may be called a Politicall
Common-wealth, or Common-wealth by *Institution*; and the former,
a Common-wealth by *Acquisition*. And first, I shall speak of a
Common-wealth by Institution.

## CHAP. XVIII

### *Of the* RIGHTS *of Soveraignes by Institution*

A *Common-wealth* is said to be *Instituted*, when a *Multitude* of
men do Agree, and *Covenant, every one, with every one*, that tó
whatsoever *Man*, or *Assembly of Men*, shall be given by the major
part, the *Right* to *Present* the Person of them all, (that is to say, to
be their *Representative*;) every one, as well he that *Voted for it*,
as he that *Voted against it*, shall *Authorise* all the Actions and
Judgements, of that Man, or Assembly of men, in the same manner,
as if they were his own, to the end, to live peaceably amongst themselves, and be protected against other men.

From this Institution of a Common-wealth are derived all the
*Rights*, and *Facultyes* of him, or them, on whom the Soveraigne
Power is conferred by the consent of the People assembled.

First, because they Covenant, it is to be understood, they are not
obliged by former Covenant to any thing repugnant hereunto. And
Consequently they that have already Instituted a Common-wealth,
being thereby bound by Covenant, to own the Actions, and Judgements of one, cannot lawfully make a new Covenant, amongst
themselves, to be obedient to any other, in any thing whatsoever,
without his permission. And therefore, they that are subjects to
a Monarch, cannot without his leave cast off Monarchy, and return
to the confusion of a disunited Multitude; nor transferre their
Person from him that beareth it, to another Man, or other Assembly

of men: for they are bound, every man to every man, to Own, and be reputed Author of all, that he that already is their Soveraigne, shall do, and judge fit to be done: so that any one man dissenting all the rest should break their Covenant made to that man, which is injustice: and they have also every man given the Sòveraignty to him that beareth their Person; and therefore if they depose him, they take from him that which is his own, and so again it is injustice. Besides, if he that attempteth to depose his Soveraign, be killed, òr punished by him for such attempt, he is author of his own punishment, as being by the Institution, Author of all his Soveraign shall do: And because it is injustice for a man to do any thing, for which he may be punished by his own authority, he is also upon that title, unjust. And whereas some men have pretended for their disobedience to their Soveraign, a new Covenant, made, not with men, but with God; this also is unjust: for there is no Covenant with God, but by mediation of some body that representeth Gods Person; which none doth but Gods Lieutenant, who hath the Soveraignty under God. But this pretence of Covenant with God, is so evident a lye, even in the pretenders own consciences, that it is not onely an act of an unjust, but also of a vile, and unmanly disposition.

Secondly, Because the Right of bearing the Person of them all, is given to him they make Soveraigne, by Covenant onely of one to another, and not of him to any of them; there can happen no breach of Covenant on the part of the Soveraigne; and consequently none of his Subjects, by any pretence of forfeiture, can be freed from his Subjection. That he which is made Soveraigne maketh no Covenant with his Subjects before-hand, is manifest; because either he must make it with the whole multitude, as one party to the Covenant; or he must make a severall Covenant with every man. With the whole, as one party, it is impossible; because as yet they are not one Person: and if he make so many severall Covenants as there be men, those Covenants after he hath the Soveraignty are voyd, because what act soever can be pretended by any one of them for breach thereof, is the act both of himselfe, and of all the rest, because done in the Person, and by the Right of every one of them in particular. Besides, if any one, or more of them, pretend a breach of the Covenant made by the Soveraigne at his Institution; and others, or one other of his Subjects, or himselfe alone, pretend there was no such breach, there is in this case, no Judge to decide the controversie: it returns therefore to the Sword again; and every man recovereth the right of Protecting himselfe by his own strength, contrary to the designe they had in the Institution. It is therefore in vain to grant Soveraignty by way of precedent Covenant. The opinion that any Monarch receiveth his Power by Covenant, that is to say on Condition, proceedeth from want of understanding this easie truth, that Covenants being but words, and breath, have no force to oblige, contain, constrain, or protect any man, but what it has from the publique Sword; that is, from the untyed hands of that Man, or Assembly of men that hath the Soveraignty, and whose actions are avouched by them all, and performed by the strength of them all, in him united.  But when an Assembly of men is made Soveraigne; then no man imagineth any such Covenant to have past in the Institution; for no man is so dull as to say, for example, the People of *Rome*, made a Covenant with the Romans, to hold the Soveraignty on such or such conditions; which not performed, the Romans might lawfully depose the Roman people.  That men see not the reason to be alike in a Monarchy, and in a Popular Government, proceedeth from the ambition of some, that are kinder to the government of an Assembly, whereof they may hope to participate, than of Monarchy, which they despair to enjoy.

Thirdly, because the major part hath by consenting voices declared a Soveraigne; he that dissented must now consent with the rest; that is, be contented to avow all the actions he shall do, or else justly be destroyed by the rest.  For if he voluntarily entered into the Congregation of them that were assembled, he sufficiently declared thereby his will (and therefore tacitely covenanted) to stand to what the major part should ordayne: and therefore if he refuse to stand thereto, or make Protestation against any of their Decrees, he does contrary to his Covenant, and therfore unjustly.  And whether he be of the Congregation, or not; and whether his consent be asked, or not, he must either submit to their decrees, or be left in the condition of warre he was in before; wherein he might without injustice be destroyed by any man whatsoever.

Fourthly, because every Subject is by this Institution Author of all the Actions, and Judgments of the Soveraigne Instituted; it followes, that whatsoever he doth, it can be no injury to any of his Subjects; nor ought he to be by any of them accused of Injustice.  For he that doth any thing by authority from another, doth therein no injury to him by whose authority he acteth: But by this Institution of a Common-wealth, every particular man is Author of all the Soveraigne doth; and consequently he that complaineth of injury from his Soveraigne, complaineth of that whereof he himselfe is Author; and therefore ought not to accuse any man but himselfe; no nor himselfe of injury; because to do injury to ones selfe, is impossible.  It is true that they that have Soveraigne power, may commit Iniquite; but not Injustice, or Injury in the proper signification.

Fiftly, and consequently to that which was sayd last, no man that hath Soveraigne power can iustly be put to death, or otherwise in any manner by his Subjects punished.  For seeing every Subject is Author of the actions of his Soveraigne; he punisheth another, for the actions committed by himselfe.

And because the End of this Institution, is the Peace and Defence of them all; and whosoever has right to the End, has right to the Means; it belongeth of Right, to whatsoever Man, or Assembly that hath the Soveraignty, to be Judge both of the meanes of Peace and Defence; and also of the hindrances, and disturbances of the same; and to do whatsoever he shall think necessary to be done, both before hand, for the preserving of Peace and Security, by prevention of Discord at home, and Hostility from abroad; and, when Peace and Security are lost, for the recovery of the same.

And therefore,

Sixtly, it is annexed to the Soveraignty, to be Judge of what Opinions and Doctrines are averse, and what conducing to Peace; and consequently, on what occasions, how farre, and what, men are to be trusted withall, in speaking to Multitudes of people; and who shall examine the Doctrines of all bookes before they be published. For the Actions of men proceed from their Opinions; and in the wel governing of Opinions, consisteth the well governing of mens Actions, in order to their Peace, and Concord. And though in matter of Doctrine, nothing ought to be regarded but the Truth; yet this is not repugnant to regulating of the same by Peace. For Doctrine repugnant to Peace, can no more be True, than Peace and Concord can be against the Law of Nature. It is true, that in a Common-wealth, where by the negligence, or unskilfullnesse of Governours, and Teachers, false Doctrines are by time generally received; the contrary Truths may be generally offensive: Yet the most sudden, and rough busling in of a new Truth, that can be, does never breake the Peace, but only somtimes awake the Warre. For those men that are so remissely governed, that they dare take up Armes, to defend, or introduce an Opinion, are still in Warre; and their condition not Peace, but only a Cessation of Armes for feare of one another; and they live as it were, in the procincts of battaile continually. It belongeth therefore to him that hath the Soveraign Power, to be Judge, or constitute all Judges of Opinions and Doctrines, as a thing necessary to Peace; therby to prevent Discord and Civill Warre.

Seventhly, is annexed to the Soveraigntie, the whole power of prescribing the Rules, whereby every man may know, what Goods he may enjoy, and what Actions he may doe, without being molested by any of his fellow Subjects: And this is it men call *Propriety*. For before constitution of Soveraign Power (as hath already been shewn) all men had right to all things; which necessarily causeth Warre: and therefore this Proprietie, being necessary to Peace, and depending on Soveraign Power, is the Act of that Power, in order to the publique peace. These Rules of Propriety (or *Meum* and *Tuum*) and of *Good, Evill, Lawfull*, and *Unlawfull* in the actions of Subjects, are the Civill Lawes; that is to say, the Lawes of each Commonwealth in particular; though the name of Civill Law be now restrained to the antient Civill Lawes of the City of *Rome*; which being the head of a great part of the World, her Lawes at that time were in these parts the Civill Law.

Eightly, is annexed to the Soveraigntie, the Right of Judicature; that is to say, of hearing and deciding all Controversies, which may arise concerning Law, either Civill, or Naturall, or concerning Fact. For without the decision of Controversies, there is no protection of

one Subject, against the injuries of another; the Lawes concerning
*Meum* and *Tuum* are in vaine; and to every man remaineth, from
the naturall and necessary appetite of his own conservation, the right
of protecting himselfe by his private strength, which is the condition
of Warre; and contrary to the end for which every Common-wealth
is instituted.

Ninthly, is annexed to the Soveraignty, the Right of making
Warre, and Peace with other Nations, and Common-wealths; that
is to say, of Judging when it is for the publique good, and how great
forces are to be assembled, armed, and payd for that end; and to
levy mony upon the Subjects, to defray the expences thereof. For
the Power by which the people are to be defended, consisteth in
their Armies; and the strength of an Army, in the union of their
strength under one Command; which Command the Soveraign
Instituted, therefore hath; because the command of the *Militia*,
without other Institution, maketh him that hath it Soveraign.
And therefore whosoever is made Generall of an Army, he that hath
the Soveraign Power is alwayes Generallissimo.

Tenthly, is annexed to the Soveraignty, the choosing of all
Counsellours, Ministers, Magistrates, and Officers, both in Peace,
and War. For seeing the Soveraign is charged with the End, which
is the common Peace and Defence; he is understood to have Power
to use such Means, as he shall think most fit for his discharge.

Eleventhly, to the Soveraign is committed the Power of Reward-
ing with riches, or honour; and of Punishing with corporall, or
pecuniary punishment, or with ignominy every Subject according
to the Law he hath formerly made; or if there be no Law made,
according as he shall judge most to conduce to the encouraging of
men to serve the Common-wealth, or deterring of them from doing
dis-service to the same.

Lastly, considering what values men are naturally apt to set upon
themselves; what respect they look for from others; and how little
they value other men; from whence continually arise amongst
them, Emulation, Quarrells, Factions, and at last Warre, to the
destroying of one another, and diminution of their strength against
a Common Enemy; It is necessary that there be Lawes of Honour,
and a publique rate of the worth of such men as have deserved, or
are able to deserve well of the Common-wealth; and that there be
force in the hands of some or others, to put those Lawes in execution.
But it hath already been shewn, that not onely the whole *Militia*,
or forces of the Common-wealth; but also the Judicature of all
Controversies, is annexed to the Soveraignty. To the Soveraign
therefore it belongeth also to give titles of Honour; and to appoint
what Order of place, and dignity, each man shall hold; and what
signes of respect, in publique or private meetings, they shall give
to one another.

These are the Rights, which make the Essence of Soveraignty;
and which are the markes, whereby a man may discern in what
Man, or Assembly of men, the Soveraign Power is placed, and

resideth. For these are incommunicable, and inseparable. The Power to coyn Mony; to dispose of the estate and persons of Infant heires; to have præemption in Markets; and all other Statute Prærogatives, may be transferred by the Soveraign; and yet the power to protect his subjects be retained. But if he transferre the *Militia*, he retains the Judicature in vain, for want of execution of the Lawes: Or if he grant away the Power of raising Mony; the *Militia* is in vain: or if he give away the government of Doctrines, men will be frighted into rebellion with the feare of Spirits. And so if we consider any one of the said Rights, we shall presently see, that the holding of all the rest, will produce no effect, in the conservation of Peace and Justice, the end for which all Commonwealths are Instituted. And this division is it, whereof it is said, *a Kingdome divided in it selfe, cannot stand*: for unlesse this division precede, division into opposite Armies can never happen. If there had not first been an opinion received of the greatest part of *England*, that these Powers were divided between the King and the Lords, and the House of Commons, the people had never been divided, and fallen into this Civill Warre; first between those that disagreed in Politiques; and after between the Dissenters about the liberty of Religion; which have so instructed men in this point of Soveraign Right, that there be few now (in *England*,) that do not see, that these Rights are inseparable, and will be so generally acknowledged, at the next return of Peace; and so continue, till their miseries are forgotten; and no longer, except the vulgar be better taught than they have hetherto been.

And because they are essentiall and inseparable Rights, it follows necessarily, that in whatsoever words any of them seem to be granted away, yet if the Soveraign Power it selfe be not in direct termes renounced, and the name of Soveraign no more given by the Grantees to him that Grants them, the Grant is voyd: for when he has granted all he can, if we grant back the Soveraignty, all is restored, as inseparably annexed thereunto.

This great Authority being Indivisible, and inseparably annexed to the Soveraignty, there is little ground for the opinion of them, that say of Soveraign Kings, though they be *singulis majores*, of greater Power than every one of their Subjects, yet they be *Universis minores*, of lesse power than them all together. For if by *all together*, they mean not the collective body as one person, then *all together*, and *every one*, signifie the same; and the speech is absurd. But if by *all together*, they understand them as one Person (which person the Soveraign bears,) then the power of all together, is the same with the Soveraigns power; and so again the speech is absurd: which absurdity they see well enough, when the Soveraignty is in an Assembly of the people; but in a Monarch they see it not; and yet the power of Soveraignty is the same in whomsoever it be placed.

And as the Power, so also the Honour of the Soveraign, ought to be greater, than that of any, or all the Subjects. For in the Soveraignty is the fountain of Honour. The dignities of Lord,

Earle, Duke, and Prince are his Creatures. As in the presence of
the Master, the Servants are equall, and without any honour at
all; So are the Subjects, in the presence of the Soveraign. And
though they shine some more, some lesse, when they are out of his
sight; yet in his presence, they shine no more than the Starres in
presence of the Sun.

But a man may here object, that the Condition of Subjects is
very miserable; as being obnoxious to the lusts, and other irregular
passions of him, or them that have so unlimited a Power in their
hands. And commonly they that live under a Monarch, think it
the fault of Monarchy; and they that live under the government of
Democracy, or other Soveraign Assembly, attribute all the inconvenience to that forme of Commonwealth; whereas the Power in
all formes, if they be perfect enough to protect them, is the same;
not considering that the estate of Man can never be without some
incommodity or other; and that the greatest, that in any forme of
Government can possibly happen to the people in generall, is scarce
sensible, in respect of the miseries, and horrible calamities, that
accompany a Civill Warre; or that dissolute condition of masterlesse men, without subjection to Lawes, and a coërcive Power to
tye their hands from rapine, and revenge: nor considering that
the greatest pressure of Soveraign Governours, proceedeth not
from any delight, or profit they can expect in the dammage, or
weakening of their Subjects, in whose vigor, consisteth their
own strength and glory; but in the restiveness of themselves, that
unwillingly contributing to their own defence, make it necessary
for their Governours to draw from them what they can in time of
Peace, that they may have means on any emergent occasion, or
sudden need, to resist, to take advantage on their Enemies. For
all men are by nature provided of notable multiplying glasses,
(that is their Passions and Selfe-love,) through which, every little
payment appeareth a great grievance; but are destitute of those
prospective glasses, (namely Morall and Civill Science,) to see a
farre off the miseries that hang over them, and cannot without such
payments be avoyded.

## CHAP. XIX

*Of the severall Kinds of* Common-wealth *by Institution, and of
Succession to the Soveraigne Power*

THE difference of Common-wealths, consisteth in the difference
of the Soveraign, or the Person representative of all and every one
of the Multitude. And because the Soveraignty is either in one
Man, or in an Assembly of more than one; and into that Assembly
either Every man hath right to enter, or not every one, but Certain
men distinguished from the rest; it is manifest, there can be but
Three kinds of Common-wealth. For the Representative must

needs be One man, or More: and if more, then it is the Assembly of All, or but of a Part.   When the Representative is One man, then is the Common-wealth a MONARCHY: when an Assembly of All that will come together, then it is a DEMOCRACY, or Popular Common-wealth: when an Assembly of a Part onely, then it is called an ARISTOCRACY.   Other kind of Common-wealth there can be none: for either One, or More, or All, must have the Soveraign Power (which I have shewn to be indivisible) entire.

There be other names of Government, in the Histories, and books of Policy; as *Tyranny*, and *Oligarchy*: But they are not the names of other Formes of Government, but of the same Formes misliked.   For they that are discontented under *Monarchy*, call it *Tyranny*; and they that are displeased with *Aristocracy*, called it *Oligarchy*: So also, they which find themselves grieved under a *Democracy*, call it *Anarchy*, (which signifies want of Government;) and yet I think no man believes, that want of Government, is any new kind of Government: nor by the same reason ought they to believe, that the Government is of one kind, when they like it, and another, when they mislike it, or are oppressed by the Governours.

It is manifest, that men who are in absolute liberty, may, if they please, give Authority to One man, to represent them every one; as well as give such Authority to any Assembly of men whatsoever; and consequently may subject themselves, if they think good, to a Monarch, as absolutely, as to any other Representative.   There-fore, where there is already erected a Soveraign Power, there can be no other Representative of the same people, but onely to certain particular ends, by the Soveraign limited.   For that were to erect two Soveraigns; and every man to have his person represented by two Actors, that by opposing one another, must needs divide that Power, which (if men will live in Peace) is indivisible; and thereby reduce the Multitude into the condition of Warre, contrary to the end for which all Soveraignty is instituted.   And therefore as it is absurd, to think that a Soveraign Assembly, inviting the People of their Dominion, to send up their Deputies, with power to make known their Advise, or Desires, should therefore hold such Deputies, rather than themselves, for the absolute Represen-tative of the people: so it is absurd also, to think the same in a Monarchy.   And I know not how this so manifest a truth, should of late be so little observed; that in a Monarchy, he that had the Soveraignty from a descent of 600 years, was alone called Soveraign, had the title of Majesty from every one of his Subjects, and was unquestionably taken by them for their King, was notwithstanding never considered as their Representative; that name without contradiction passing for the title of those men, which at his com-mand were sent up by the people to carry their Petitions, and give him (if he permitted it) their advise.   Which may serve as an admonition, for those that are the true, and absolute Representative of a People, to instruct men in the nature of that Office, and to take

heed how they admit of any other generall Representation upon
any occasion whatsoever, if they mean to discharge the trust
committed to them.

The difference between these three kindes of Commonwealth,
consisteth not in the difference of Power; but in the difference of
Convenience, or Aptitude to produce the Peace, and Security of
the people; for which end they were instituted. And to compare
Monarchy with the other two, we may observe; First, that whosoever beareth the Person of the people, or is one of that Assembly
that bears it, beareth also his own naturall Person. And though he
be carefull in his politique Person to procure the common interest;
yet he is more, or no lesse carefull to procure the private good of
himselfe, his family, kindred and friends; and for the most part,
if the publique interest chance to crosse the private, he preferrs
the private: for the Passions of men, are commonly more potent
than their Reason. From whence it follows, that where the publique
and private interest are most closely united, there is the publique
most advanced. Now in Monarchy, the private interest is the same
with the publique. The riches, power, and honour of a Monarch
arise onely from the riches, strength and reputation of his Subjects.
For no King can be rich, nor glorious, nor secure; whose Subjects
are either poore, or contemptible, or too weak through want or
dissention, to maintain a war against their enemies: Whereas
in a Democracy, or Aristocracy, the publique prosperity con-
ferres not so much to the private fortune of one that is corrupt, or
ambitious, as doth many times a perfidious advice, a treacherous
action, or a Civill warre.

Secondly, that a Monarch receiveth counsell of whom, when, and
where he pleaseth; and consequently may heare the opinion of men
versed in the matter about which he deliberates, of what rank or
quality soever, and as long before the time of action, and with as
much secrecy, as he will. But when a Soveraigne Assembly has
need of Counsell, none are admitted, but such as have a Right
thereto from the beginning; which for the most part are of those
who have beene versed more in the acquisition of Wealth than of
Knowledge; and are to give their advice in long discourses, which
may, and do commonly excite men to action, but not governe them
in it. For the *Understanding* is by the flame of the Passions, never
enlightned, but dazled: Nor is there any place, or time, wherein
an Assemblie can receive Counsell with secrecie, because of their
owne Multitude.

Thirdly, that the Resolutions of a Monarch, are subject to no
other Inconstancy, than that of Humane Nature; but in Assemblies,
besides that of Nature, there ariseth an Inconstancy from the
Number. For the absence of a few, that would have the Resolution
once taken, continue firme, (which may happen by security, negligence, or private impediments,) or the diligent appearance of a few
of the contrary opinion, undoes to day, all that was concluded
yesterday.

Fourthly, that a Monarch cannot disagree with himselfe, out of envy, or interest; but an Assembly may; and that to such a height, as may produce a Civill Warre:

Fifthly, that in Monarchy there is this inconvenience; that any Subject, by the power of one man, for the enriching of a favourite or flatterer, may be deprived of all he possesseth; which I confesse is a great and inevitable inconvenience. But the same may as well happen, where the Soveraigne Power is in an Assembly: For their power is the same; and they are as subject to evill Counsell, and to be seduced by Orators, as a Monarch by Flatterers; and becoming one an others Flatterers, serve one anothers Covetousnesse and Ambition by turnes. And whereas the Favorites of Monarchs, are few, and they have none els to advance but their owne Kindred; the Favorites of an Assembly, are many; and the Kindred much more numerous, than of any Monarch. Besides, there is no Favourite of a Monarch, which cannot as well succour his friends, as hurt his enemies: But Orators, that is to say, Favourites of Soveraigne Assemblies, though they have great power to hurt, have little to save. For to accuse, requires lesse Eloquence (such is mans Nature) than to excuse; and condemnation, than absolution more resembles Justice.

Sixtly, that it is an inconvenience in Monarchie, that the Soveraigntie may descend upon an Infant, or one that cannot discerne between Good and Evill: and consisteth in this, that the use of his Power, must be in the hand of another Man, or of some Assembly of men, which are to governe by his right, and in his name; as Curators, and Protectors of his Person, and Authority. But to say there is inconvenience, in putting the use of the Soveraign Power, into the hand of a Man, or an Assembly of men; is to say that all Government is more Inconvenient, than Confusion, and Civill Warre. And therefore all the danger that can be pretended, must arise from the Contention of those, that for an office of so great honour, and profit, may become Competitors. To make it appear, that this inconvenience, proceedeth not from that forme of Government we call Monarchy, we are to consider, that the precedent Monarch, hath appointed who shall have the Tuition of his Infant Successor, either expressely by Testament, or tacitly, by not controlling the Custome in that case received: And then such inconvenience (if it happen) is to be attributed, not to the Monarchy, but to the Ambition, and Injustice of the Subjects: which in all kinds of Government, where the people are not well instructed in their Duty, and the Rights of Soveraignty, is the same. Or else the precedent Monarch, hath not at all taken order for such Tuition; And then the Law of Nature hath provided this sufficient rule, That the Tuition shall be in him, that hath by Nature most interest in the preservation of the Authority of the Infant, and to whom least benefit can accrue by his death, or diminution. For seeing every man by nature seeketh his own benefit, and promotion; to put an Infant into the power of those, that can promote themselves, by his destruction, or dammage, is not Tuition, but Trechery. So that sufficient provision being taken, against all just quarrell, about the Government under a Child, if any contention arise to the disturbance of the publique Peace, it is not to be attributed to the forme of Monarchy, but to the ambition of Subjects, and ignorance of their Duty. On the other side, there is no great Common-wealth, the Soveraignty whereof is in a great Assembly, which is not, as to consultations of Peace, and Warre, and making of Lawes, in the same condition, as if the Government were in a Child. For as a Child wants the judgement to dissent from counsell given him, and is thereby necessitated to take the advise of them, or him, to whom he is committed: So an Assembly wanteth the liberty, to dissent from the counsell of the major part, be it good, or bad. And as a Child has need of a Tutor, or Protector, to preserve his Person, and Authority: So also (in great Common-wealths,) the Soveraign Assembly, in all great dangers and troubles, have need of *Custodes libertatis*; that is of Dictators, or Protectors of their Authoritie; which are as much as Temporary Monarchs; to whom for a time, they may commit the entire exercise of their Power; and have (at the end of that timē) been oftner deprived thereof, than Infant Kings, by their Protectors, Regents, or any other Tutors.

Though the Kinds of Soveraigntie be, as I have now shewn, but three; that is to say, Monarchie, where One Man has it; or Democracie, where the generall Assembly of Subjects hath it; or Aristocracie, where it is in an Assembly of certain persons nominated, or otherwise distinguished from the rest: Yet he that shall consider the particular Common-wealthes that have been, and are in the world, will not perhaps easily reduce them to three, and may thereby be inclined to think there be other Formes, arising from these mingled together. As for example, Elective King-domes; where Kings have the Soveraigne Power put into their hands for a time; or Kingdomes, wherein the King hath a power limited: which Governments, are nevertheles by most Writers called Monarchie. Likewise if a Popular, or Aristocraticall Common-wealth, subdue an Enemies Countrie, and govern the same, by a President, Procurator, or other Magistrate; this may seeme perhaps at first sight, to be a Democraticall, or Aristocraticall Government. But it is not so. For Elective Kings, are not Soveraignes, but Ministers of the Soveraigne; nor limited Kings Soveraignes, but Ministers of them that have the Soveraigne Power: Nor are those Provinces which are in subjection to a Democracie, or Aristocracie of another Common-wealth, Democratically, or Aristocratically governed, but Monarchically.

And first, concerning an Elective King, whose power is limited to his life, as it is in many places of Christendome at this day; or to certaine Yeares or Moneths, as the Dictators power amongst the Romans; If he have Right to appoint his Successor, he is no more Elective but Hereditary. But if he have no Power to elect his Successor, then there is some other Man, or Assembly known, which after his decease may elect a new, or else the Common-wealth dieth, and dissolveth with him, and returneth to the condition of Warre. If it be known who have the power to give the Soveraigntie after his death, it is known also that the Soveraigntie was in them before: For none have right to give that which they have not right to possesse, and keep to themselves, if they think good. But if there be none that can give the Soveraigntie, after the decease of him that was first elected; then has he power, nay he is obliged by the Law of Nature, to provide, by establishing his Successor, to keep those that had trusted him with the Government, from relapsing into the miserable condition of Civill warre. And consequently he was, when elected, a Soveraign absolute.

Secondly, that King whose power is limited, is not superior to. him, or them that have the power to limit it; and he that is not superiour, is not supreme; that is to say not Soveraign. The Soveraignty therefore was alwaies in that Assembly which had the Right to Limit him; and by consequence the government not Monarchy, but either Democracy, or Aristocracy; as of old time in *Sparta*; where the Kings had a priviledge to lead their Armies; but the Soveraignty was in the *Ephori*.

Thirdly, whereas heretofore the Roman People, governed the land of *Judea* (for example) by a President; yet was not *Judea* therefore a Democracy; because they were not governed by any Assembly, into the which, any of them, had right to enter; nor by an Aristocracy; because they were not governed by any Assembly, into which, any man could enter by their Election: but they were governed by one Person, which though as to the people of *Rome* was an Assembly of the people, or Democracy; yet as to people of *Judea*, which had no right at all of participating in the government, was a Monarch. For though where the people are governed by an Assembly, chosen by themselves out of their own number, the government is called a Democracy, or Aristocracy; yet when they are governed by an Assembly, not of their own choosing, 'tis a Monarchy; not of *One* man, over another man; but of one people, over another people.

Of all these Formes of Government, the matter being mortall, so that not onely Monarchs, but also whole Assemblies dy, it is necessary for the conservation of the peace of men, that as there was order taken for an Artificiall Man, so there be order also taken, for an Artificiall Eternity of life; without which, men that are governed by an Assembly, should return into the condition of Warre in every age; and they that are governed by One man, as soon as their Governour dyeth. This Artificiall Eternity, is that which men call the Right of *Succession*.

There is no perfect forme of Government, where the disposing of the Succession is not in the present Soveraign. For if it be in any other particular Man, or private Assembly, it is in a person subject, and may be assumed by the Soveraign at his pleasure; and consequently the Right is in himselfe. And if it be in no particular man, but left to a new choyce; then is the Common-wealth dissolved; and the Right is in him that can get it; contrary to the intention of them that did Institute the Common-wealth, for their perpetuall, and not temporary security.

In a Democracy, the whole Assembly cannot faile, unlesse the Multitude that are to be governed faile. And therefore questions of the right of Succession, have in that forme of Government no place at all.

In an Aristocracy, when any of the Assembly dyeth, the election of another into his room belongeth to the Assembly, as the Soveraign, to whom belongeth the choosing of all Counsellours, and Officers. For that which the Representative doth, as Actor, every one of the Subjects doth, as Author. And though the Soveraign Assembly, may give Power to others, to elect new men, for supply of their court; yet it is still by their Authority, that the Election is made; and by the same it may (when the publique shall require it) be recalled.

The greatest difficultie about the right of Succession, is in Monarchy: And the difficulty ariseth from this, that at first sight, it is not manifest who is to appoint the Successor; nor many times, who it is whom he hath appointed. For in both these cases, there is required a more exact ratiocination, than every man is accustomed to use. As to the question, who shall appoint the Successor, of a Monarch that hath the Soveraign Authority; that is to say, who shall determine of the right of Inheritance, (for Elective Kings and Princes have not the Soveraign Power in propriety, but in use only,) we are to consider, that either he that is in possession, has right to dispose of the Succession, or else that right is again in the dissolved Multitude. For the death of him that hath the Soveraign power in propriety, leaves the Multitude without any Soveraign at all; that is, without any Representative in whom they should be united, and be capable of doing any one action at all: And therefore they are incapable of Election of any new Monarch; every man having equall right to submit himselfe to such as he thinks best able to protect him; or if he can, protect himselfe by his owne sword, which is a returne to Confusion, and to the condition of a War of every man against every man, contrary to the end for which Monarchy had its first Institution. Therfore it is manifest, that by the Institution of Monarchy, the disposing of the Successor, is alwaies left to the Judgment and Will of the present Possessor.

And for the question (which may arise sometimes) who it is that the Monarch in possession, hath designed to the succession and inheritance of his power; it is determined by his expresse Words, and Testament; or by other tacite signes sufficient.

By expresse Words, or Testament, when it is declared by him in his life time, *viva voce*, or by Writing; as the first Emperours of *Rome* declared who should be their Heires. For the word Heire does not of it selfe imply the Children, or nearest Kindred of a man; but whomsoever a man shall any way declare, he would have to

succeed him in his Estate.   If therefore a Monarch declare expresly,
that such a man shall be his Heire, either by Word or Writing, then
is that man immediatly after the decease of his Predecessor,
Invested in the right of being Monarch.

But where Testament, and expresse Words are wanting, other
naturall signes of the Will are to be followed: whereof the one is
Custome.   And therefore where the Custome is, that the next of
Kindred absolutely succeedeth, there also the next of Kindred hath
right to the Succession;  for that, if the will of him that was in
posession had been otherwise, he might easily have declared the
same in his life time.   And likewise where the Custome is, that the
next of the Male Kindred succeedeth, there also the right of Succession is in the next of the Kindred Male, for the same reason.
And so it is if the Custome were to advance the Female.   For whatsoever Custome a man may by a word controule, and does not,
it is a naturall signe he would have that Custome stand.

But where neither Custome, nor Testament hath preceded, there
it is to be understood, First, that a Monarchs will is, that the government remain Monarchicall;   because he hath approved that
government, in himselfe.   Secondly, that a Child of his own, Male,
or Female, be preferred before any other;  because men are presumed
to be more enclined by nature, to advance their own children, than
the children of other men;  and of their own, rather a Male than a
Female;  because men, are naturally fitter than women, for actions
of labour and danger.   Thirdly, where his own Issue faileth, rather
a Brother than a stranger;  and so still the neerer in bloud, rather
than the more remote;  because it is alwayes presumed that the
neerer of kin, is the neerer in affection;  and 'tis evident that a man
receives alwayes, by reflexion, the most honour from the greatnesse
of his neerest kindred.

But if it be lawful for a Monarch to dispose of the Succession by
words of Contract, or Testament, men may perhaps object a great
inconvenience: for he may sell, or give his Right of governing to a
stranger;  which, because strangers (that is, men not used to live
under the same government, nor speaking the same language) do
commonly undervalue one another, may turn to the oppression of
his Subjects;  which is indeed a great inconvenience: but it proceedeth not necessarily from the subjection to a strangers government, but from the unskilfulnesse of the Governours, ignorant of
the true rules of Politiques.   And therefore the Romans when they
had subdued many Nations, to make their Government digestible,
were wont to take away that grievance, as much as they thought
necessary, by giving sometimes to whole Nations, and sometimes
to Principall men of every Nation they conquered, not onely the
Privileges, but also the Name of Romans;  and took many of them
into the Senate, and Offices of charge, even in the Roman City.
And this was it our most wise King, King *James*, aymed at, in
endeavouring the Union of his two Realms of *England* and *Scotland*.
Which if he could have obtained, had in all likelihood prevented

the Civill warres, which make both those Kingdomes, at this present, miserable. It is not therefore any injury to the people, for a Monarch to dispose of the Succession by Will; though by the fault of many Princes, it hath been sometimes found inconvenient. Of the lawfulnesse of it, this also is an argument, that whatsoever inconvenience can arrive by giving a Kingdome to a stranger, may arrive also by so marrying with strangers, as the Right of Succession may descend upon them: yet this by all men is accounted lawfull.

## CHAP. XX

### *Of Dominion* PATERNALL, *and* DESPOTICALL

A *Common-wealth by Acquisition*, is that, where the Soveraign Power is acquired by Force; And it is acquired by force, when men singly, or many together by plurality of voyces, for fear of death, or bonds, do authorise all the actions of that Man, or Assembly, that hath their lives and liberty in his Power.

And this kind of Dominion, or Soveraignty, differeth from Soveraignty by Institution, onely in this, That men who choose their Soveraign, do it for fear of one another, and not of him whom they Institute: But in this case, they subject themselves, to him they are afraid of. In both cases they do it for fear: which is to be noted by them, that hold all such Covenants, as proceed from fear of death, or violence, voyd: which if it were true, no man, in any kind of Common-wealth, could be obliged to Obedience. It is true, that in a Common-wealth once Instituted, or acquired, Promises proceeding from fear of death, or violence, are no Covenants, nor obliging, when the thing promised is contrary to the Lawes; But the reason is not, because it was made upon fear, but because he that promiseth, hath no right in the thing promised. Also, when he may lawfully performe, and doth not, it is not the Invalidity of the Covenant, that absolveth him, but the Sentence of the Soveraign. Otherwise, whensoever a man lawfully promiseth, he unlawfully breaketh: But when the Soveraign, who is the Actor, acquitteth him, then he is acquitted by him that extorted the promise, as by the Author of such absolution.

But the Rights, and Consequences of Soveraignty, are the same in both. His Power cannot, without his consent, be transferred to another: He cannot Forfeit it: He cannot be Accused by any of his Subjects, of Injury: He cannot be Punished by them: He is Judge of what is necessary for Peace; and Judge of Doctrines: He is Sole Legislator; and Supreme Judge of Controversies; and of the times, and Occasions of Warre, and Peace: to him it belongeth to choose Magistrates, Counsellours, Commanders, and all other Officers, and Ministers; and to determine of Rewards, and Punishments, Honour, and Order. The reasons whereof, are

the same which are alledged in the precedent Chapter, for the same
Rights, and Consequences of Soveraignty by Institution.

Dominion is acquired two wayes; By Generation, and by Conquest. The right of Dominion by Generation, is that, which the
Parent hath over his Children; and is called PATERNALL. And is
not so derived from the Generation, as if therefore the Parent had
Dominion over his Child because he begat him; but from the Childs
Consent, either expresse, or by other sufficient arguments declared.
For as to the Generation, God hath ordained to man a helper; and
there be alwayes two that are equally Parents: the Dominion
therefore over the Child, should belong equally to both; and he be
equally subject to both, which is impossible; for no man can obey
two Masters. And whereas some have attributed the Dominion
to the Man onely, as being of the more excellent Sex; they mis-
reckon in it. For there is not alwayes that difference of strength,
or prudence between the man and the woman, as that the right
can be determined without War. In Common-wealths, this controversie is decided by the Civill Law: and for the most part, (but
not alwayes) the sentence is in favour of the Father; because for
the most part Common-wealths have been erected by the Fathers,
not by the Mothers of families. But the question lyeth now in
the state of meer Nature; where there are supposed no lawes of
Matrimony; no lawes for the Education of Children; but the Law
of Nature, and the naturall inclination of the Sexes, one to another,
and to their children. In this condition of meer Nature, either the
Parents between themselves dispose of the dominion over the Child
by Contract; or do not dispose thereof at all. If they dispose
thereof, the right passeth according to the Contract. We find in
History that the *Amazons* Contracted with the Men of the neighbouring Countries, to whom they had recourse for issue, that the
issue Male should be sent back, but the Female remain with themselves: so that the dominion of the Females was in the Mother.

If there be no Contract, the Dominion is in the Mother. For in
the condition of meer Nature, where there are no Matrimoniall
lawes, it cannot be known who is the Father, unlesse it be declared
by the Mother: and therefore the right of Dominion over the Child
dependeth on her will, and is consequently hers. Again, seeing
the Infant is first in the power of the Mother, so as she may either
nourish, or expose it; if she nourish it, it oweth its life to the
Mother; and is therefore obliged to obey her, rather than any
other; and by consequence the Dominion over it is hers. But if
she expose it, and another find, and nourish it, the Dominion is in
him that nourisheth it. For it ought to obey him by whom it is
preserved; because preservation of life being the end, for which
one man becomes subject to another, every man is supposed to
promise obedience, to him, in whose power it is to save, or destroy
him.

If the Mother be the Fathers subject, the Child, is in the Fathers
power: and if the Father be the Mothers subject, (as when a Sove-

raign Queen marrieth one of her subjects,) the Child is subject to the Mother; because the Father also is her subject.

If a man and a woman, Monarches of two severall Kingdomes, have a Child, and contract concerning who shall have the Dominion of him, the Right of the Dominion passeth by the Contract. If they contract not, the Dominion followeth the Dominion of the place of his residence. For the Soveraign of each Country hath Dominion over all that reside therein.

He that hath the Dominion over the Child, hath Dominion also over the Children of the Child; and over their Childrens Children. For he that hath Dominion over the person of a man, hath Dominion over all that is his; without which, Dominion were but a Title, without the effect.

The Right of Succession to Paternall Dominion, proceedeth in the same manner, as doth the Right of Succession to Monarchy; of which I have already sufficiently spoken in the precedent chapter.

Dominion acquired by Conquest, or Victory in war, is that which some Writers call DESPOTICALL, from Δεσπότης which signifieth a *Lord*, or *Master*; and is the Dominion of the Master over his Servant. And this Dominion is then acquired to the Victor, when the Vanquished, to avoyd the present stroke of death, covenanteth either in expresse words, or by other sufficient signes of the Will, that so long as his life, and the liberty of his body is allowed him, the Victor shall have the use thereof, at his pleasure. And after such Covenant made, the Vanquished is a SERVANT, and not before: for by the word *Servant* (whether it be derived from *Servire*, to Serve, or from *Servare*, to Save, which I leave to Grammarians to dispute) is not meant a Captive, which is kept in prison, or bonds, till the owner of him that took him, or bought him of one that did, shall consider what to do with him: (for such men, (commonly called Slaves,) have no obligation at all; but may break their bonds, or the prison; and kill, or carry away captive their Master, justly:) but one, that being taken, hath corporall liberty allowed him; and upon promise not to run away, nor to do violence to his Master, is trusted by him.

It is not therefore the Victory, that giveth the right of Dominion over the Vanquished, but his own Covenant. Nor is he obliged because he is Conquered; that is to say, beaten, and taken, or put to flight; but because he commeth in, and Submitteth to the Victor; Nor is the Victor obliged by an enemies rendring him-selfe, (without promise of life,) to spare him for this his yeelding to discretion; which obliges not the Victor longer, than in his own discretion hee shall think fit.

And that which men do, when they demand (as it is now called) *Quarter*, (which the Greeks called Ζωγρία, *taking alive*,) is to evade the present fury of the Victor, by Submission, and to compound for their life, with Ransome, or Service: and therefore he that hath Quarter hath not his life given, but deferred till farther deliberation; For it is not an yeelding on condition of life, but to discretion. And then onely is his life in security, and his service due, when the Victor hath trusted him with his corporall liberty. For Slaves that work in Prisons, or Fetters, do it not of duty, but to avoyd the cruelty of their task-masters.

The Master of the Servant, is Master also of all he hath; and may exact the use thereof; that is to say, of his goods, of his labour, of his servants, and of his children, as often as he shall think fit. For he holdeth his life of his Master, by the covenant of obedience; that is, of owning, and authorising whatsoever the Master shall do. And in case the Master, if he refuse, kill him, or cast him into bonds, or otherwise punish him for his disobedience, he is himselfe the author of the same; and cannot accuse him of injury.

In summe, the Rights and Consequences of both *Paternall* and *Despoticall* Dominion, are the very same with those of a Soveraign by Institution; and for the same reasons: which reasons are set down in the precedent chapter. So that for a man that is Monarch of divers Nations, whereof he hath, in one the Soveraignty by Institution of the people assembled, and in another by Conquest, that is by the submission of each particular, to avoyd death or bonds; to demand of one Nation more than of the other, from the title of Conquest, as being a Conquered Nation, is an act of ignorance of the Rights of Soveraignty. For the Soveraign is absolute over both alike; or else there is no Soveraignty at all; and so every man may Lawfully protect himselfe, if he can, with his own sword, which is the condition of war.

By this it appears, that a great Family if it be not part of some Common-wealth, is of it self, as to the Rights of Soveraignty, a little Monarchy; whether that Family consist of a man and his children; or of a man and his servants; or of a man, and his children, and servants together: wherein the Father or Master is the Soveraign. But yet a Family is not properly a Common-wealth; unlesse it be of that power by its own number, or by other opportunities, as not to be subdued without the hazard of war. For where a number of men are manifestly too weak to defend themselves united, every one may use his own reason in time of danger, to save his own life, either by flight, or by submission to the enemy, as hee shall think best; in the same manner as a very small company of souldiers, surprised by an army, may cast down their armes, and demand quarter, or run away, rather than be put to the sword. And thus much shall suffice; concerning what I find by speculation, and deduction, of Soveraign Rights, from the nature, need, and designes of men, in erecting of Common-wealths, and putting themselves under Monarchs or Assemblies, entrusted with power enough for their protection.

Let us now consider what the Scripture teacheth in the same point. To *Moses*, the children of *Israel* say thus. [1]*Speak thou to us, and we will heare thee ; but let not God speak to us, lest we dye.* This is absolute obedience to *Moses*. Concerning the Right of

[1] Exod. 20. 19.

Kings, God himself by the mouth of *Samuel*, saith, ¹ *This shall be the Right of the King you will have to reigne over you.* He shall take *your sons, and set them to drive his Chariots, and to be his horsemen, and to run before his chariots ; and gather in his harvest ; and to make his engines of War, and Instruments of his chariots ; and shall take your daughters to make perfumes, to be his Cookes, and Bakers.* He *shall take your fields, your vine-yards, and your olive-yards, and give them to his servants.* He shall take the tyth of your corne and wine, *and give it to the men of his chamber, and to his other servants.* He *shall take your man-servants, and your maid-servants, and the choice of your youth, and employ them in his businesse.* He shall take the *tyth of your flocks ; and you shall be his servants.* This is absolute power, and summed up in the last words, *you shall be his servants.* Againe, when the people heard what power their King was to have, yet they consented thereto, and say thus, ² *We will be as all other nations, and our King shall judge our causes, and goe before us, to conduct our wars.* Here is confirmed the Right that Soveraigns have, both to the *Militia,* and to all *Judicature*; in which is conteined as absolute power, as one man can possibly transferre to another. Again, the prayer of King *Salomon* to God, was this. ³ *Give to thy servant understanding, to judge thy people, and to discerne between Good and Evill.* It belongeth therefore to the Soveraigne to bee *Judge,* and to præscribe the Rules of *discerning Good and Evill*: which Rules are Lawes; and therefore in him is the Legislative Power. *Saul* sought the life of *David*; yet when it was in his power to slay *Saul,* and his Servants would have done it, *David* forbad them, saying, ⁴ *God forbid I should do such an act against my Lord, the anoynted of God.* For obedience of servants St. *Paul* saith, ⁵ *Servants obey your masters in All things*; and, ⁶ *Children obey your Parents in All things.* There is simple obedience in those that are subject to Paternall or Despoticall Dominion. Again, ⁷ *The Scribes and Pharisees sit in Moses chayre, and therefore All that they shall bid you observe, that observe and do.* There again is simple obedience. And St. *Paul,* ⁸ *Warn them that they subject themselves to Princes, and to those that are in Authority, & obey them.* This obedience is also simple. Lastly, our Saviour himselfe acknowledges, that men ought to pay such taxes as are by Kings imposed, where he sayes, *Give to Cæsar that which is Cæsars*; and payed such taxes himselfe. And that the Kings word, is sufficient to take any thing from any Subject, when there is need; and that the King is Judge of that need: For he himselfe, as King of the Jewes, commanded his Disciples to take the Asse, and Asses Colt to carry him into *Jerusalem,* saying, ⁹ *Go into the Village over against you, and you shall find a shee Asse tyed, and her Colt with her, unty them, and bring them to me. And if any man ask you, what you mean by it, Say the Lord hath need of them : And they will let them go.* They

---

¹ 1 Sam. 8. 11, 12, &c.　　² Verse 19, &c.　　⁸ 1 Kings 3. 9.
⁴ 1 Sam. 24. 9.　　⁵ Coll. 3. 20.　　⁶ Verse 22.
⁷ Math. 23. 2, 3.　　⁸ Tit. 3. 2.　　⁹ Mat. 21. 2, 3.

will not ask whether his necessity be a sufficient title; nor whether he be judge of that necessity; but acquiesce in the will of the Lord.

To these places may be added also that of *Genesis*, [1] *You shall be as Gods, knowing Good and Evill.* And verse 11. *Who told thee that thou wast naked ? hast thou eaten of the tree, of which I commanded thee thou shouldest not eat ?* For the Cognisance or Judicature of *Good* and *Evill*, being forbidden by the name of the fruit of the tree of Knowledge, as a triall of *Adams* obedience; The Divel to enflame the Ambition of the woman, to whom that fruit already seemed beautifull, told her that by tasting it, they should be as Gods, knowing *Good* and *Evill*. Whereupon having both eaten, they did indeed take upon them Gods office, which is Judicature of Good and Evill; but acquired no new ability to distinguish between them aright. And whereas it is sayd, that having eaten, they saw they were naked; no man hath so interpreted that place, as if they had been formerly blind, and saw not their own skins: the meaning is plain, that it was then they first judged their nakednesse (wherein it was Gods will to create them) to be uncomely; and by being ashamed, did tacitely censure God himselfe. And thereupon God saith, *Hast thou eaten, &c.* as if he should say, doest thou that owest me obedience, take upon thee to judge of my Commandements? Whereby it is cleerly, (though Allegorically,) signified, that the Commands of them that have the right to command, are not by their Subjects to be censured, nor disputed.

So that it appeareth plainly, to my understanding, both from Reason, and Scripture, that the Soveraign Power, whether placed in One Man, as in Monarchy, or in one Assembly of men, as in Popular, and Aristocraticall Common-wealths, is as great, as possibly men can be imagined to make it. And though of so unlimited a Power, men may fancy many evill consequences, yet the consequences of the want of it, which is perpetuall warre of every man against his neighbour, are much worse. The condition of man in this life shall never be without Inconveniences; but there happeneth in no Common-wealth any great Inconvenience, but what proceeds from the Subjects disobedience, and breach of those Covenants, from which the Common-wealth hath its being. And whosoever thinking Soveraign Power too great, will seek to make it lesse; must subject himselfe, to the Power, that can limit it; that is to say, to a greater.

The greatest objection is, that of the Practise; when men ask, where, and when, such Power has by Subjects been acknowledged. But one may ask them again, when, or where has there been a Kingdome long free from Sedition and Civill Warre. In those Nations, whose Common-wealths have been long-lived, and not been destroyed, but by forraign warre, the Subjects never did dispute of the Soveraign Power. But howsoever, an argument from the Practise of men, that have not sifted to the bottom, and with exact reason weighed the causes, and nature of Common-wealths, and

[1] Gen. 3. 5.

suffer daily those miseries, that proceed from the ignorance thereof, is invalid. For though in all places of the world, men should lay the foundation of their houses on the sand, it could not thence be inferred, that so it ought to be. The skill of making, and maintaining Common-wealths, consisteth in certain Rules, as doth Arithmetique and Geometry; not (as Tennis-play) on Practise onely: which Rules, neither poor men have the leisure, nor men that have had the leisure, have hitherto had the curiosity, or the method to find out.

## CHAP. XXI

### Of the LIBERTY of Subjects

LIBERTY, or FREEDOME, signifieth (properly) the absence of Opposition; (by Opposition, I mean externall Impediments of motion;) and may be applyed no lesse to Irrationall, and Inanimate creatures, than to Rationall. For whatsoever is so tyed, or environed, as it cannot move, but within a certain space, which space is determined by the opposition of some externall body, we say it hath not Liberty to go further. And so of all living creatures, whilest they are imprisoned, or restrained, with walls, or chayns; and of the water whilest it is kept in by banks, or vessels, that otherwise would spread it selfe into a larger space, we use to say, they are not at Liberty, to move in such manner, as without those externall impediments they would. But when the impediment of motion, is in the constitution of the thing it selfe, we use not to say, it wants the Liberty; but the Power to move; as when a stone lyeth still, or a man is fastned to his bed by sicknesse.

And according to this proper, and generally received meaning of the word, *A FREE-MAN, is he, that in those things, which by his strength and wit he is able to do, is not hindred to doe what he has a will to.* But when the words *Free*, and *Liberty*, are applyed to any thing but *Bodies*, they are abused; for that which is not subject to Motion, is not subject to Impediment: And therefore, when 'tis said (for example) The way is Free, no Liberty of the way is signified, but of those that walk in it without stop. And when we say a Guift is Free, there is not meant any Liberty of the Guift, but of the Giver, that was not bound by any law, or Covenant to give it. So when we *speak Freely*, it is not the Liberty of voice, or pronunciation, but of the man, whom no law hath obliged to speak otherwise then he did. Lastly, from the use of the word *Free-Will*, no Liberty can be inferred of the will, desire, or inclination, but the Liberty of the man; which consisteth in this, that he finds no stop, in doing what he has the will, desire, or inclination to doe.

Feare, and Liberty are consistent; as when a man throweth his goods into the Sea for *feare* the ship should sink, he doth it neverthelesse very willingly, and may refuse to doe it if he will: It is therefore the action, of one that was *free*: so a man sometimes pays his debt, only for *feare* of Imprisonment, which because no body hindred him from detaining, was the action of a man at *liberty*. And generally all actions which men doe in Common-wealths, for *feare* of the law, are actions, which the doers had *liberty* to omit.

*Liberty* and *Necessity* are consistent: As in the water, that hath not only *liberty*, but a *necessity* of descending by the Channel; so likewise in the Actions which men voluntarily doe: which, because they proceed from their will, proceed from *liberty*; and yet, because every act of mans will, and every desire, and inclination proceedeth from some cause, and that from another cause, in a continuall chaine, (whose first link is in the hand of God the first of all causes,) they proceed from *necessity*. So that to him that could see the connexion of those causes, the *necessity* of all mens voluntary actions, would appeare manifest. And therefore God, that seeth, and disposeth all things, seeth also that the *liberty* of man in doing what he will, is accompanied with the *necessity* of doing that which God will, & no more, nor lesse. For though men may do many things, which God does not command, nor is therefore Author of them; yet they can have no passion nor appetite to any thing, of which appetite Gods will is not the cause. And did not his will assure the *necessity* of mans will, and consequently of all that on mans will dependeth, the *liberty* of men would be a contradiction, and impediment to the omnipotence and *liberty* of God. And this shall suffice, (as to the matter in hand) of that natural *liberty*, which only is properly called *liberty*.

But as men, for the atteyning of peace, and conservation of themselves thereby, have made an Artificiall Man, which we call a Common-wealth; so also have they made Artificial Chains, called *Civill Lawes*, which they themselves, by mutuall covenants, have fastned at one end, to the lips of that Man, or Assembly, to whom they have given the Soveraigne Power; and at the other end to their own Ears. These Bonds in their own nature but weak, may neverthelesse be made to hold, by the danger, though not by the difficulty of breaking them.

In relation to these Bonds only it is, that I am to speak now, of the *Liberty* of *Subjects*. For seeing there is no Common-wealth in the world, wherein there be Rules enough set down, for the regulating of all the actions, and words of men, (as being a thing impossible:) it followeth necessarily, that in all kinds of actions, by the laws prætermitted, men have the Liberty, of doing what their own reasons shall suggest, for the most profitable to themselves. For if wee take Liberty in the proper sense, for corporall Liberty; that is to say, freedome from chains, and prison, it were very absurd for men to clamor as they doe, for the Liberty they so manifestly enjoy. Againe, if we take Liberty, for an exemption from Lawes, it is no lesse absurd, for men to demand as they doe, that Liberty, by which all other men may be masters of their lives. And yet as absurd as it is, this is it they demand; not knowing that the Lawes are of no power to protect them, without a Sword in the hands of a man, or men, to cause those laws to be put in execution. The Liberty of a Subject, lyeth therefore only in those things, which in regulating their actions, the Soveraign hath prætermitted: such as is the Liberty to buy, and sell, and otherwise contract with one another; to choose their own aboad, their own diet, their own trade of life, and institute their children as they themselves think fit; & the like.

Neverthelesse we are not to understand, that by such Liberty, the Soveraign Power of life, and death, is either abolished, or limited. For it has been already shewn, that nothing the Soveraign Representative can doe to a Subject, on what pretence soever, can properly be called Injustice, or Injury; because every Subject is Author of every act the Soveraign doth; so that he never wanteth Right to any thing, otherwise, than as he himself is the Subject of God, and bound thereby to observe the laws of Nature. And therefore it may, and doth often happen in Common-wealths, that a Subject may be put to death, by the command of the Soveraign Power; and yet neither doe the other wrong: As when *Jeptha* caused his daughter to be sacrificed: In which, and the like cases, he that so dieth, had Liberty to doe the action, for which he is neverthelesse, without Injury put to death. And the same holdeth also in a Soveraign Prince, that putteth to death an Innocent Subject. For though the action be against the law of Nature, as being contrary to Equitie, (as was the killing of *Uriah*, by *David*;) yet it was not an Injurie to *Uriah*; but to *God*. Not to *Uriah*, because the right to doe what he pleased, was given him by *Uriah* himself: And yet to *God*, because *David* was *Gods* Subject; and prohibited all Iniquitie by the law of Nature. Which distinction, *David* himself, when he repented the fact, evidently confirmed, saying, *To thee only have I sinned*. In the same manner, the people of *Athens*, when they banished the most potent of their Common-wealth for ten years, thought they committed no Injustice; and yet they never questioned what crime he had done; but what hurt he would doe: Nay they commanded the banishment of they knew not whom; and every Citizen bringing his Oystershell into the market place, written with the name of him he desired should be banished, without actuall accusing him, sometimes banished an *Aristides*, for his reputation of Justice; And sometimes a scurrilous Jester, as *Hyperbolous*, to make a Jest of it. And yet a man cannot say, the Soveraign People of *Athens* wanted right to banish them; or an *Athenian* the Libertie to Jest, or to be Just.

The Libertie, whereof there is so frequent, and honourable mention, in the Histories, and Philosophy of the Antient Greeks, and Romans, and in the writings, and discourse of those that from them have received all their learning in the Politiques, is not the Libertie of Particular men; but the Libertie of the Common-wealth: which is the same with that, which every man then should have, if there were no Civil Laws, nor Common-wealth at all. And the effects of it also be the same. For as amongst masterlesse men, there is perpetuall war, of every man against his neighbour; no inheritance, to transmit to the Son, nor to expect from the Father; no propriety of Goods, or Lands; no security; but a full and absolute Libertie in every Particular man: So in States, and Common-wealths not dependent on one another, every Common-wealth, (not every man) has an absolute Libertie, to doe what it shall judge (that is to say, what that Man, or Assemblie that representeth it, shall judge) most conducing to their benefit. But withall, they live in the condition of a perpetuall war, and upon the confines of battel, with their frontiers armed, and canons planted against their neighbours round about. The *Athenians*, and *Romanes* were free; that is, free Common-wealths: not that any particular men had the Libertie to resist their own Representative; but that their Representative had the Libertie to resist, or invade other people. There is written on the Turrets of the city of *Luca* in great characters at this day, the word *LIBERTAS*; yet no man can thence inferre, that a particular man has more Libertie, or Immunitie from the service of the Commonwealth there, than in *Constantinople*. Whether a Common-wealth be Monarchicall, or Popular, the Freedome is still the same.

But it is an easy thing, for men to be deceived, by the specious name of Libertie; and for want of Judgement to distinguish, mistake that for their Private Inheritance, and Birth right, which is the right of the Publique only. And when the same errour is confirmed by the authority of men in reputation for their writings in this subject, it is no wonder if it produce sedition, and change of Government. In these westerne parts of the world, we are made to receive our opinions concerning the Institution, and Rights of Common-wealths, from *Aristotle*, *Cicero*, and other men, Greeks and Romanes, that living under Popular States, derived those Rights, not from the Principles of Nature, but transcribed them into their books, out of the Practise of their own Common-wealths, which were Popular; as the Grammarians describe the Rules of Language, out of the Practise of the time; or the Rules of Poetry, out of the Poems of *Homer* and *Virgil*. And because the Athenians were taught, (to keep them from desire of changing their Government,) that they were Freemen, and all that lived under Monarchy were slaves; therefore *Aristotle* puts it down in his *Politiques*, (lib. 6. cap. 2.) *In democracy, Liberty is to be supposed: for 'tis commonly held, that no man is Free in any other Government.* And as *Aristotle*; so *Cicero*, and other Writers have grounded their Civill doctrine, on the opinions of the Romans, who were taught to hate Monarchy, at first, by them that having deposed their Soveraign, shared amongst them the Soveraignty of *Rome*; and afterwards by their Successors. And by reading of these Greek, and Latine Authors, men from their childhood have gotten a habit (under a false shew of Liberty,) of favouring tumults, and of licentious controlling the actions of their Soveraigns; and again of controlling those controllers, with the effusion of so much blood; as I think I may truly say, there was never any thing so deerly bought, as these Western parts have bought the learning of the Greek and Latine tongues.

To come now to the particulars of the true Liberty of a Subject; that is to say, what are the things, which though commanded by the Soveraign, he may nevertheless, without Injustice, refuse to do; we are to consider, what Rights we passe away, when we make a Common-wealth; or (which is all one,) what Liberty we deny our selves, by owning all the Actions (without exception) of the Man, or Assembly we make our Soveraign. For in the act of our *Submission,* consisteth both our *Obligation,* and our *Liberty*; which must therefore be inferred by arguments taken from thence; there being no Obligation on any man, which ariseth not from some Act of his own; for all men equally, are by Nature Free. And because such arguments, must either be drawn from the expresse words, *I Authorise all his Actions,* or from the Intention of him that submitteth himselfe to his Power, (which Intention is to be understood by the End for which he so submitteth;) The Obligation, and Liberty of the Subject, is to be derived, either from those Words, (or others equivalent;) or else from the End of the Institution of Soveraignty; namely, the Peace of the Subjects within themselves, and their Defence against a common Enemy.

First therefore, seeing Soveraignty by Institution, is by Covenant of every one to every one; and Soveraignty by Acquisition, by Covenants of the Vanquished to the Victor, or Child to the Parent; It is manifest, that every Subject has Liberty in all those things, the right whereof cannot by Covenant be transferred. I have shewn before in the 14. Chapter, that Covenants, not to defend a mans own body, are voyd. Therefore,

If the Soveraign command a man (though justly condemned,) to kill, wound, or mayme himselfe; or not to resist those that assault him; or to abstain from the use of food, ayre, medicine, or any other thing, without which he cannot live; yet hath that man the Liberty to disobey.

If a man be interrogated by the Soveraign, or his Authority, concerning a crime done by himselfe, he is not bound (without assurance of Pardon) to confesse it; because no man (as I have shewn in the same Chapter) can be obliged by Covenant to accuse himselfe.

Again, the Consent of a Subject to Soveraign Power, is contained in these words, *I Authorise, or take upon me, all his actions*; in which there is no restriction at all, of his own former naturall Liberty: For by allowing him to *kill me,* I am not bound to kill my selfe when he commands me. 'Tis one thing to say, *Kill me, or my fellow, if you please*; another thing to say, *I will kill my selfe, or my fellow.* It followeth therefore, that

No man is bound by the words themselves, either to kill himselfe, or any other man; And consequently, that the Obligation a man may sometimes have, upon the Command of the Soveraign to execute any dangerous, or dishonourable Office, dependeth not on the Words of our Submission; but on the Intention; which is to be understood by the End thereof. When therefore our refusall to obey, frustrates the End for which the Soveraignty was ordained; then there is no Liberty to refuse: otherwise there is.

Upon this ground, a man that is commanded as a Souldier to fight against the enemy, though his Soveraign have Right enough to punish his refusall with death, may neverthelesse in many cases refuse, without Injustice; as when he substituteth a sufficient Souldier in his place: for in this case he deserteth not the service of the Common-wealth. And there is allowance to be made for naturall timorousnesse, not onely to women, (of whom no such dangerous duty is expected,) but also to men of feminine courage. When Armies fight, there is on one side, or both, a running away; yet when they do it not out of trechery, but fear, they are not esteemed to do it unjustly, but dishonourably. For the same reason, to avoyd battell, is not Injustice, but Cowardise. But he that inrowleth himselfe a Souldier, or taketh imprest mony, taketh away the excuse of a timorous nature; and is obliged, not onely to go to the battell, but also not to run from it, without his Captaines leave. And when the Defence of the Common-wealth, requireth at once the help of all that are able to bear Arms, every one is obliged; because otherwise the Institution of the Common-wealth, which they have not the purpose, or courage to preserve, was in vain.

To resist the Sword of the Common-wealth, in defence of another man, guilty, or innocent, no man hath Liberty; because such Liberty, takes away from the Soveraign, the means of Protecting us; and is therefore destructive of the very essence of Government. But in case a great many men together, have already resisted the Soveraign Power unjustly, or committed some Capitall crime, for which every one of them expecteth death, whether have they not the Liberty then to joyn together, and assist, and defend one another? Certainly they have: For they but defend their lives, which the Guilty man may as well do, as the Innocent. There was indeed injustice in the first breach of their duty; Their bearing of Arms subsequent to it, though it be to maintain what they have done, is no new unjust act. And if it be onely to defend their persons, it is not unjust at all. But the offer of pardon taketh from them, to whom it is offered, the plea of self-defence, and maketh their perseverance in assisting, or defending the rest, unlawfull.

As for other Lyberties, they depend on the Silence of the Law. In cases where the Soveraign has prescribed no rule, there the Subject hath the Liberty to do, or forbeare, according to his own discretion. And therefore such Liberty is in some places more, and in some lesse; and in some times more, in other times lesse, according as they that have the Soveraignty shall think most convenient. As for Example, there was a time, when in *England* a man might enter in to his own Land, (and dispossesse such as wrongfully possessed it,) by force. But in after-times, that Liberty of Forcible Entry, was taken away by a Statute made (by the King) in Parliament. And in some places of the world, men have the Liberty of many wives: in other places, such Liberty is not allowed.

If a Subject have a controversie with his Soveraigne, of debt, or of right of possession of lands or goods, or concerning any service required at his hands, or concerning any penalty, corporall, or pecuniary, grounded on a precedent Law: he hath the same Liberty, to sue for his right, as if it were against a Subject; and before such Judges, as are appointed by the Sovereign. For seeing the Soveraign demandeth by force of a former Law, and not by vertue of his Power; he declareth thereby, that he requireth no more, than shall appear to be due by that Law. The sute therefore is not contrary to the will of the Soveraign; and consequently the Subject hath the Liberty to demand the hearing of his Cause; and sentence, according to that Law. But if he demand, or take any thing by pretence of his Power; there lyeth, in that case, no action of Law: for all that is done by him in Vertue of his Power, is done by the Authority of every Subject, and conequently, he that brings an action against the Soveraign brings it against himselfe.

If a Monarch, or Soveraign Assembly, grant a Liberty to all, or any of his Subjects, which Grant standing, he is disabled to provide for their safety, the Grant is voyd; unlesse he directly renounce, or tranferre the Soveraignty to another. For in that he might openly, (if it had been his will,) and in plain termes, have renounced, or transferred it, and did not; it is to be understood it was not his will; but that the Grant proceeded from ignorance of the repugnancy between such a Liberty and the Soveraign Power: and therefore the Soveraignty is still retayned; and consequently all those Powers, which are necessary to the exercising thereof; such as are the Power of Warre, and Peace, of Judicature, of appointing Officers, and Councellours, of levying Mony, and the rest named in the 18th Chapter.

The Obligation of Subjects to the Soveraign, is understood to last as long, and no longer, than the power lasteth, by which he is able to protect them. For the right men have by Nature to protect themselves, when none else can protect them, can by no Covenant be relinquished. The Soveraignty is the Soule of the Common-wealth; which once departed from the Body, the members doe no more receive their motion from it. The end of Obedience is Protection; which, wheresoever a man seeth it, either in his own, or in anothers sword, Nature applyeth his obedience to it, and his endeavour to maintain it. And though Soveraignty, in the intention of them that make it, be immortall; yet is it in its own nature, not only subject to violent death, by forreign war; but also through the ignorance, and passions of men, it hath in it, from the very institution, many seeds of a naturall mortality, by Intestine Discord.

If a Subject be taken prisoner in war; or his person, or his means of life be within the Guards of the enemy, and hath his life and corporall Libertie given him, on condition to be Subject to the Victor, he hath Libertie to accept the condition; and having accepted it, is the subject of him that took him; because he had no other way to preserve himself. The case is the same, if he be deteined on the same termes, in a forreign country. But if a man be held in prison, or bonds, or is not trusted with the libertie of his bodie; he cannot be understood to be bound by Covenant to subjection; and therefore may, if he can, make his escape by any means whatsoever.

If a Monarch shall relinquish the Soveraignty, both for himself, and his heires; His Subjects returne to the absolute Libertie of Nature; because, though Nature may declare who are his Sons, and who are the nerest of his Kin; yet it dependeth on his own will, (as hath been said in the precedent chapter,) who shall be his Heyr. If therefore he will have no Heyre, there is no Soveraignty, no Subjection. The case is the same, if he dye without known Kindred, and without declaration of his Heyre. For then there can no Heire be known, and consequently no Subjection be due.

If the Soveraign Banish his Subject; during the Banishment, he is not Subject. But he that is sent on a message, or hath leave to travell, is still Subject; but it is, by Contract between Soveraigns, not by vertue of the covenant of Subjection. For whosoever entreth into anothers dominion, is Subject to all the Laws thereof; unlesse he have a privilege by the amity of the Soveraigns, or by speciall licence.

If a Monarch subdued by war, render himself Subject to the Victor; his Subjects are delivered from their former obligation, and become obliged to the Victor. But if he be held prisoner, or have not the liberty of his own Body; he is not understood to have given away the Right of Soveraigntie; and therefore his Subjects are obliged to yield obedience to the Magistrates formerly placed, governing not in their own name, but in his. For, his Right remaining, the question is only of the Administration; that is to say, of the Magistrates and Officers; which, if he have not means to name, he is supposed to approve those, which he himself had formerly appointed.

## CHAP. XXII

### Of SYSTEMES *Subject, Politicall, and Private*

HAVING spoken of the Generation, Forme, and Power of a Common-wealth, I am in order to speak next of the parts thereof. And first of Systemes, which resemble the similar parts, or Muscles of a Body naturall. By SYSTEMES; I understand any numbers of men joyned in one Interest, or one Businesse. Of which, some are *Regular*, and some *Irregular*. *Regular* are those, where one Man, or Assembly of men, is constituted Representative of the whole number. All other are *Irregular*.

Of Regular, some are *Absolute*, and *Independent*, subject to none
but their own Representative: such are only Common-wealths;
Of which I have spoken already in the 5. last precedent chapters.
Others are Dependent; that is to say, Subordinate to some Soveraign
Power, to which every one, as also their Representative is *Subject*.

Of Systemes subordinate, some are *Politicall*, and some *Private*.
*Politicall* (otherwise Called *Bodies Politique*, and *Persons in Law*,)
are those, which are made by authority from the Soveraign Power
of the Common-wealth. *Private*, are those, which are constituted
by Subjects amongst themselves, or by authoritie from a stranger.
For no authority derived from forraign power, within the Dominion
of another, is Publique there, but Private.

And of Private Systemes, some are *Lawfull*; some *Unlawfull*:
*Lawfull*, are those which are allowed by the Common-wealth:
all other are *Unlawfull*. *Irregular* Systemes, are those which having
no Representative, consist only in concourse of People; which if not
forbidden by the Common-wealth, nor made on evill designe,
(such as are conflux of People to markets, or shews, or any other
harmlesse end,) are Lawfull. But when the Intention is evill, or
(if the number be considerable) unknown, they are Unlawfull.

In Bodies Politique, the power of the Representative is alwaies
Limited: And that which prescribeth the Limits thereof, is the
Power Soveraign. For Power Unlimited, is absolute Soveraignty.
And the Soveraign, in every Commonwealth, is the absolute
Representative of all the subjects; and therefore no other, can be
Representative of any part of them, but so far forth, as he shall give
leave: And to give leave to a Body Politique of Subjects, to have
an absolute Representative to all intents and purposes, were to
abandon the government of so much of the Commonwealth, and to
divide the Dominion, contrary to their Peace and Defence, which the
Soveraign cannot be understood to doe, by any Grant, that does
not plainly, and directly discharge them of their subjection. For
consequences of words, are not the signes of his will, when other
consequences are signes of the contrary; but rather signes of errour,
and misreckonning; to which all mankind is too prone.

The bounds of that Power, which is given to the Representative
of a Bodie Politique, are to be taken notice of, from two things.
One is their Writt, or Letters from the Soveraign: the other is the
Law of the Common-wealth.

For though in the Institution or Acquisition of a Common-wealth,
which is independent, there needs no Writing, because the Power
of the Representative has there no other bounds, but such as are set
out by the unwritten Law of Nature; yet in subordinate bodies,
there are such diversities of Limitation necessary, concerning their
businesses, times, and places, as can neither be remembred without
Letters, nor taken notice of, unlesse such Letters be Patent, that
they may be read to them, and withall sealed, or testified, with the
Seales, or other permanent signes of the Authority Soveraign.

And because such Limitation is not alwaies easie, or perhaps

possible to be described in writing; the ordinary Lawes, common
to all Subjects, must determine, what the Representative may
lawfully do, in all Cases, where the Letters themselves are silent.
And therefore

In a Body Politique, if the Representative be one man, whatsoever
he does in the Person of the Body, which is not warranted in his
Letters, nor by the Lawes, is his own act, and not the act of the
Body, nor of any other Member thereof besides himselfe: Because
further than his Letters, or the Lawes limit, he representeth no
mans person, but his own. But what he does according to these,
is the act of every one: For of the Act of the Soveraign every one is
Author, because he is their Representative unlimited; and the act
of him that recedes not from the Letters of the Soveraign, is the act
of the Soveraign, and therefore every member of the Body is Author
of it.

But if the Representative be an Assembly; whatsoever that
Assembly shall Decree, not warranted by their Letters, or the Lawes,
is the act of the Assembly, or Body Politique, and the act of every
one by whose Vote the Decree was made; but not the act of any
man that being present Voted to the contrary; nor of any man
absent, unlesse he Voted it by procuration. It is the act of the
Assembly, because Voted by the major part; and if it be a crime,
the Assembly may be punished, as farre-forth as it is capable, as
by dissolution, or forfeiture of their Letters, (which is to such
artificiall, and fictitious Bodies, capitall,) or (if the Assembly have
a Common stock, wherein none of the Innocent Members have
propriety,) by pecuniary Mulct. For from corporall penalties
Nature hath exempted all Bodies Politique. But they that gave
not their Vote, are therefore Innocent, because the Assembly
cannot Represent any man in things unwarranted by their Letters,
and consequently are not involved in their Votes.

If the person of the Body Politique being in one man, borrow
mony of a stranger, that is, of one that is not of the same Body,
(for no Letters need limit borrowing, seeing it is left to mens own
inclinations to limit lending) the debt is the Representatives. For
if he should have Authority from his Letters, to make the
members pay what he borroweth, he should have by consequence
the Soveraignty of them; and therefore the grant were either voyd,
as proceeding from Errour, commonly incident to humane Nature,
and an unsufficient signe of the will of the Granter; or if it be
avowed by him, then is the Representer Soveraign, and falleth not
under the present question, which is onely of Bodies subordinate.
No member therefore is obliged to pay the debt so borrowed, but
the Representative himselfe: because he that lendeth it, being a
stranger to the Letters, and to the qualification of the Body, under-
standeth those onely for his debtors, that are engaged; and seeing
the Representer can ingage himselfe, and none else, has him onely
for Debtor; who must therefore pay him, out of the common stock
(if there be any), or (if there be none) out of his own estate.

If he come into debt by Contract, or Mulct, the case is the same.

But when the Representative is an Assembly, and the debt to a stranger; all they, and onely they are responsible for the debt, that gave their votes to the borrowing of it, or to the Contract that made it due, or to the fact for which the Mulct was imposed; because every one of those in voting did engage himselfe for the payment: For he that is author of the borrowing, is obliged to the payment, even of the whole debt, though when payd by any one, he be discharged.

But if the debt be to one of the Assembly, the Assembly onely is obliged to the payment, out of their common stock (if they have any:) For having liberty of Vote, if he Vote the Mony, shall be borrowed, he Votes it shall be payd; If he Vote it shall not be borrowed, or be absent, yet because in lending, he voteth the borrowing, he contradicteth his former Vote, and is obliged by the later, and becomes both borrower and lender, and consequently cannot demand payment from any particular man, but from the common Treasure onely; which fayling he hath no remedy, nor complaint, but against himselfe, that being privy to the acts of the Assembly, and to their means to pay, and not being enforced, did neverthelesse through his own folly lend his mony.

It is manifest by this, that in Bodies Politique subordinate and subject to a Soveraign Power, it is sometimes not onely lawfull, but expedient, for a particular man to make open protestation against the decrees of the Representative Assembly, and cause their dissent to be Registred, or to take witnesse of it; because otherwise they may be obliged to pay debts contracted, and be responsible for crimes committed by other men: But in a Soveraign Assembly, that liberty is taken away, both because he that protesteth there, denies their Soveraignty; and also because whatsoever is commanded by the Soveraign Power, is as to the Subject (though not so alwayes in the sight of God) justified by the Command; for of such command every Subject is the Author.

The variety of Bodies Politique, is almost infinite: for they are not onely distinguished by the severall affaires, for which they are constituted, wherein there is an unspeakable diversitie; but also by the times, places and numbers, subject to many limitations. And as to their affaires, some are ordained for Government; As first, the Government of a Province may be committed to an Assembly of men, wherein all resolutions shall depend on the Votes of the major part; and then this Assembly is a Body Politique, and their power limited by Commission. This word Province signifies a charge, or care of businesse, which he whose businesse it is, committeth to another man, to be administred for, and under him; and therefore when in one Common-wealth there be divers Countries, that have their Lawes distinct one from another, or are farre distant in place, the Administration of the Government being committed to divers persons, those Countries, where the Soveraign is not resident, but governs by Commission, are called Provinces. But of the government of a Province, by an Assembly residing in the Province it selfe, there be few examples. The Romans who had the Soveraignty of many Provinces; yet governed them alwaies by Presidents, and Prætors; and not by Assemblies, as they governed the City of *Rome*, and Territories adjacent. In like manner, when there were Colonies sent from *England*, to Plant *Virginia*, and *Sommer-Ilands*; though the government of them here, were committed to Assemblies in *London*, yet did those Assemblies never commit the Government under them to any Assembly there; but did to each Plantation send one Governour; For though every man, where he can be present by Nature, desires to participate of government; yet where they cannot be present, they are by Nature also enclined, to commit the Government of their common Interest rather to a Monarchicall, then a Popular form of Government: which is also evident in those men that have great private estates; who when they are unwilling to take the paines of administring the businesse that belongs to them, choose rather to trust one Servant, then an Assembly either of their friends or servants. But howsoever it be in fact, yet we may suppose the Government of a Province, or Colony committed to an Assembly: and when it is, that which in this place I have to say, is this; that whatsoever debt is by that Assembly contracted; or whatsoever unlawfull Act is decreed, is the Act onely of those that assented, and not of any that dissented, or were absent, for the reasons before alledged. Also that an Assembly residing out of the bounds of that Colony whereof they have the government, cannot execute any power over the persons, or goods of any of the Colonie, to seize on them for debt, or other duty, in any place without the Colony it selfe, as having no Jurisdiction, nor Authoritie elsewhere, but are left to the remedie, which the Law of the place alloweth them. And though the Assembly have right, to impose a Mulct upon any of their members, that shall break the Lawes they make; yet out of the Colonie it selfe, they have no right to execute the same. And that which is said here, of the Rights of an Assembly, for the government of a Province, or a Colony, is appliable also to an Assembly for the Government of a Town, an University, or a College, or a Church, or for any other Government over the persons of men.

And generally, in all Bodies Politique, if any particular member conceive himself Injuried by the Body it self, the Cognisance of his cause belongeth to the Soveraign, and those the Soveraign hath ordained for Judges in such causes, or shall ordaine for that particular cause; and not to the Body it self. For the whole Body is in this case his fellow subject, which in a Soveraign Assembly, is otherwise: for there, if the Soveraign be not Judge, though in his own cause, there can be no Judge at all.

In a Bodie Politique, for the well ordering of forraigne Traffique, the most commodious Representative is an Assembly of all the members; that is to say, such a one, as every one that adventureth his mony, may be present at all the Deliberations, and Resolutions of the Body, if they will themselves. For proof whereof, we are to consider the end, for which men that are Merchants, and may buy and sell, export, and import their Merchandise according to their own discretions, doe nevertheless bind themselves up in one Corporation. It is true, there be few Merchants, that with the Merchandise they buy at home, can fraight a Ship, to export it; or with that they buy abroad, to bring it home; and have therefore need to joyn together in one Society; where every man may either participate of the gaine, according to the proportion of his adventure; or take his own, and sell what he transports, or imports, at such prices as he thinks fit. But this is no Body Politique, there being no Common Representative to oblige them to any other Law, than that which is common to all other subjects. The End of their Incorporating, is to make their gaine the greater; which is done two wayes; by sole buying, and sole selling, both at home, and abroad. So that to grant to a Company of Merchants to be a Corporation, or Body Politique, is to grant them a double Monopoly, whereof one is to be sole buyers; another to be sole sellers. For when there is a Company incorporate for any particular forraign Country, they only export the Commodities vendible in that Country; which is sole buying at home, and sole selling abroad. For at home there is but one buyer, and abroad but one that selleth: both which is gainfull to the Merchant, because thereby they buy at home at lower, and sell abroad at higher rates: And abroad there is but one buyer of forraign Merchandise, and but one that sels them at home; both which againe are gainfull to the adventurers.

Of this double Monopoly one part is disadvantageous to the people at home, the other to forraigners. For at home by their sole exportation they set what price they please on the husbandry, and handy-works of the people; and by the sole importation, what price they please of all forraign commodities the people have need of; both which are ill for the people. On the contrary, by the sole selling of the native commodities abroad, and sole buying the forraign commodities upon the place, they raise the price of those, and abate the price of these, to the disadvantage of the forraigner: For where but one selleth, the Merchandise is the dearer; and where but one buyeth the cheaper: Such Corporations therefore are no other than Monopolies; though they would be very profitable for a Common-wealth, if being bound up into one body in forraigne Markets they were at liberty at home, every man to buy, and sell at what price he could.

The end then of these Bodies of Merchants, being not a Common benefit to the whole Body, (which have in this case no common stock but what is deducted out of the particular adventures, for building, buying, victualling and manning of Ships,) but the particular gaine of every adventurer, it is reason that every one be acquainted with the employment of his own; that is, that every one be of the Assembly, that shall have the power to order the same; and be acquainted with their accounts. And therefore the Representative of such a Body must be an Assembly, where every member of the Body may be present at the consultations, if he will.

If a Body Politique of Merchants, contract a debt to a stranger by the act of their Representative Assembly, every Member is lyable by himself for the whole. For a stranger can take no notice of their private Lawes, but considereth them as so many particular men, obliged every one to the whole payment, till payment made by one dischargeth all the rest: But if the debt be to one of the Company, the creditor is debter for the whole to himself, and cannot therefore demand his debt, but only from the common stock, if there be any.

If the Common-wealth impose a Tax upon the Body, it is understood to be layd upon every Member proportionably to his particular adventure in the Company. For there is in this case no other common stock, but what is made of their particular adventures.

If a Mulct be layd upon the Body for some unlawfull act, they only are lyable by whose votes the act was decreed, or by whose assistance it was executed; for in none of the rest is there any other crime but being of the Body; which if a crime, (because the Body was ordeyned by the authority of the Common-wealth,) is not his.

If one of the Members be indebted to the Body, he may be sued by the Body; but his goods cannot be taken, nor his person imprisoned by the authority of the Body; but only by Authority of the Common-wealth: for if they can doe it by their own Authority, they can by their own Authority give judgement that the debt is due; which is as much as to be Judge in their own Cause.

These Bodies made for the government of Men, or of Traffique, be either perpetuall, or for a time prescribed by writing. But there be Bodies also whose times are limited, and that only by the nature of their businesse. For example, if a Soveraign Monarch, or a Soveraign Assembly, shall think fit to give command to the towns, and other severall parts of their territory, to send to him their Deputies, to enforme him of the condition, and necessities of the Subjects, or to advise with him for the making of good Lawes, or for any other cause, as with one Person representing the whole Country, such Deputies having a place and time of meeting assigned them, are there, and at that time, a Body Politique, representing every Subject of that Dominion; but it is onely for such matters as shall be propounded unto them by that Man, or Assembly, that by the Soveraign Authority sent for them; and when it shall be declared that nothing more shall be propounded, nor debated by them, the Body is dissolved. For if they were the absolute Representative of the people, then were it the Soveraign Assembly; and so there would be two Soveraign Assemblies, or two Soveraigns, over the same people; which cannot consist with their Peace. And therefore where there is once a Soveraignty, there can be no absolute Representation of the people, but by it. And for the limits of how farre such a Body shall represent the whole People, they are set forth in the Writing by which they were sent for. For the People cannot choose their Deputies to other intent, than is in the Writing directed to them from their Soveraign expressed.

Private Bodies Regular, and Lawfull, are those that are constituted without Letters, or other written Authority, saving the Lawes common to all other Subjects. And because they be united in one Person Representative, they are held for Regular; such as are all Families, in which the Father, or Master ordereth the whole Family. For he obligeth his Children, and Servants, as farre as the Law permitteth, though not further, because none of them are bound to obedience in those actions, which the Law hath forbidden to be done. In all other actions, during the time they are under domestique government, they are subject to their Fathers, and Masters, as to their immediate Soveraigns. For the Father, and Master being before the Institution of Common-wealth, absolute Soveraigns in their own Families, they lose afterward no more of their Authority, than the Law of the Common-wealth taketh from them.

Private Bodies Regular, but Unlawfull, are those that unite themselves into one person Representative, without any publique Authority at all; such as are the Corporations of Beggars, Theeves and Gipsies, the better to order their trade of begging, and stealing; and the Corporations of men, that by Authority from any forraign Person, unite themselves in anothers Dominion, for the easier propagation of Doctrines, and for making a party, against the Power of the Common-wealth.

Irregular Systemes, in their nature, but Leagues, or sometimes meer concourse of people, without union to any particular designe, not by obligation of one to another, but proceeding onely from a similitude of wills and inclinations, become Lawfull, or Unlawfull, according to the lawfulnesse, or unlawfulnesse of every particular mans designe therein: And his designe is to be understood by the occasion.

The Leagues of Subjects, (because Leagues are commonly made for mutuall defence,) are in a Common-wealth (which is no more than a League of all the Subjects together) for the most part unnecessary, and savour of unlawfull designe; and are for that cause Unlawfull, and go commonly by the name of Factions, or Conspiracies. For a League being a connexion of men by Covenants, if there be no power given to any one Man, or Assembly (as in the condition of meer Nature) to compell them to performance, is so long onely valid, as there ariseth no just cause of distrust: and therefore Leagues between Common-wealths, over whom there is no humane Power established, to keep them all in awe, are not onely lawfull, but also profitable for the time they last. But Leagues of the Subjects of one and the same Common-wealth, where every one may obtain his right by means of the Soveraign Power, are unnecessary to the maintaining of Peace and Justice, and (in case the designe of them be evill, or Unknown to the Common-wealth) unlawfull. For all uniting of strength by private men, is, if for evill intent, unjust; if for intent unknown, dangerous to the Publique, and unjustly concealed.

If the Soveraign Power be in a great Assembly, and a number of men, part of the Assembly, without authority, consult a part, to contrive the guidance of the rest; This is a Faction, or Conspiracy unlawfull, as being a fraudulent seducing of the Assembly for their particular interest. But if he, whose private interest is to be debated, and judged in the Assembly, make as many friends as he can; in him it is no Injustice; because in this case he is no part of the Assembly. And though he hire such friends with mony, (unlesse there be an expresse Law against it,) yet it is not Injustice. For sometimes, (as mens manners are,) Justice cannot be had without mony; and every man may think his own cause just, till it be heard, and judged.

In all Common-wealths, if a private man entertain more servants, than the government of his estate, and lawfull employment he has for them requires, it is Faction, and unlawfull. For having the protection of the Common-wealth, he needeth not the defence of private force. And whereas in Nations not thoroughly civilized, severall numerous Families have lived in continuall hostility, and invaded one another with private force; yet it is evident enough, that they have done unjustly; or else that they had no Common-wealth.

And as Factions for Kindred, so also Factions for Government of Religion, as of Papists, Protestants, &c. or of State, as Patricians, and Plebeians of old time in *Rome*, and of Aristocraticalls and Democraticalls of old time in *Greece*, are unjust, as being contrary to the peace and safety of the people, and a taking of the Sword out of the hand of the Soveraign.

Concourse of people, is an Irregular Systeme, the lawfulnesse, or unlawfulnesse, whereof dependeth on the occasion, and on the number of them that are assembled. If the occasion be lawfull, and manifest, the Concourse is lawfull; as the usuall meeting of men at Church, or at a publique Shew, in usuall numbers: for if the numbers be extraordinarily great, the occasion is not evident; and consequently he that cannot render a particular and good account of his being amongst them, is to be judged conscious of an unlawfull, and tumultuous designe. It may be lawfull for a thousand men, to joyn in a Petition to be delivered to a Judge, or Magistrate; yet if a thousand men come to present it, it is a tumultuous Assembly; because there needs but one or two for that purpose. But in such cases as these, it is not a set number that makes the Assembly Unlawfull, but such a number, as the present Officers are not able to suppresse, and bring to Justice.

When an unusuall number of men, assemble against a man whom they accuse; the Assembly is an Unlawfull tumult; because they may deliver their accusation to the Magistrate by a few, or by one man. Such was the case of St. *Paul* at *Ephesus*; where *Demetrius*, and a great number of other men, brought two of *Pauls* companions before the Magistrate, saying with one Voyce, *Great is Diana of the Ephesians*; which was their way of demanding Justice against them for teaching the people such doctrine, as was against their Religion, and Trade. The occasion here, considering the Lawes of that People, was just; yet was their Assembly Judged Unlawfull, and the Magistrate reprehended them for it, in these words, [1]*If Demetrius and the other work-men can accuse any man, of any thing, there be Pleas, and Deputies, let them accuse one another. And if you have any other thing to demand, your case may be judged in an Assembly Lawfully called. For we are in danger to be accused for this dayes sedition, because, there is no cause by which any man can render any reason of this Concourse of People.* Where he calleth an Assembly, whereof men can give no just account, a Sedition, and such as they could not answer for. And this is all I shall say concerning *Systemes*, and Assemblyes of People, which may be compared (as I said,) to the Similar parts of mans Body; such as be Lawfull, to the Muscles; such as are Unlawfull, to Wens, Biles, and Apostemes, engendred by the unnaturall conflux of evill humours.

## CHAP. XXIII

### *Of the* PUBLIQUE MINISTERS *of Soveraign Power*

IN the last Chapter I have spoken of the Similar parts of a Common-wealth: In this I shall speak of the parts Organicall, which are Publique Ministers.

A PUBLIQUE MINISTER, is he, that by the Soveraign, (whether a Monarch, or an Assembly,) is employed in any affaires, with Authority to represent in that employment, the Person of the Common-wealth. And whereas every man, or assembly that hath Soveraignty, representeth two Persons, or (as the more common phrase is) has two Capacities, one Naturall, and another Politique, (as a Monarch, hath the person not onely of the Common-wealth but also of a man; and a Soveraign Assembly hath the Person not onely of the Common-wealth, but also of the Assembly); they that be servants to them in their naturall Capacity, are not Publique Ministers; but those onely that serve them in the Administration of the Publique businesse. And therefore neither Ushers, nor Sergeants, nor other Officers that waite on the Assembly, for no other purpose, but for the commodity of the men assembled, in an Aristocracy, or Democracy; nor Stewards, Chamberlains, Cofferers, or any other Officers of the household of a Monarch, are Publique Ministers in a Monarchy.

Of Publique Ministers, some have charge committed to them of a generall Administration, either of the whole Dominion, or of a part thereof. Of the whole, as to a Protector, or Regent, may bee committed by the Predecessor of an Infant King, during his minority, the whole Administration of his Kingdome. In which case, every

[1] Acts 19. 40.

Subject, is so far obliged to obedience, as the Ordinances he shall make, and the commands he shall give be in the Kings name, and not inconsistent with his Soveraigne Power.　Of a part, or Province; as when either a Monarch, or a Soveraign Assembly, shall give the generall charge thereof to a Governour, Lieutenant, Præfect or Vice-Roy:　And in this case also, every one of that Province, is obliged to all he shall doe in the name of the Soveraign, and that not incompatible, with the Soveraigns Right.　For such Protectors, Vice-Roys, and Governors, have no other right, but what depends on the Soveraigns Will; and no Commission that can be given them, can be interpreted for a Declaration of the will to transferre the Soveraignty, without expresse and perspicuous words to that purpose.　And this kind of Publique Ministers resembleth the Nerves, and Tendons that move the severall limbs of a body naturall.

Others have speciall Administration; that is to say, charges of some speciall businesse, either at home, or abroad:　As at home; First, for the Oeconomy of a Common-wealth, They that have Authority concerning the *Treasure*, as Tributes, Impositions, Rents, Fines, or whatsoever publique revenue, to collect, receive, issue, or take the Accounts thereof, are Publique Ministers:　Ministers, because they serve the Person Representative, and can doe nothing against his Command, nor without his Authority:　Publique, because they serve him in his Politicall Capacity.

Secondly, they that have Authority concerning the *Militia*; to have the custody of Armes, Forts, Ports; to Levy, Pay, or Conduct Souldiers; or to provide for any necessary thing for the use of war, either by Land or Sea, are publique Ministers.　But a Souldier without Command, though he fight for the Common-wealth, does not therefore represent the Person of it; because there is none to represent it to.　For every one that hath command, represents it to them only whom he commandeth.

They also that have authority to teach, or to enable others to teach the people their duty to the Soveraign Power, and instruct them in the knowledge of what is just, and unjust, thereby to render them more apt to live in godlinesse, and in peace amongst themselves and resist the publique enemy, are Publique Ministers:　Ministers, in that they doe it not by their own Authority, but by anothers; and Publique, because they doe it (or should doe it) by no Authority, but that of the Soveraign.　The Monarch, or the Soveraign Assembly only hath immediate Authority from God, to teach and instruct the people; and no man but the Soveraign, receiveth his power *Dei gratiâ* simply; that is to say, from the favour of none but God:　All other, receive theirs from the favour and providence of God, and their Soveraigns; as in a Monarchy *Dei gratiâ & Regis*; or *Dei providentiâ & voluntate Regis*.

They also to whom Jurisdiction is given, are Publique Ministers. For in their Seats of Justice they represent the person of the Soveraign; and their Sentence, is his Sentence; For (as hath been before declared) all Judicature is essentially annexed to the Soveraignty;

and therefore all other Judges are but Ministers of him, or them that have the Soveraign Power. And as Controversies are of two sorts, namely of *Fact* and of *Law*; so are Judgements, some of Fact, some of Law: And consequently in the same controversie, there may be two Judges, one of Fact, another of Law.

And in both these controversies, there may arise a controversie between the party Judged, and the Judge; which because they be both Subjects to the Soveraign, ought in Equity to be Judged by men agreed on by consent of both; for no man can be Judge in his own cause. But the Soveraign is already agreed on for Judge by them both, and is therefore either to heare the Cause, and determine it himself, or appoint for Judge such as they shall both agree on. And this agreement is then understood to be made between them divers wayes; as first, if the Defendant be allowed to except against such of his Judges, whose interest maketh him suspect them, (for as to the Complaynant he hath already chosen his own Judge,) those which he excepteth not against, are Judges he himself agrees on. Secondly, if he appeale to any other Judge, he can appeale no further; for his appeale is his choice. Thirdly, if he appeale to the Soveraign himself, and he by himself, or by Delegates which the parties shall agree on, give Sentence; that Sentence is finall: for the Defendant is Judged by his own Judges, that is to say, by himself.

These properties of just and rationall Judicature considered, I cannot forbeare to observe the excellent constitution of the Courts of Justice, established both for Common, and also for Publique Pleas in *England*. By Common Pleas, I meane those, where both the Complaynant and Defendant are Subjects: and by Publique, (which are also called Pleas of the Crown) those, where the Complaynant is the Soveraign. For whereas there were two orders of men, whereof one was Lords, the other Commons; The Lords had this Priviledge, to have for Judges in all Capitall crimes, none but Lords; and of them, as many as would be present; which being ever acknowledged as a Priviledge of favour, their Judges were none but such as they had themselves desired. And in all controversies, every Subject (as also in civill controversies the Lords) had for Judges, men of the Country where the matter in controversie lay; against which he might make his exceptions, till at last twelve men without exception being agreed on, they were Judged by those twelve. So that having his own Judges, there could be nothing alledged by the party, why the sentence should not be finall. These publique persons, with Authority from the Soveraign Power, either to Instruct, or Judge the people, are such members of the Commonwealth, as may fitly be compared to the organs of Voice in a Body naturall.

Publique Ministers are also all those, that have Authority from the Soveraign, to procure the Execution of Judgements given; to publish the Soveraigns Commands; to suppresse Tumults; to apprehend, and imprison Malefactors; and other acts tending to the conservation of the Peace. For every act they doe by such Authority, is the act of the Common-wealth; and their service, answerable to that of the Hands, in a Bodie naturall.

Publique Ministers abroad, are those that represent the Person of their own Soveraign, to forraign States. Such are Ambassadors, Messengers, Agents, and Heralds, sent by publique Authoritie, and on publique Businesse.

But such as are sent by Authoritie only of some private partie of a troubled State, though they be received, are neither Publique, nor Private Ministers of the Common-wealth; because none of their actions have the Common-wealth for Author. Likewise, an Ambassador sent from a Prince, to congratulate, condole, or to assist, at a solemnity, though the Authority be Publique; yet because the businesse is Private, and belonging to him in his naturall capacity; is a Private person. Also if a man be sent into another Country, secretly to explore their counsels, and strength; though both the Authority, and the Businesse be Publique; yet because there is none to take notice of any Person in him, but his own; he is but a Private Minister; but yet a Minister of the Common-wealth; and may be compared to an Eye in the Body naturall. And those that are appointed to receive the Petitions or other informations of the People, and are as it were the publique Eare, are Publique Ministers, and represent their Soveraign in that office.

Neither a Counsellor (nor a Councell of State, if we consider it with no Authority of Judicature or Command, but only of giving Advice to the Soveraign when it is required, or of offering it when it is not required, is a Publique Person. For the Advice is addressed to the Soveraign only, whose person cannot in his own presence, be represented to him, by another. But a Body of Counsellors, are never without some other Authority, either of Judicature, or of immediate Administration: As in a Monarchy, they represent the Monarch, in delivering his Commands to the Publique Ministers: In a Democracy, the Councell, or Senate propounds the Result of their deliberations to the people, as a Councell; but when they appoint Judges, or heare Causes, or give Audience to Ambassadors, it is in the quality of a Minister of the People: And in an Aristocracy the Councell of State is the Soveraign Assembly it self; and gives counsell to none but themselves.

## CHAP. XXIV

*Of the* NUTRITION, *and* PROCREATION *of a Common-wealth*

THE NUTRITION of a Common-wealth consisteth, in the *Plenty*, and *Distribution* of *Materials* conducing to Life: In *Concoction*, or *Preparation*; and (when concocted) in the *Conveyance* of it, by convenient conduits, to the Publique use.

As for the Plenty of Matter, it is a thing limited by Nature, to those commodities, which from (the two breasts of our common Mother) Land, and Sea, God usually either freely giveth, or for labour selleth to man-kind.

For the Matter of this Nutriment, consisting in Animals, Vegetals, and Minerals, God hath freely layd them before us, in or neer to the face of the Earth; so as there needeth no more but the labour, and industry of receiving them. Insomuch as Plenty dependeth (next to Gods favour) meerly on the labour and industry of men.

This Matter, commonly called Commodities, is partly *Native*, and partly *Forraign*: *Native*, that which is to be had within the Territory of the Common-wealth: *Forraign*, that which is imported from without. And because there is no Territory under the Dominion of one Common-wealth, (except it be of very vast extent,) that produceth all things needfull for the maintenance, and motion of the whole Body; and few that produce not something more than necessary; the superfluous commodities to be had within, become no more superfluous, but supply these wants at home, by importation of that which may be had abroad, either by Exchange, or by just Warre, or by Labour: for a mans Labour also is a commodity exchangeable for benefit, as well as any other thing: And there have been Common-wealths that having no more Territory, than hath served them for habitation, have neverthelesse, not onely maintained, but also encreased their Power, partly by the labour of trading from one place to another, and partly by selling the Manifactures, whereof the Materials were brought in from other places.

The Distribution of the Materials of this Nourishment, is the constitution of *Mine*, and *Thine*, and *His*; that is to say, in one word *Propriety*; and belongeth in all kinds of Common-wealth to the Soveraign Power. For where there is no Common-wealth, there is (as hath been already shewn) a perpetuall warre of every man against his neighbour; And therefore every thing is his that getteth it, and keepeth it by force; which is neither *Propriety*, nor *Community*; but *Uncertainty*. Which is so evident, that even *Cicero*, (a passionate defender of Liberty,) in a publique pleading, attributeth all Propriety to the Law Civil, *Let the Civill Law*, saith he, *be once abandoned, or but negligently guarded, (not to say oppressed,) and there is nothing, that any man can be sure to receive from his*

*Ancestor, or leave to his Children.* And again; *Take away the Civill Law, and no man knows what is his own, and what another mans.* Seeing therefore the Introduction of *Propriety* is an effect of Common-wealth; which can do nothing but by the Person that Represents it, it is the act onely of the Soveraign; and consisteth in the Lawes, which none can make that have not the Soveraign Power. And this they well knew of old, who called that Νόμος, (that is to say, *Distribution,*) which we call Law; and defined Justice, by *distributing* to every man *his own.*

In this Distribution, the First Law, is for Division of the Land it selfe: wherein the Soveraign assigneth to every man a portion, according as he, and not according as any Subject, or any number of them, shall judge agreeable to Equity, and the Common Good. The Children of Israel, were a Common-wealth in the Wildernesse: but wanted the commodities of the Earth, till they were masters of the Land of Promise; which afterward was divided amongst them, not by their own discretion, but by the discretion of *Eleazar* the Priest, and *Joshua* their Generall: who when there were twelve Tribes, making them thirteen by subdivision of the Tribe of *Joseph*; made neverthelesse but twelve portions of the Land; and ordained for the Tribe of *Levi* no land; but assigned them the tenth part of the whole fruits; which division was therefore Arbitrary. And though a People comming into possession of a Land by warre, do not alwaies exterminate the antient Inhabitants, (as did the Jewes,) but leave to many, or most, or all of them their estates; yet it is manifest they hold them afterwards, as of the Victors distribution; as the people of *England* held all theirs of *William* the *Conquerour.*

From whence we may collect, that the propriety which a subject hath in his lands, consisteth in a right to exclude all other subjects from the use of them; and not to exclude their Soveraign, be it an Assembly, or a Monarch. For seeing the Soveraign, that is to say, the Common-wealth (whose Person he representeth,) is understood to do nothing but in order to the common Peace and Security, this Distribution of lands, is to be understod as done in order to the same: And consequently, whatsoever Distribution he shall make in prejudice thereof, is contrary to the will of every subject, that committed his Peace, and safety to his discretion, and conscience; and therefore by the will of every one of them, is to be reputed voyd. It is true, that a Soveraign Monarch, or the greater part of a Soveraign Assembly, may ordain the doing of many things in pursuit of their Passions, contrary to their own consciences, which is a breach of trust, and of the Law of Nature; but this is not enough to authorise any subject, either to make warre upon, or so much as to accuse of Injustice, or any way to speak evill of their Soveraign; because they have authorised all his actions, and in bestowing the Soveraign Power, made them their own. But in what cases the Commands of Soveraigns are contrary to Equity, and the Law of Nature, is to be considered hereafter in another place.

In the Distribution of land, the Common-wealth it selfe, may be conceived to have a portion, and possesse, and improve the same by their Representative; and that such portion may be made sufficient, to susteine the whole expence to the common Peace, and defence necessarily required: Which were very true if there could be any Representative conceived free from humane passions, and infirmities. But the nature of men being as it is, the setting forth of Publique Land, or of any certaine Revenue for the Common-wealth, is in vaine; and tendeth to the dissolution of Government, and to the condition of meere Nature, and War, as soon as ever the Soveraign Power falleth into the hands of a Monarch, or of an Assembly, that are either too negligent of mony, or too hazardous in engaging the publique stock, into a long, or costly war. Common-wealths can endure no Diet: For seeing their expence is not limited by their own appetite, but by externall Accidents, and the appetites of their neighbours, the Publique Riches cannot be limited by other limits, than those which the emergent occasions shall require. And whereas in *England*, there were by the Conquerour, divers Lands reserved to his own use, (besides Forrests, and Chases, either for his recreation, or for preservation of Woods,) and divers services reserved on the Land he gave his Subjects; yet it seems they were not reserved for his Maintenance in his Publique, but in his Naturall capacity: For he, and his Successors did for all that, lay Arbitrary Taxes on all Subjects Land, when they judged it necessary. Or if those publique Lands and Services, were ordained as a sufficient maintenance of the Common-wealth, it was contrary to the scope of the Institution; being (as it appeared by those ensuing Taxes) insufficient, and (as it appeares by the late small Revenue of the Crown) Subject to Alienation, and Diminution. It is therefore in vaine, to assign a portion to the Common-wealth; which may sell, or give it away; and does sell, and give it away when tis done by their Representative.

As the Distribution of Lands at home; so also to assigne in what places, and for what commodities, the Subject shall traffique abroad, belongeth to the Soveraign. For if it did belong to private persons to use their own descretion therein, some of them would bee drawn for gaine, both to furnish the enemy with means to hurt the Common-wealth, and hurt it themselves, by importing such things, as pleasing mens appetites, be neverthelesse noxious, or at least unprofitable to them. And therefore it belongeth to the Common-wealth, (that is, to the Soveraign only,) to approve, or disapprove both of the places, and matter of forraign Traffique.

Further, seeing it is not enough to the Sustentation of a Common-wealth, that every man have a propriety in a portion of Land, or in some few commodities, or a naturall property in some usefull art, and there is no art in the world, but is necessary either for the being, or well being almost of every particular man; it is necessary, that men distribute that which they can spare, and transferre their propriety therein, mutually one to another, by exchange, and mutuall contract. And therefore it belongeth to the Common-wealth, (that is to say, to the Soveraign,) to appoint in what manner, all kinds of contract between Subjects, (as buying, selling, exchanging, borrowing, lending, letting, and taking to hire,) are to bee made; and by what words, and signes they shall be understood for valid.  And for the Matter, and Distribution of the Nourishment, to the severall Members of the Common-wealth, thus much (considering the modell of the whole worke) is sufficient.

By Concoction, I understand the reducing of all commodities, which are not presently consumed, but reserved for Nourishment in time to come, to some thing of equall value, and withall so portable, as not to hinder the motion of men from place to place; to the end a man may have in what place soever, such Nourishment as the place affordeth.  And this is nothing else but Gold, and Silver, and Mony.  For Gold and Silver, being (as it happens) almost in all Countries of the world highly valued, is a commodious measure of the value of all things else between Nations; and Mony (of what matter soever coyned by the Soveraign of a Common-wealth,) is a sufficient measure of the value of all things else, between the Subjects of that Common-wealth.  By the means of which measures, all commodities, Moveable, and Immoveable, are made to accompany a man, to all places of his resort, within and without the place of his ordinary residence; and the same passeth from Man to Man, within the Common-wealth; and goes round about, Nourishing (as it passeth) every part thereof; In so much as this Concoction, is as it were the Sanguification of the Common-wealth: For naturall Bloud is in like manner made of the fruits of the Earth; and circulating, nourisheth by the way, every Member of the Body of Man.

And because Silver and Gold, have their value from the matter it selfe; they have first this privilege, that the value of them cannot be altered by the power of one, nor of a few Common-wealths; as being a common measure of the commodities of all places.  But base Mony, may easily be enhansed, or abased.  Secondly, they have the priviledge to make Common-wealths move, and stretch out their armes, when need is, into forraign Countries; and supply, not only private Subjects that travell, but also whole Armies with Provision.  But that Coyne, which is not considerable for the Matter, but for the Stamp of the place, being unable to endure change of ayr, hath its effect at home only; where also it is subject to the change of Laws, and thereby to have the value diminished, to the prejudice many times of those that have it.

The Conduits, and Wayes by which it is conveyed to the Publique use, are of two sorts; One, that Conveyth it to the Publique Coffers; The other, that Issueth the same out againe for publique payments.  Of the first sort, are Collectors, Receivers, and Treasurers; of the second are the Treasurers againe, and the Officers appointed for payment of severall publique or private Ministers.  And in this also, the Artificiall Man maintains his resemblance with the Naturall; whose Veins receiving the Bloud from the severall

Parts of the Body, carry it to the Heart; where being made Vitall, the Heart by the Arteries sends it out again, to enliven, and enable for motion all the Members of the same.

The Procreation, or Children of a Common-wealth, are those we call *Plantations*, or *Colonies*; which are numbers of men sent out from the Common-wealth, under a Conductor, or Governour, to inhabit a Forraign Country, either formerly voyd of Inhabitants, or made voyd then, by warre. And when a Colony is setled, they are either a Common-wealth of themselves, discharged of their subjection to their Soveraign that sent them, (as hath been done by many Common-wealths of antient time,) in which case the Common-wealth from which they went, was called their Metropolis, or Mother, and requires no more of them, then Fathers require of the Children, whom they emancipate, and make free from their domestique government, which is Honour, and Friendship; or else they remain united to the Metropolis, as were the Colonies of the people of *Rome*; and then they are no Common-wealths themselves, but Provinces, and parts of the Common-wealth that sent them. So that the Right of Colonies (saving Honour, and League with their Metropolis,) dependeth wholly on their Licence, or Letters, by which their Soveraign authorised them to Plant.

## CHAP. XXV

### *Of* COUNSELL

How fallacious it is to judge of the nature of things, by the ordinary and inconstant use of words, appeareth in nothing more, than in the confusion of Counsels, and Commands, arising from the Imperative manner of speaking in them both, and in many other occasions besides. For the words *Doe this*, are the words not onely of him that Commandeth; but also of him that giveth Counsell; and of him that Exhorteth; and yet there are but few, that see not, that these are very different things; or that cannot distinguish between them, when they perceive who it is that speaketh, and to whom the Speech is directed, and upon what occasion. But finding those phrases in mens writings, and being not able, or not willing to enter into a consideration of the circumstances, they mistake sometimes the Precepts of Counsellours, for the Precepts of them that Command; and sometimes the contrary; according as it best agreeth with the conclusions they would inferre, or the actions they approve. To avoyd which mistakes, and render to those termes of Commanding, Counselling, and Exhorting, their proper and distinct significations. I define them thus.

COMMAND is where a man saith, *Doe this*, or *Doe not this*, without expecting other reason than the Will of him that sayes it. From this it followeth manifestly, that he that Commandeth, pretendeth

thereby his own Benefit: For the reason of his Command is his own |
Will onely, and the proper object of every mans Will, is some Good
to himselfe.

COUNSELL, is where a man saith, *Doe*, or *Doe not this*, and deduceth
his reasons from the benefit that arriveth by it to him to whom he
saith it. And from this it is evident, that he that giveth Counsell,
pretendeth onely (whatsoever he intendeth) the good of him, to
whom he giveth it.

Therefore between Counsell and Command, one great difference
is, that Command is directed to a mans own benefit; and Counsell
to the benefit of another man. And from this ariseth another
difference, that a man may be obliged to do what he is Commanded;
as when he hath convenanted to obey: But he cannot be obliged
to do as he is Counselled, because the hurt of not following it, is his
own; or if he should covenant to follow it, then is the Counsell
turned into the nature of a Command. A third difference between
them is, that no man can pretend a right to be of another mans
Counsell; because he is not to pretend benefit by it to himselfe:
but to demand right to Counsell another, argues a will to know his
designes, or to gain some other Good to himselfe; which (as I said
before) is of every mans will the proper object.

This also is incident to the nature of Counsell; that whatsoever
it be, he that asketh it, cannot in equity accuse, or punish it: For
to ask Counsell of another, is to permit him to give such Counsell
as he shall think best; And consequently, he that giveth counsell
to his Soveraign, (whether a Monarch, or an Assembly) when he
asketh it, cannot in equity be punished for it, whether the same be
conformable to the opinion of the most, or not, so it be to the
Proposition in debate. For if the sense of the Assembly can be
taken notice of, before the Debate be ended, they should neither
ask, nor take any further Counsell; For the Sense of the Assembly,
is the Resolution of the Debate, and End of all Deliberation. And
Generally he that demandeth Counsell, is Author of it; and therefore
cannot punish it; and what the Soveraign cannot, no man else can.
But if one Subject giveth Counsell to another, to do any thing
contrary to the Lawes, whether that Counsell proceed from evill
intention, or from ignorance onely, it is punishable by the Common-
wealth; because ignorance of the Law, is no good excuse, where
every man is bound to take notice of the Lawes to which he is
subject.

EXHORTATION, and DEHORTATION, is Counsell, accompanied with
signes in him that giveth it, of vehement desire to have it followed;
or to say it more briefly, *Counsell vehemently pressed.* For he that
Exhorteth, doth not deduce the consequences of what he adviseth
to be done, and tye himselfe therein to the rigour of true reasoning;
but encourages him he Counselleth, to Action: As he that Dehorteth,
deterreth him from it. And therefore they have in their speeches,
a regard to the common Passions, and opinions of men, in deducing
their reasons: and make use of Similitudes, Metaphors, Examples,

and other tooles of Oratory, to perswade their Hearers of the Utility, Honour, or Justice of following their advise.

From whence may be inferred, First, that Exhortation and Dehortation, is directed to the Good of him that giveth the Counsell, not of him that asketh it, which is contrary to the duty of a Counsellour; who (by the definition of Counsell) ought to regard, not his own benefit, but his whom he adviseth. And that he directeth his Counsell to his own benefit, is manifest enough, by the long and vehement urging, or by the artificiall giving thereof; which being not required of him, and consequently proceeding from his own occasions, is directed principally to his own benefit, and but accidentarily to the good of him that is Counselled, or not at all.

Secondly, that the use of Exhortation and Dehortation lyeth onely, where a man is to speak to a Multitude; because when the Speech is addressed to one, he may interrupt him, and examine his reasons more rigorously, than can be done in a Multitude; which are too many to enter into Dispute, and Dialogue with him that speaketh indifferently to them all at once.

Thirdly, that they that Exhort and Dehort, where they are required to give Counsell, are corrupt Counsellours, and as it were bribed by their own interest. For though the Counsell they give be never so good; yet he that gives it, is no more a good Counsellour, than he that giveth a Just Sentence for a reward, is a Just Judge. But where a man may lawfully Command, as a Father in his Family, or a Leader in an Army, his Exhortations and Dehortations, are not onely lawfull, but also necessary, and laudable: But then they are no more Counsells, but Commands; which when they are for Execution of soure labour; sometimes necessity, and alwayes humanity requireth to be sweetned in the delivery, by encouragement, and in the tune and phrase of Counsell, rather then in harsher language of Command.

Examples of the difference between Command and Counsell, we may take from the formes of Speech that expresse them in Holy Scripture. *Have no other Gods but me; Make to thy selfe no graven Image; Take not Gods name in vain; Sanctifie the Sabbath; Honour thy Parents; Kill not; Steale not,* &c. are Commands; because the reason for which we are to obey them, is drawn from the will of God our King, whom we are obliged to obey. But these words, *Sell all thou hast; give it to the poore; and follow me,* are Counsell; because the reason for which we are to do so, is drawn from our own benefit; which is this, that we shall have *Treasure in Heaven.* These words, *Go into the Village over against you, and you shall find an Asse tyed, and her Colt: loose her, and bring her to me,* are a Command: for the reason of their fact is drawn from the will of their Master: but these words, *Repent, and be Baptized in the Name of Jesus,* are Counsell; because the reason why we should so do, tendeth not to any benefit of God Almighty, who shall still be King in what manner soever we rebell; but of our selves, who have no other means of avoyding the punishment hanging over us for our sins.

As the difference of Counsell from Command, hath been now deduced from the nature of Counsell, consisting in a deducing of the benefit, or hurt that may arise to him that is to be Counselled, by the necessary or probable consequences of the action he propoundeth; so may also the differences between *apt*, and *inept* Counsellours be derived from the same. For Experience, being but Memory of the consequences of like actions formerly observed, and Counsell but the Speech whereby that experience is made known to another; the Vertues, and Defects of Counsell, are the same with the Vertues, and Defects Intellectuall: And to the Person of a Common-wealth, his Counsellours serve him in the place of Memory, and Mentall Discourse. But with this resemblance of the Common-wealth, to a naturall man, there is one dissimilitude joyned, of great importance; which is, that a naturall man receiveth his experience, from the naturall objects of sense, which work upon him without passion, or interest of their own; whereas they that give Counsell to the Representative person of a Common-wealth, may have, and have often their particular ends, and passions, that render their Counsells alwayes suspected, and many times unfaithfull. And therefore we may set down for the first condition of a good Counsellour, *That his Ends, and Interest, be not inconsistent with the Ends and Interest of him he Counselleth.*

Secondly, Because the office of a Counsellour, when an action comes into deliberation, is to make manifest the consequences of it, in such manner, as he that is Counselled may be truly and evidently informed; he ought to propound his advise, in such forme of speech, as may make the truth most evidently appear; that is to say, with as firme ratiocination, as significant and proper language, and as briefly, as the evidence will permit. And therefore *rash, and unevident Inferences*; (such as are fetched onely from Examples, or authority of Books, and are not arguments of what is good, or evill, but witnesses of fact, or of opinion,) *obscure, confused, and ambiguous Expressions, also all metaphoricall Speeches, tending to the stirring up of Passion*, (because such reasoning, and such expressions, are usefull onely to deceive, or to lead him we Counsell towards other ends than his own) *are repugnant to the Office of a Counsellour.*

Thirdly, Because the Ability of Counselling proceedeth from Experience, and long study; and no man is presumed to have experience in all those things that to the Administration of a great Common-wealth are necessary to be known, *No man is presumed to be a good Counsellour, but in such Businesse, as he hath not onely been much versed in, but hath also much meditated on, and considered.* For seeing the businesse of a Common-wealth is this, to preserve the people in Peace at home, and defend them against forraign Invasion, we shall find, it requires great knowledge of the disposition of Man-kind, of the Rights of Governemnt, and of the nature of Equity, Law, Justice, and Honour, not to be attained without study; And of the Strength, Commodities, Places both of their own Country, and their Neighbours; as also of the inclinations, and designes of all Nations that may any way annoy them. And this is not attained to, without much experience. Of which things, not onely the whole summe, but every one of the particulars requires the age, and observation of a man in years, and of more than ordinary study. The wit required for Counsel, as I have said before (Chap. 8.) is Judgement. And the differences of men in that point come from different education, of some to one kind of study, or businesse, and of others to another. When for the doing of any thing, there be Infallible rules, (as in Engines, and Edifices, the rules of Geometry,) all the experience of the world cannot equal his Counsell, that has learnt, or found out the Rule. And when there is no such Rule, he that hath most experience in that particular kind of businesse, has therein the best Judgement, and is the best Counsellour.

Fourthly, to be able to give Counsell to a Common-wealth, in a businesse that hath reference to another Common-wealth, *It is necessary to be acquainted with the Intelligences, and Letters* that come from thence, *and with all the records of Treaties, and other transactions of State* between them; which none can doe, but such as the Representative shall think fit. By which we may see, that they who are not called to Counsell, can have no good Counsell in such cases to obtrude.

Fifthly, Supposing the number of Counsellors equall, a man is better Counselled by hearing them apart, then in an Assembly; and that for many causes. First, in hearing them apart, you have the advice of every man; but in an Assembly many of them deliver their advise with *I*, or *No*, or with their hands, or feet, not moved by their own sense, but by the eloquence of another, or for feare of displeasing some that have spoken, or the whole Assembly, by contradiction; or for feare of appearing duller in apprehension, than those that have applauded the contrary opinion. Secondly, in an Assembly of many, there cannot choose but be some whose interests are contrary to that of the Publique; and these their Interests make passionate, and Passion eloquent, and Eloquence drawes others into the same advice. For the Passions of men, which asunder are moderate, as the heat of one brand; in Assembly are like many brands, that enflame one another, (especially when they blow one another with Orations) to the setting of the Common-wealth on fire, under pretence of Counselling it. Thirdly, in hearing every man apart, one may examine (when there is need) the truth, or probability of his reasons, and of the grounds of the advise he gives, by frequent interruptions, and objections; which cannot be done in an Assembly, where (in every difficult question) a man is rather astonied, and dazled with the variety of discourse upon it, than informed of the course he ought to take. Besides, there cannot be an Assembly of many, called together for advice, wherein there be not some, that have the ambition to be thought eloquent,

and also learned in the Politiques; and give not their advice with
care of the businesse propounded, but of the applause of their
motly orations, made of the divers colored threds, or shreds of
Authors; which is an Impertinence at least, that takes away the
time of serious Consultation, and in the secret way of Counselling
apart, is easily avoided. Fourthly, in Deliberations that ought
to be kept secret, (whereof there be many occasions in Publique
Businesse,) the Counsells of many, and especially in Assemblies,
are dangerous; And therefore great Assemblies are necessitated
to commit such affaires to lesser numbers, and of such persons as
are most versed, and in whose fidelity they have most confidence.

To conclude, who is there that so far approves the taking of
Counsell from a great Assembly of Counsellours, that wisheth for,
or would accept of their pains, when there is a question of marrying
his Children, disposing of his Lands, governing his Household, or
managing his private Estate, especially if there be amongst them
such as wish not his prosperity? A man that doth his businesse
by the help of many and prudent Counsellours, with every one
consulting apart in his proper element, does it best, as he that useth
able Seconds at Tennis play, placed in their proper stations. He
does next best, that useth his own Judgement only; as he that has
no Second at all. But he that is carried up and down to his businesse
in a framed Counsell, which cannot move but by the plurality of
consenting opinions, the execution whereof is commonly (out of
envy, or interest) retarded by the part dissenting, does it worst of
all, and like one that is carried to the ball, though by good Players,
yet in a Wheele-barrough, or other frame, heavy of it self, and
retarded also by the inconcurrent judgements, and endeavours of
them that drive it; and so much the more, as they be more that set
their hands to it; and most of all, when there is one, or more amongst
them, that desire to have him lose. And though it be true, that
many eys see more then one; yet it is not to be understood of many
Counsellours; but then only, when the finall Resolution is in one
man. Otherwise, because many eyes see the same thing in divers
lines, and are apt to look asquint towards their private benefit;
they that desire not to misse their marke, though they look about
with two eyes, yet they never ayme but with one; And therefore
no great Popular Common-wealth was ever kept up; but either by
a forraign Enemy that united them; or by the reputation of some
one eminent Man amongst them; or by the secret Counsell of a
few; or by the mutuall feare of equall factions; and not by the
open Consultations of the Assembly. And as for very little Common-
wealths, be they Popular, or Monarchicall, there is no human
wisdome can uphold them, longer then the Jealousy lasteth of their
potent Neighbours.

## CHAP. XXVI

### *Of* CIVILL LAWES

BY CIVILL LAWES, I understand the Lawes, that men are there-fore bound to observe, because they are Members, not of this, or that Common-wealth in particular, but of a Common-wealth. For the knowledge of particular Lawes belongeth to them, that professe the study of the Lawes of their severall Countries; but the know-ledge of Civill Law in generall, to any man. The antient Law of *Rome* was called their *Civil Law*, from the word *Civitas*, which signifies a Common-wealth: And those Countries, which having been under the Roman Empire, and governed by that Law, retaine still such part thereof as they think fit, call that part the Civill Law, to distinguish it from the rest of their own Civill Lawes. But that is not it I intend to speak of here; my designe being not to shew what is Law here, and there; but what is Law; as *Plato, Aristotle, Cicero,* and divers others have done, without taking upon them the profession of the study of the Law.

And first it is manifest, that Law in generall, is not Counsell, but Command; nor a Command of any man to any man; but only of him, whose Command is addressed to one formerly obliged to obey him. And as for Civill Law, it addeth only the name of the person Commanding, which is *Persona Civitatis,* the Person of the Common-wealth.

Which considered, I define Civill Law in this manner. CIVILL LAW, *Is to every Subject, those Rules, which the Common-wealth hath Commanded him, by Word, Writing, or other sufficient Sign of the Will, to make use of, for the Distinction of Right, and Wrong; that is to say, of what is contrary, and what is not contrary to the Rule.*

In which definition, there is nothing that is not at first sight evident. For every man seeth, that some Lawes are addressed to all the Subjects in generall; some to particular Provinces; some to particular Vocations; and some to particular Men; and are therefore Lawes, to every of those to whom the Command is directed; and to none else. As also, that Lawes are the Rules of Just, and Unjust; nothing being reputed Unjust, that is not contrary to some Law. Likewise, that none can make Lawes but the Common-wealth; because our Subjection is to the Common-wealth only: and that Commands, are to be signified by sufficient Signs; because a man knows not otherwise how to obey them. And therefore, whatsoever can from this definition by necessary consequence be deduced, ought to be acknowledged for truth. Now I deduce from it this that followeth.

1. The Legislator in all Common-wealths, is only the Soveraign, be he one Man, as in a Monarchy, or one Assembly of men, as in

a Democracy or Aristocracy. For the Legislator, is he that maketh the Law. And the Common-wealth only, præscribes, and commandeth the observation of those rules, which we call Law: Therefore the Common-wealth is the Legislator. But the Common-wealth is no Person, nor has capacity to doe any thing, but by the Representative, (that is, the Soveraign;) and therefore the Soveraign is the sole Legislator. For the same reason, none can abrogate a Law made, but the Soveraign; because a Law is not abrogated, but by another Law, that forbiddeth it to be put in execution.

2. The Soveraign of a Common-wealth, be it an Assembly, or one Man, is not Subject to the Civill Lawes. For having power to make, and repeale Lawes, he may when he pleaseth, free himselfe from that subjection, by repealing those Lawes that trouble him, and making of new; and consequently he was free before. For he is free, that can be free when he will: Nor is it possible for any person to be bound to himselfe; because he that can bind, can release; and therefore he that is bound to himselfe onely, is not bound.

3. When long Use obtaineth the authority of a Law, it is not the Length of Time that maketh the Authority, but the Will of the Soveraign signified by his silence, (for Silence is sometimes an argument of Consent;) and it is no longer Law, then the Soveraign shall be silent therein. And therefore if the Soveraign shall have a question of Right grounded, not upon his present Will, but upon the Lawes, formerly made; the Length of Time shal bring no prejudice to his Right; but the question shal be judged by Equity. For many unjust Actions, and unjust Sentences, go uncontrolled a longer time, than any man can remember. And our Lawyers account no Customes Law, but such as are reasonable, and that evill Customes are to be abolished: But the Judgement of what is reasonable, and of what is to be abolished, belongeth to him that maketh the Law, which is the Soveraign Assembly, or Monarch.

4. The Law of Nature, and the Civill Law, contain each other, and are of equall extent. For the Lawes of Nature, which consist in Equity, Justice, Gratitude, and other morall Vertues on these depending, in the condition of meer Nature (as I have said before in the end of the 15th Chapter,) are not properly Lawes, but qualities that dispose men to peace, and to obedience. When a Common-wealth is once settled, then are they actually Lawes, and not before; as being then the commands of the Common-wealth; and therefore also Civill Lawes: For it is the Soveraign Power that obliges men to obey them. For in the differences of private men, to declare, what is Equity, what is Justice, and what is morall Vertue, and to make them binding, there is need of the Ordinances of Soveraign Power, and Punishments to be ordained for such as shall break them; which Ordinances are therefore part of the Civill Law. The Law of Nature therefore is a part of the Civill Law in all Common-wealths of the world. Reciprocally also, the Civill Law is a part of the Dictates of Nature. For Justice, that is to say, Perfor-

mance of Covenant, and giving to every man his own, is a Dictate of the Law of Nature. But every subject in a Common-wealth, hath covenanted to obey the Civill Law, (either one with another, as when they assemble to make a common Representative, or with the Representative it selfe one by one, when subdued by the Sword they promise obedience, that they may receive life;) And therefore Obedience to the Civill Law is part also of the Law of Nature. Civill, and Naturall Law are not different kinds, but different parts of Law; whereof one part being written, is called Civill, the other unwritten, Naturall. But the Right of Nature, that is, the naturall Liberty of man, may by the Civill Law be abridged, and restrained: nay, the end of making Lawes, is no other, but such Restraint; without the which there cannot possibly be any Peace. And Law was brought into the world for nothing else, but to limit the naturall liberty of particular men, in such manner, as they might not hurt, but assist one another, and joyn together against a common Enemy.

5. If the Soveraign of one Common-wealth, subdue a People that have lived under other written Lawes, and afterwards govern them by the same Lawes, by which they were governed before; yet those Lawes are the Civill Lawes of the Victor, and not of the Vanquished Common-wealth. For the Legislator is he, not by whose authority the Lawes were first made, but by whose authority they now continue to be Lawes. And therefore where there be divers Provinces, within the Dominion of a Common-wealth, and in those Provinces diversity of Lawes, which commonly are called the Customes of each severall Province, we are not to understand that such Customes have their force, onely from Length of Time; but that they were antiently Lawes written, or otherwise made known, for the Constitutions, and Statutes of their Soveraigns; and are now Lawes, not by vertue of the Præscription of time, but by the Constitutions of their present Soveraigns. But if an unwritten Law, in all the Provinces of a Dominion, shall be generally observed, and no iniquity appear in the use thereof; that Law can be no other but a Law of Nature, equally obliging all man-kind.

6. Seeing then all Lawes, written, and unwritten, have their Authority, and force, from the Will of the Common-wealth; that is to say, from the Will of the Representative; which in a Monarchy is the Monarch, and in other Common-wealths the Soveraign Assembly; a man may wonder from whence proceed such opinions, as are found in the Books of Lawyers of eminence in severall Common-wealths, directly, or by consequence making the Legislative Power depend on private men, or subordinate Judges. As for example, *That the Common Law, hath no Controuler but the Parlament*; which is true onely where a Parlament has the Soveraign Power, and cannot be assembled, nor dissolved, but by their own discretion. For if there be a right in any else to dissolve them, there is a right also to controule them, and consequently to controule their controulings. And if there be no such right, then the Controuler of Lawes is not *Parlamentum*, but *Rex in Parlamento*. And

where a Parlament is Soveraign, if it should assemble never so many, or so wise men, from the Countries subject to them, for whatsoever cause; yet there is no man will believe, that such an Assembly hath thereby acquired to themselves a Legislative Power. *Item*, that the two arms of a Commonwealth, *are Force, and Justice ; the first whereof is in the King ; the other deposited in the hands of the Parlament.* As if a Common-wealth could consist, where the Force were in any hand, which Justice had not the Authority to command and govern.

7. That Law can never be against Reason, our Lawyers are agreed; and that not the Letter, (that is, every construction of it,) but that which is according to the Intention of the Legislator, is the Law. And it is true: but the doubt is, of whose Reason it is, that shall be received for Law. It is not meant of any private Reason; for then there would be as much contradiction in the Lawes, as there is in the Schooles; nor yet, (as Sr. *Ed. Coke* makes it,) an *Artificiall perfection of Reason, gotten by long study, observation, and experience,* (as his was.) For it is possible long study may encrease, and confirm erroneous Sentences: and where men build on false grounds, the more they build, the greater is the ruine: and of those that study, and observe with equall time, and diligence, the reasons and resolutions are, and must remain discordant: and therefore it is not that *Juris prudentia*, or wisedome of subordinate Judges; but the Reason of this our Artificiall Man the Common-wealth, and his Command, that maketh Law: And the Common-wealth being in their Representative but one Person, there cannot easily arise any contradiction in the Lawes; and when there doth, the same Reason is able, by interpretation or alteration, to take it away. In all Courts of Justice, the Soveraign (which is the Person of the Common-wealth,) is he that Judgeth: The subordinate Judge, ought to have regard to the reason, which moved his Soveraign to make such Law, that his Sentence may be according thereunto; which then is his Soveraigns Sentence; otherwise it is his own, and an unjust one.

8. From this, that the Law is a Command, and a Command consisteth in declaration, or manifestation of the will of him that commandeth, by voyce, writing, or some other sufficient argument of the same, we may understand, that the Command of the Common-wealth, is Law onely to those, that have means to take notice of it. Over naturall fooles, children, or mad-men there is no Law, no more than over brute beasts; nor are they capable of the title of just, or unjust; because they had never power to make any covenant, or to understand the consequences thereof; and consequently never took upon them to authorise the actions of any Soveraign, as they must do that make to themselves a Common-wealth And as those from whom Nature, or Accident hath taken away the notice of all Lawes in generall; so also every man, from whom any accident, not proceeding from his own default, hath taken away the means to take notice of any particular Law, is excused, if he observe it

not; And to speak properly, that Law is no Law to him. It is therefore necessary, to consider in this place, what arguments, and signes be sufficient for the knowledge of what is the Law; that is to say, what is the will of the Soveraign, as well in Monarchies, as in other formes of government.

And first, if it be a Law that obliges all the Subjects without exception, and is not written nor otherwise published in such places as they may take notice thereof, it is a Law of Nature. For whatsoever men are to take knowledge of for Law, not upon other mens words, but every one from his own reasons, must be such as is agreeable to the reason of all men; which no Law can be, but the Law of Nature. The Lawes of Nature therefore need not any publishing, nor Proclamation; as being contained in this one Sentence, approved by all the world, *Do not that to another, which thou thinketh unreasonable to be done by another to thy selfe.*

Secondly, if it be a Law that obliges only some condition of men, or one particular man, and be not written, nor published by word, then also it is a Law of Nature; and known by the same arguments, and signs, that distinguish those in such a condition, from other Subjects. For whatsoever Law is not written, or some way published by him that makes it Law, can be known no way, but by the reason of him that is to obey it; and is therefore also a Law not only Civill, but Naturall. For Example, if the Soveraign employ a Publique Minister, without written Instructions what to doe; he is obliged to take for Instructions the Dictates of Reason; As if he make a Judge, The Judge is to take notice, that his Sentence ought to be according to the reason of his Soveraign, which being alwaies understood to be Equity, he is bound to it by the Law of Nature: Or if an Ambassador, he is (in all things not conteined in his written Instructions) to take for Instruction that which Reason dictates to be most conducing to his Soveraigns interest; and so all of other Ministers of the Soveraignty, publique and private. All which Instructions of naturall Reason may be comprehended under one name of *Fidelity*; which is a branch of naturall Justice.

The Law of Nature excepted, it belongeth to the essence of all other Lawes, to be made known, to every man that shall be obliged to obey them, either by word, or writing, or some other act, known to proceed from the Soveraign Authority. For the will of another, cannot be understood, but by his own word, or act, or by conjecture taken from his scope and purpose; which in the person of the Common-wealth, is to be supposed alwaies consonant to Equity and Reason. And in antient time, before letters were in common use, the Lawes were many times put into verse; that the rude people taking pleasure in singing, or reciting them, might the more easily reteine them in memory. And for the same reason *Solomon* adviseth a man, to bind the ten Commandements [1] upon his ten fingers. And for the Law which *Moses* gave to the people of *Israel* at the renewing of the Covenant,[2] he biddeth them to teach it their

[1] Prov. 7. 3.    [2] Deut. 11. 19.

Children, by discoursing of it both at home, and upon the way; at going to bed, and at rising from bed; and to write it upon the posts, and dores of their houses; and [1] to assemble the people, man, woman, and child, to heare it read.

Nor is it enough the Law be written, and published; but also that there be manifest signs, that it proceedeth from the will of the Soveraign. For private men, when they have, or think they have force enough to secure their unjust designes, and convoy them safely to their ambitious ends, may publish for Lawes what they please, without, or against the Legislative Authority. There is therefore requisite, not only a Declaration of the Law, but also sufficient signes of the Author, and Authority. The Author, or Legislator is supposed in every Common-wealth to be evident, because he is the Soveraign, who having been Constituted by the consent of every one, is supposed by every one to be sufficiently known. And though the ignorance, and security of men be such, for the most part, as that when the memory of the first Constitution of their Common-wealth is worn out, they doe not consider, by whose power they use to be defended against their enemies, and to have their industry protected, and to be righted when injury is done them; yet because no man that considers, can make question of it, no excuse can be derived from the ignorance of where the Soveraignty is placed. And it is a Dictate of Naturall Reason, and consequently an evident Law of Nature, that no man ought to weaken that power, the protection whereof he hath himself demanded, or wittingly received against others. Therefore of who is Soveraign, no man, but by his own fault, (whatsoever evill men suggest,) can make any doubt. The difficulty consisteth in the evidence of the Authority derived from him; The removing whereof, dependeth on the knowledge of the publique Registers, publique Counsels, publique Ministers, and publique Seales; by which all Lawes are sufficiently verified; Verifyed, I say, not Authorised: for the Verification, is but the Testimony and Record; not the Authority of the Law; which consisteth in the Command of the Soveraign only.

If therefore a man have a question of Injury, depending on the Law of Nature; that is to say, on common Equity; the Sentence of the Judge, that by Commission hath Authority to take cognisance of such causes, is a sufficient Verification of the Law of Nature in that individuall case. For though the advice of one that professeth the study of the Law, be usefull for the avoyding of contention; yet it is but advice: tis the Judge must tell men what is Law, upon the hearing of the Controversy.

But when the question is of injury, or crime, upon a written Law; every man by recourse to the Registers, by himself, or others, may (if he will) be sufficiently enformed, before he doe such injury, or commit the crime, whither it be an injury, or not: Nay he ought to doe so: For when a man doubts whether the act he goeth about, be just, or injust; and may informe himself, if he will; the doing is

[1] Deut. 31. 12.

unlawfull. In like manner, he that supposeth himself injured, in a case determined by the written Law, which he may by himself, or others see and consider; if he complaine before he consults with the Law, he does unjustly, and bewrayeth a disposition rather to vex other men, than to demand his own right.

If the question be of Obedience to a publique Officer; To have seen his Commission, with the Publique Seale, and heard it read; or to have had the means to be informed of it, if a man would, is a sufficient Verification of his Authority. For every man is obliged to doe his best endeavour, to informe himself of all written Lawes, that may concerne his own future actions.

The Legislator known; and the Lawes, either by writing, or by the light of Nature, sufficiently published; there wanteth yet another very materiall circumstance to make them obligatory. For it is not the Letter, but the Intendment, or Meaning; that is to say, the authentique Interpretation of the Law (which is the sense of the Legislator,) in which the nature of the Law consisteth; And therefore the Interpretation of all Lawes dependeth on the Authority Soveraign; and the Interpreters can be none but those, which the Soveraign, (to whom only the Subject oweth obedience) shall appoint. For else, by the craft of an Interpreter, the Law may be made to beare a sense, contrary to that of the Soveraign; by which means the Interpreter becomes the Legislator.

All Lawes, written, and unwritten, have need of Interpretation. The unwritten Law of Nature, though it be easy to such, as without partiality, and passion, make use of their naturall reason, and therefore leaves the violaters thereof without excuse; yet considering there be very few, perhaps none, that in some cases are not blinded by self love, or some other passion, it is now become of all Laws the most obscure; and has consequently the greatest need of able Interpreters. The written Laws, if they be short, are easily misinterpreted, from the divers significations of a word, or two: if long they be more obscure by the diverse significations of many words: in so much as no written Law, delivered in few, or many words, can be well understood, without a perfect understanding of the finall causes, for which the Law was made; the knowledge of which finall causes is in the Legislator. To him therefore there can not be any knot in the Law, insoluble; either by finding out the ends, to undoe it by; or else by making what ends he will, (as *Alexander* did with his sword in the Gordian knot,) by the Legislative power; which no other Interpreter can doe.

The Interpretation of the Lawes of Nature, in a Common-wealth, dependeth not on the books of Morall Philosophy. The Authority of writers, without the Authority of the Common-wealth, maketh not their opinions Law, be they never so true. That which I have written in this Treatise, concerning the Morall Vertues, and of their necessity, for the procuring, and maintaining peace, though it bee evident Truth, is not therefore presently Law; but because in all Common-wealths in the world, it is part of the Civill Law: For though it be naturally reasonable; yet it is by the Soveraigne Power that it is Law: Otherwise, it were a great errour, to call the Lawes of Nature unwritten Law; whereof wee see so many volumes published, and in them so many contradictions of one another, and of themselves.

The Interpretation of the Law of Nature, is the Sentence of the Judge constituted by the Soveraign Authority, to heare and determine such controversies, as depend thereon; and consisteth in the application of the Law to the present case. For in the act of Judicature, the Judge doth no more but consider, whither the demand of the party, be consonant to naturall reason, and Equity; and the Sentence he giveth, is therefore the Interpretation of the Law of Nature; which Interpretation is Authentique; not because it is his private Sentence; but because he giveth it by Authority of the Soveraign, whereby it becomes the Soveraigns Sentence; which is Law for that time, to the parties pleading.

But because there is no Judge Subordinate, nor Soveraign, but may erre in a Judgement of Equity; if afterward in another like case he find it more consonant to Equity to give a contrary Sentence, he is obliged to doe it. No mans error becomes his own Law; nor obliges him to persist in it. Neither (for the same reason) becomes it a Law to other Judges, though sworn to follow it. For though a wrong Sentence given by authority of the Soveraign, if he know and allow it, in such Lawes as are mutable, be a constitution of a new Law, in cases, in which every little circumstance is the same; yet in Lawes immutable, such as are the Lawes of Nature, they are no Lawes to the same, or other Judges, in the like cases for ever after. Princes succeed one another; and one Judge passeth, another commeth; nay, Heaven and Earth shall passe; but not one title of the Law of Nature shall passe; for it is the Eternall Law of God. Therefore all the Sentences of precedent Judges that have ever been, cannot all together make a Law contrary to naturall Equity: Nor any Examples of former Judges, can warrant an unreasonable Sentence, or discharge the present Judge of the trouble of studying what is Equity (in the case he is to Judge,) from the principles of his own naturall reason. For example sake, 'Tis against the Law of Nature, *To punish the Innocent*; and Innocent is he that acquitteth himselfe Judically, and is acknowledged for Innocent by the Judge. Put the case now, that a man is accused of a capitall crime, and seeing the power and malice of some enemy, and the frequent corruption and partiality of Judges, runneth away for feare of the event, and afterwards is taken, and brought to a legall triall, and maketh it sufficiently appear, he was not guilty of the crime, and being thereof acquitted, is neverthelesse condemned to lose his goods; this is a manifest condemnation of the Innocent. I say therefore, that there is no place in the world, where this can be an interpretation of a Law of Nature, or be made a Law by the Sentences of precedent Judges, that had done the same. For he that judged it first, judged unjustly; and no Injustice can be a pattern of Judgement to succeeding Judges. A written Law may forbid innocent men to fly, and they may be punished for flying: But that flying for feare of injury, should be taken for presumption of guilt, after a man is already absolved of the crime Judicially, is contrary to the nature of a Presumption, which hath no place after Judgement given. Yet this is set down by a great Lawyer for the common Law of *England*. *If a man* (saith he) *that is Innocent, be accused of Felony, and for feare flyeth for the same; albeit he judicially acquitteth himselfe of the Felony ; yet if it be found that he fled for the Felony, he shall notwithstanding his Innocency, Forfeit all his goods, chattells, debts, and duties. For as to the Forfeiture of them, the Law will admit no proofe against the Presumption in Law, grounded upon his flight.* Here you see, *An Innocent man, Judicially acquitted, notwithstanding his Innocency,* (when no written Law forbad him to fly) after his acquittall, *upon a Presumption in Law,* condemned to lose all the goods he hath. If the Law ground upon his flight a Presumption of the fact, (which was Capitall,) the Sentence ought to have been Capitall: if the Presumption were not of the Fact, for what then ought he to lose his goods? This therefore is no Law of *England*; nor is the condemnation grounded upon a Presumption of Law, but upon the Presumption of the Judges. It is also against Law, to say that no Proofe shall be admitted against a Presumption of Law. For all Judges, Soveraign and subordinate, if they refuse to heare Proofe, refuse to do Justice: for though the Sentence be Just, yet the Judges that condemn without hearing the Proofes offered, are Unjust Judges, and their Presumption is but Prejudice; which no man ought to bring with him to the Seat of Justice, whatsoever precedent judgements, or examples he shall pretend to follow. There be other things of this nature, wherein mens Judgements have been perverted, by trusting to Precedents: but this is enough to shew, that though the Sentence of the Judge, be a Law to the party pleading, yet it is no Law to any Judge, that shall succeed him in that Office.

In like manner, when question is of the Meaning of written Lawes, he is not the Interpreter of them that writeth a Commentary upon them. For Commentaries are commonly more subject to cavill, than the Text; and therefore need other Commentaries; and so there will be no end of such Interpretation. And therefore unlesse there be an Interpreter authorised by the Soveraign, from which the subordinate Judges are not to recede, the Interpreter can be no other than the ordinary Judges, in the same manner, as they are in cases of the unwritten Law; and their Sentences are to be taken by them that plead, for Lawes in that particular case; but not to bind other Judges, in like cases to give like judgements. For a Judge may erre in the Interpretation even of written Lawes; but no errour of a subordinate Judge, can change the Law, which is the generall Sentence of the Soveraigne.

In written Lawes, men use to make a difference between the Letter, and the Sentence of the Law: And when by the Letter, is meant whatsoever can be gathered from the bare words, 'tis well distinguished.  For the significations of almost all words, are either in themselves, or in the metaphoricall use of them, ambiguous; and may be drawn in argument, to make many senses; but there is onely one sense of the Law.  But if by the Letter, be meant the literall sense, then the Letter, and the Sentence or intention of the Law, is all one.  For the literall sense is that, which the Legislator intended, should by the letter of the Law be signified.  Now the Intention of the Legislator is alwayes supposed to be Equity: For it were a great contumely for a Judge to think otherwise of the Soveraigne.  He ought therefore, if the Word of the Law doe not fully authorise a reasonable Sentence, to supply it with the Law of Nature; or if the case be difficult, to respit Judgement till he have received more ample authority.  For Example, a written Law ordaineth, that he which is thrust out of his house by force, shall be restored by force: It happens that a man by negligence leaves his house empty, and returning is kept out by force, in which case there is no speciall Law ordained.  It is evident, that this case is contained in the same Law: for else there is no remedy for him at all; which is to be supposed against the Intention of the Legislator.  Again, the word of the Law, commandeth to Judge according to the Evidence: A man is accused falsly of a fact, which the Judge saw himself done by another; and not by him that is accused.  In this case neither shall the Letter of the Law be followed to the condemnation of the Innocent, nor shall the Judge give Sentence against the evidence of the Witnesses; because the Letter of the Law is to the contrary: but procure of the Soveraign that another be made Judge, and himself Witnesse.  So that the incommodity that follows the bare words of a written Law, may lead him to the Intention of the Law, whereby to interpret the same the better; though no Incommodity can warrant a Sentence against the Law.  For every Judge of Right, and Wrong, is not Judge of what is Commodious, or Incommodious to the Common-wealth.

The abilities required in a good Interpreter of the Law, that is to say, in a good Judge, are not the same with those of an Advocate; namely the study of the Lawes.  For a Judge, as he ought to take notice of the Fact, from none but the Witnesses; so also he ought to take notice of the Law, from nothing but the Statutes, and Constitutions of the Soveraign, alledged in the pleading, or declared to him by some that have authority from the Soveraign Power to declare them; and need not take care before-hand, what hee shall Judge; for it shall bee given him what hee shall say concerning the Fact, by Witnesses; and what hee shall say in point of Law, from those that shall in their pleadings shew it, and by authority interpret it upon the place.  The Lords of Parlament in *England* were Judges, and most difficult causes have been heard and determined by them; yet few of them were much versed in the study of the Lawes, and fewer had made profession of them: and though they consulted with Lawyers, that were appointed to be present there for that purpose; yet they alone had the authority of giving Sentence. In like manner, in the ordinary trialls of Right, Twelve men of the common People, are the Judges, and give Sentence, not onely of the Fact, but of the Right; and pronounce simply for the Complaynant, or for the Defendant; that is to say, are Judges not onely of the Fact, but also of the Right: and in a question of crime, not onely determine whether done, or not done; but also whether it be *Murder, Homicide, Felony, Assault,* and the like, which are determinations of Law: but because they are not supposed to know the Law of themselves, there is one that hath Authority to enforme them of it, in the particular case they are to Judge of. But yet if they judge not according to that he tells them, they are not subject thereby to any penalty; unlesse it be made appear, they did it against their consciences, or had been corrupted by reward.

The things that make a good Judge, or good Interpreter of the Lawes, are, first, *A right understanding* of that principall Law of Nature called *Equity*; which depending not on the reading of other mens Writings, but on the goodnesse of a mans own naturall Reason, and Meditation, is presumed to be in the most, that have had most leisure, and had the most inclination to meditate thereon. Secondly, *Contempt of unnecessary Riches,* and Preferments. Thirdly *To be able in judgement to devest himselfe of all feare, anger, hatred, love, and compassion.* Fourthly, and lastly, *Patience to heare; diligent attention in hearing; and memory to retain, digest and apply what he hath heard.*

The difference and division of the Lawes, has been made in divers manners, according to the different methods, of those men that have written of them. For it is a thing that dependeth not on Nature, but on the scope of the Writer; and is subservient to every mans proper method. In the Institutions of *Justinian,* we find seven sorts of Civill Lawes. 1. The *Edicts, Constitutions,* and *Epistles of the Prince,* that is, of the Emperour; because the whole power of the people was in him. Like these, are the Proclamations of the Kings of *England.*

2. *The Decrees of the whole people of Rome* (comprehending the Senate,) when they were put to the Question by the *Senate.* These were Lawes, at first, by the vertue of the Soveraign Power residing in the people; and such of them as by the Emperours were not abrogated, remained Lawes by the Authority Imperiall. For all Lawes that bind, are understood to be Lawes by his authority that has power to repeale them. Somewhat like to these Lawes, are the Acts of Parliament in England.

3. *The Decrees of the Common People* (excluding the Senate,) when they were put to the question by the *Tribune* of the people. For such of them as were not abrogated by the Emperours, remained Lawes by the Authority Imperiall. Like to these, were the Orders of the House of Commons in *England.*

4. *Senatûs consulta,* the *Orders of the Senate*; because when the people of *Rome* grew so numerous, as it was inconvenient to assemble

them; it was thought fit by the Emperour, that men should Consult the Senate, in stead of the people: And these have some resemblance with the Acts of Counsell.

5. *The Edicts of Prætors*, and (in some Cases) of the *Ædiles*: such as are the Chiefe Justices in the Courts of *England*.

6. *Responsa Prudentum*; which were the Sentences, and Opinions of those Lawyers, to whom the Emperour gave Authority to interpret the Law, and to give answer to such as in matter of Law demanded their advice; which Answers, the Judges in giving Judgement were obliged by the Constitutions of the Emperour to observe: And should be like the Reports of Cases Judged, if other Judges be by the Law of *England* bound to observe them.   For the Judges of the Common Law of *England*, are not properly Judges, but *Juris Consulti*; of whom the Judges, who are either the Lords, or Twelve men of the Country, are in point of Law to ask advice.

7. Also, *Unwritten Customes*, (which in their own nature are an imitation of Law,) by the tacite consent of the Emperour, in case they be not contrary to the Law of Nature, are very Lawes.

Another division of Lawes, is into *Naturall* and *Positive*.   *Naturall* are those which have been Lawes from all Eternity; and are called not onely *Naturall*, but also *Morall* Lawes; consisting in the Morall Vertues, as Justice, Equity, and all habits of the mind that conduce to Peace, and Charity; of which I have already spoken in the fourteenth and fifteenth Chapters.

*Positive*, are those which have not been from Eternity; but have been made Lawes by the Will of those that have had the Soveraign Power over others; and are either written, or made known to men, by some other argument of the Will of their Legislator.

Again, of Positive Lawes, some are *Humane*, some *Divine :* And of Humane positive lawes, some are *Distributive*, some *Penal*. *Distributive* are those that determine the Rights of the Subjects, declaring to every man what it is, by which he acquireth and holdeth a propriety in lands, or goods, and a right or liberty of action: and these speak to all the Subjects.   *Penal* are those, which declare, what Penalty shall be inflicted on those that violate the Law; and speak to the Ministers and Officers ordained for execution.   For though every one ought to be informed of the Punishments ordained beforehand for their transgression; neverthelesse the Command is not addressed to the Delinquent, (who cannot be supposed will faithfully punish himselfe,) but to publique Ministers appointed to see the Penalty executed.   And these Penal Lawes are for the most part written together with the Lawes Distributive; and are some-times called Judgements.   For all Lawes are generall J dgements, or Sentences of the Legislator, as also every particular Judgement, is a Law to him, whose case is Judged.

*Divine Positive Lawes* (for Naturall Lawes being Eternall, and Universall, are all Divine,) are those, which being the Command-ments of God, (not from all Eternity, nor universally addressed to all men, but onely to a certain people, or to certain persons,) are declared for such, by those whom God hath authorised to declare them. But this Authority of man to declare what be these Positive Lawes of God, how can it be known? God may command a man by a supernaturall way, to deliver Lawes to other men. But because it is of the essence of Law, that he who is to be obliged, be assured of the Authority of him that declareth it, which we cannot naturally take notice to be from God, *How can a man without supernaturall Revelation be assured of the Revelation received by the declarer?* and *how can he be bound to obey them?* For the first question, how a man can be assured of the Revelation of another, without a Revelation particularly to himselfe, it is evidently impossible: For though a man may be induced to believe such Revelation, from the Miracles they see him doe, or from seeing the Extraordinary sanctity of his life, or from seeing the Extraordinary wisedome, or Extraordinary felicity of his Actions, all which are marks of God[s] extraordinary favour; yet they are not assured evidences of speciall Revelation. Miracles are Marvellous workes: but that which is marvellous to one, may not be so to another. Sanctity may be feigned; and the visible felicities of this world, are most often the work of God by Naturall, and ordinary causes. And therefore no man can infallibly know by naturall reason, that another has had a supernaturall revelation of Gods will; but only a beliefe; every one (as the signes thereof shall appear greater, or lesser) a firmer, or a weaker belief.

But for the second, how he can be bound to obey them; it is not so hard. For if the Law declared, be not against the Law of Nature (which is undoubtedly Gods Law) and he undertake to obey it, he is bound by his own act; bound I say to obey it, but not bound to believe it: for mens beliefe, and interiour cogitations, are not subject to the commands, but only to the operation of God, ordinary, or extraordinary. Faith of Supernaturall Law, is not a fulfilling, but only an assenting to the same; and not a duty that we exhibite to God, but a gift which God freely giveth to whom he pleaseth; as also Unbelief is not a breach of any of his Lawes; but a rejection of them all, except the Laws Naturall. But this that I say, will be made yet cleerer, by the Examples, and Testimonies concerning this point in holy Scripture. The Covenant God made with *Abraham* (in a Supernaturall manner) was thus, *This is the Covenant which thou shalt observe between Me and Thee and thy Seed after thee,* *Abrahams* Seed had not this revelation, nor were yet in being; yet they are a party to the Covenant, and bound to obey what *Abraham* should declare to them for Gods Law; which they could not be, but in vertue of the obedience they owed to their Parents; who (if they be Subject to no other earthly power, as here in the case of *Abraham*) have Soveraign power over their children, and servants. Againe, where God saith to *Abraham, In thee shall all Nations of the earth be blessed: For I know thou wilt command thy children, and thy house after thee to keep the way of the Lord, and to observe Righteousnesse and Judgement,* it is manifest, the obedience of his Family, who had no Revelation, depended on their former obligation to obey their

Soveraign.  At Mount *Sinai Moses* only went up to God; the people were forbidden to approach on paine of death; yet were they bound to obey all that *Moses* declared to them for Gods Law.  Upon what ground, but on this submission of their own, *Speak thou to us, and we will heare thee ; but let not God speak to us, lest we dye ?*  By which two places it sufficiently appeareth, that in a Common-wealth, a subject that has no certain and assured Revelation particularly to himself concerning the Will of God, is to obey for such, the Command of the Common-wealth: for if men were at liberty, to take for Gods Commandements, their own dreams, and fancies, or the dreams and fancies of private men; scarce two men would agree upon what is Gods Commandement; and yet in respect of them, every man would despise the Commandements of the Common-wealth.  I conclude therefore, that in all things not contrary to· the Morall Law, (that is to say, to the Law of Nature,) all Subjects are bound to obey that for divine Law, which is declared to be so, by the Lawes of the Common-wealth.  Which also is evident to any mans reason; for whatsoever is not against the Law of Nature, may be made Law in the name of them that have the Soveraign power; and there is no reason men should be the lesse obliged by it, when tis propounded in the name of God.  Besides, there is no place in the world where men are permitted to pretend other Commandments of God, than are declared for such by the Common-wealth.  Christian States punish those that revolt· from Christian Religion, and all other States, those that set up any Religion by them forbidden.  For in whatsoever is not regulated by the Common-wealth, tis Equity (which is the Law of Nature, and therefore an eternall Law of God) that every man equally enjoy his liberty.

There is also another distinction of Laws, into *Fundamentall,* and *not Fundamentall*: but I could never see in any Author, what a Fundamentall Law signifieth.  Nevertheless one may very reasonably distinguish Laws in that manner.

For a Fundamentall Law in every Common-wealth is that, which being taken away, the Common-wealth faileth, and is utterly dissolved; as a building whose Foundation is destroyed.  And therefore a Fundamentall Law is that, by which Subjects are bound to uphold whatsoever power is given to the Soveraign, whether a Monarch, or a Soveraign Assembly, without which the Common-wealth cannot stand; such as is the power of War and Peace, of Judicature, of Election of Officers, and of doing whatsoever he shall think necessary for the Publique good.  Not Fundamentall is that, the abrogating whereof, draweth not with it the dissolution of the Common-Wealth; such as are the Lawes concerning Controversies between subject and subject.  Thus much of the Division of Lawes.

I find the words *Lex Civilis*, and *Jus Civile*, that is to say, *Law* and *Right Civil*, promiscuously used for the same thing, even in the most learned Authors; which nevertheless ought not to be so.  For *Right* is *Liberty*, namely that Liberty which the Civil Law leaves us: But *Civill Law* is an *Obligation*; and takes from us the Liberty which the Law of Nature gave us. Nature gave a Right to every man to secure himselfe by his own strength, and to invade a suspected neighbour, by way of prevention: but the Civill Law takes away that Liberty, in all cases where the protection of the Law may be safely stayd for. Insomuch as *Lex* and *Jus*, are as different as *Obligation* and *Liberty*.

Likewise *Lawes* and *Charters* are taken promiscuously for the same thing. Yet Charters are Donations of the Soveraign; and not Lawes, but exemptions from Law. The phrase of a Law is *Jubeo, Injungo, I command,* and *Enjoyn:* the phrase of a Charter is *Dedi, Concessi, I have Given, I have Granted:* but what is given or granted, to a man, is not forced upon him, by a Law. A Law may be made to bind All the Subjects of a Common-wealth: a Liberty, or Charter is only to One man, or some One part of the people. For to say all the people of a Common-wealth, have Liberty in any case whatsoever; is to say, that in such case, there hath been no Law made; or else having been made, is now abrogated.

## CHAP. XXVII.

### *Of* CRIMES, EXCUSES, *and* EXTENUATIONS

A *Sinne,* is not onely a Transgression of a Law, but also any Contempt of the Legislator. For such Contempt, is a breach of all his Lawes at once. And therefore may consist, not onely in the *Commission* of a Fact, or in the Speaking of Words by the Lawes forbidden, or in the *Omission* of what the Law commandeth, but also in the *Intention,* or purpose to transgresse. For the purpose to breake the Law, is some degree of Contempt of him, to whom it belongeth to see it executed. To be delighted in the Imagination onely, of being possessed of another mans goods, servants, or wife, without any intention to take them from him by force, or fraud, is no breach of the Law, that sayth, *Thou shalt not covet:* nor is the pleasure a man may have in imagining, or dreaming of the death of him, from whose life be expecteth nothing but dammage, and displeasure, a Sinne; but the resolving to put some Act in execution, that tendeth thereto. For to be pleased in the fiction of that, which would please a man if it were reall, is a Passion so adhærent to the Nature both of man, and every other living creature, as to make it a Sinne, were to make Sinne of being a man. The consideration of this, has made me think them too severe, both to themselves, and others, that maintain, that the First motions of the mind, (though checked with the fear of God) be Sinnes. But I confesse it is safer to erre on that hand, than on the other.

A CRIME, is a sinne, consisting in the Committing (by Deed, or Word) of that which the Law forbiddeth, or the Omission of what it hath commanded.  So that every Crime is a sinne;  but not every sinne a Crime.  To intend to steale, or kill, is a sinne, though it never appeare in Word, or Fact:  for God that seeth the thoughts of man, can lay it to his charge:  but till it appear by some thing done, or said, by which the intention may be argued by a humane Judge, it hath not the name of Crime:  which distinction the Greeks observed, in the word ἁμάρτημα, and ἔγκλημα, or αἰτία;  whereof the former, (which is translated *Sinne*) signifieth any swarving from the Law whatsoever;  but the two later, (which are translated *Crime*,) signifie that sinne onely, whereof one man may accuse another.  But of Intentions, which never appear by any outward act, there is no place for humane accusation.  In like manner the Latines by *Peccatum*, which is *Sinne*, signifie all manner of deviation from the Law;  but by *Crimen*, (which word they derive from *Cerno*, which signifies to perceive,) they mean onely such sinnes, as may be made appear before a Judge;  and therfore are not meer Intentions.

From this relation of Sinne to the Law, and of Crime to the Civill Law, may be inferred, First, that where Law ceaseth, Sinne ceaseth. But because the Law of Nature is eternall, Violation of Covenants, Ingratitude, Arrogance, and all Facts contrary to any Morall vertue, can never cease to be Sinne.  Secondly, that the Civill Law ceasing, Crimes cease:  for there being no other Law remaining, but that of Nature, there is no place for Accusation;  every man being his own Judge, and accused onely by his own Conscience, and cleared by the Uprightnesse of his own Intention.  When therefore his Intention is Right, his fact is no Sinne:  if otherwise, his fact is Sinne;  but not Crime.  Thirdly, That when the Soveraign Power ceaseth, Crime also ceaseth:  for where there is no such Power, there is no protection to be had from the Law;  and therefore every one may protect himself by his own power:  for no man in the Institution of Soveraign Power can be supposed to give away the Right of preserving his own body;  for the safety whereof all Soveraignty was ordained.  But this is to be understood onely of those, that have not themselves contributed to the taking away of the Power that protected them: for that was a Crime from the beginning.

The source of every Crime, is some defect of the Understanding; or some errour in Reasoning;  or some sudden force of the Passions. Defect in the Understanding, is *Ignorance*;  in Reasoning, *Erroneous Opinion*.  Again, Ignorance is of three sorts;  of the *Law*, and of the *Soveraign*, and of the *Penalty*.  Ignorance of the Law of Nature Excuseth no man;  because every man that hath attained to the use of Reason, is supposed to know, he ought not to do to another, what he would not have done to himselfe.  Therefore into what place soever a man shall come, if he do any thing contrary to that Law, it is a Crime.  If a man come from the *Indies* hither, and perswade men here to receive a new Religion, or teach them any thing that tendeth to disobedience of the Lawes of this Country, though he be never so well perswaded of the truth of what he teacheth, he commits a Crime, and may be justly punished for the same, not onely because his doctrine is false, but also because he does that which he would not approve in another, namely, that comming from hence, he should endeavour to alter the Religion there. But ignorance of the Civill Law, shall Excuse a man in a strange Country, till it be declared to him; because, till then no Civill Law is binding.

In the like manner, if the Civill Law of a mans own Country, be not so sufficiently declared, as he may know it if he will; nor the Action against the Law of Nature; the Ignorance is a good Excuse: In other cases Ignorance of the Civill Law, Excuseth not.

Ignorance of the Soveraign Power, in the place of a mans ordinary residence, Excuseth him not; because he ought to take notice of the Power, by which he hath been protected there.

Ignorance of the Penalty, where the Law is declared, Excuseth no man: For in breaking the Law, which without a fear of penalty to follow, were not a Law, but vain words, he undergoeth the penalty, though he know not what it is; because, whosoever voluntarily doth any action, accepteth all the known consequences of it; but Punishment is a known consequence of the violation of the Lawes, in every Common-wealth; which punishment, if it be determined already by the Law, he is subject to that; if not, then is he subject to Arbitrary punishment. For it is reason, that he which does Injury, without other limitation than that of his own Will, should suffer punishment without other limitation, than that of his Will whose Law is thereby violated.

But when a penalty, is either annexed to the Crime in the Law it selfe, or hath been usually inflicted in the like cases; there the Delinquent is Excused from a greater penalty. For the punishment foreknown, if not great enough to deterre men from the action, is an invitement to it: because when men compare the benefit of their Injustice, with the harm of their punishment, by necessity of Nature they choose that which appeareth best for themselves: and therefore when they are punished more than the Law had formerly determined, or more than others were punished for the same Crime; it is the Law that tempted, and deceiveth them.

No Law, made after a Fact done, can make it a Crime: because if the Fact be against the Law of Nature, the Law was before the Fact; and a Positive Law cannot be taken notice of, before it be made; and therefore cannot be Obligatory. But when the Law that forbiddeth a Fact, is made before the Fact be done; yet he that doth the Fact, is lyable to the Penalty ordained after, in case no lesser Penalty were made known before, neither by Writing, nor by Example, for the reason immediately before alledged.

From defect in Reasoning, (that is to say, from Errour,) men are prone to violate the Lawes, three wayes. First, by Presumption of false Principles: as when men from having observed how in all places, and in all ages, unjust Actions have been authorised, by the force, and victories of those who have committed them; and that potent men, breaking through the Cob-web Lawes of their Country, the weaker sort, and those that have failed in their Enterprises, have been esteemed the onely Criminals; have thereupon taken for Principles, and grounds of their Reasoning, *That Justice is but a vain word : That whatsoever a man can get by his own Industry, and hazard, is his own : That the Practice of all Nations cannot be unjust : That Examples of former times are good Arguments of doing the like again*; and many more of that kind: Which being granted, no Act in it selfe can be a Crime, but must be made so (not by the Law, but) by the successe of them that commit it; and the same Fact be vertuous, or vicious, as Fortune pleaseth; so that what *Marius* makes a Crime, *Sylla* shall make meritorious, and *Cæsar* (the same Lawes standing) turn again into a Crime, to the perpetuall disturbance of the Peace of the Common-wealth.

Secondly, by false Teachers, that either mis-interpret the Law of Nature, making it thereby repugnant to the Law Civill; or by teaching for Lawes, such Doctrines of their own, or Traditions of former times, as are inconsistent with the duty of a Subject.

Thirdly, by Erroneous Inferences from True Principles; which happens commonly to men that are hasty, and præcipitate in concluding, and resolving what to do; such as are they, that have both a great opinion of their own understanding, and believe that things of this nature require not time and study, but onely common experience, and a good naturall wit; whereof no man thinks himselfe unprovided: whereas the knowledge, of Right and Wrong, which is no lesse difficult, there is no man will pretend to, without great and long study. And of those defects in Reasoning, there is none that can Excuse (though some of them may Extenuate) a Crime, in any man, that pretendeth to the administration of his own private businesse; much lesse in them that undertake a publique charge; because they pretend to the Reason, upon the want whereof they would ground their Excuse.

Of the Passions that most frequently are the causes of Crime, one, is Vain-glory, or a foolish over-rating of their own worth; as if difference of worth, were an effect of their wit, or riches, or bloud, or some other naturall quality, not depending on the Will of those that have the Soveraign Authority. From whence proceedeth a Presumption that the punishments ordained by the Lawes, and extended generally to all Subjects, ought not to be inflicted on them, with the same rigour they are inflicted on the poor, obscure, and simple men, comprehended under the name of the *Vulgar*.

Therefore it happeneth commonly, that such as value themselves by the greatnesse of their wealth, adventure on Crimes, upon hope of escaping punishment, by corrupting publique Justice, or obtaining Pardon by Mony, or other rewards.

And that such as have multitude of Potent Kindred; and popular men, that have gained reputation amongst the Multitude, take courage to violate the Lawes, from a hope of oppressing the Power, to whom it belongeth to put them in execution.

And that such as have a great, and false opinion of their own Wisedome, take upon them to reprehend the actions, and call in question the Authority of them that govern, and so to unsettle the Lawes with their publique discourse, as that nothing shall be a Crime, but what their own designes require should be so. It happeneth also to the same men, to be prone to all such Crimes, as consist in Craft, and in deceiving of their Neighbours; because they think their designes are too subtile to be perceived. These I say are effects of a false presumption of their own Wisdome. For of them that are the first movers in the disturbance of Common-wealths; (which can never happen without a Civill Warre,) very few are left alive long enough, to see their new Designes established: so that the benefit of their Crimes, redoundeth to Posterity, and such as would least have wished it: which argues they were not so wise, as they thought they were. And those that deceive upon hope of not being observed, do commonly deceive themselves, (the darknesse in which they believe they lye hidden, being nothing else but their own blindnesse;) and are no wiser than Children, that think all hid, by hiding their own eyes.

And generally all vain-glorious men, (unlesse they be withall timorous,) are subject to Anger; as being more prone than others to interpret for contempt, the ordinary liberty of conversation: And there are few Crimes that may not be produced by Anger.

As for the Passions, of Hate, Lust, Ambition, and Covetousnesse, what Crimes they are apt to produce, is so obvious to every mans experience and understanding, as there needeth nothing to be said of them, saving that they are infirmities, so annexed to the nature, both of man, and all other living creatures, as that their effects cannot be hindred, but by extraordinary use of Reason, or a constant severity in punishing them. For in those things men hate, they find a continuall, and unavoydable molestation; whereby either a mans patience must be everlasting, or he must be eased by removing the power of that which molesteth him: the former is difficult; the later is many times impossible, without some violation of the Law. Ambition, and Covetousnesse are Passions also that are perpetually incumbent, and pressing; whereas Reason is not perpetually present, to resist them; and therefore whensoever the hope of impunity appears, their effects proceed. And for Lust, what it wants in the lasting, it hath in the vehemence, which sufficeth to weigh down the apprehension of all easie, or uncertain punishments.

Of all Passions, that which enclineth men least to break the Lawes, is Fear. Nay, (excepting some generous natures,) it is the onely thing, (when there is apparence of profit, or pleasure by breaking the Lawes,) that makes men keep them. And yet in many cases a Crime may be committed through Feare.

For not every Fear justifies the Action it produceth, but the fear onely of corporeall hurt, which we call *Bodily Fear*, and from which a man cannot see how to be delivered, but by the action. A man is assaulted, fears present death, from which he sees not how to escape, but by wounding him that assaulteth him; If he wound him to death, this is no Crime; because no man is supposed at the making of a Common-wealth, to have abandoned the defence of his life, or limbes, where the Law cannot arrive time enough to his assistance. But to kill a man, because from his actions, or his threatnings, I may argue he will kill me when he can, (seeing I have time, and means to demand protection, from the Soveraign Power,) is a Crime. Again, a man receives words of disgrace, or some little injuries (for which they that made the Lawes, had assigned no punishment, nor thought it worthy of a man that hath the use of Reason, to take notice of,) and is afraid, unlesse he revenge it, he shall fall into contempt, and consequently be obnoxious to the like injuries from others; and to avoyd this, breaks the Law, and protects himselfe for the future, by the terrour of his private revenge. This is a Crime: For the hurt is not Corporeall, but Phantasticall, and (though in this corner of the world, made sensible by a custome not many years since begun, amongst young and vain men,) so light, as a gallant man, and one that is assured of his own courage, cannot take notice of. Also a man may stand in fear of Spirits, either through his own superstition, or through too much credit given to other men, that tell him of strange Dreams and Visions; and thereby be made believe they will hurt him, for doing, or omitting divers things, which neverthelesse, to do or omit, is contrary to the Lawes; And that which is so done, or omitted, is not to be Excused by this fear; but is a Crime. For (as I have shewn before in the second Chapter) Dreams be naturally but the fancies remaining in sleep, after the impressions our Senses had formerly received waking; and when men are by any accident unassured they have slept, seem to be reall Visions; and therefore he that presumes to break the Law upon his own, or anothers Dream, or pretended Vision, or upon other Fancy of the power of Invisible Spirits, than is permitted by the Common-wealth, leaveth the Law of Nature, which is a certain offence, and followeth the imagery of his own, or another private mans brain, which he can never know whether it signifieth any thing, or nothing, nor whether he that tells his Dream, say true, or lye; which if every private man should have leave to do, (as they must by the Law of Nature, if any one have it) there could no Law be made to hold, and so all Common-wealth would be dissolved.

From these different sources of Crimes, it appeares already, that all Crimes are not (as the Stoicks of old time maintained) of the same allay. There is place, not only for Excuse, by which that which seemed a Crime, is proved to be none at all; but also for Extenuation, by which the Crime, that seemed great, is made lesse. For though all Crimes doe equally deserve the name of Injustice, as all deviation from a strait line is equally crookednesse which the Stoicks rightly observed; yet it does not follow that all Crimes are equally unjust, no more than that all crooked lines are equally crooked; which the Stoicks not observing, held it as great a Crime, to kill a Hen, against the Law, as to kill ones Father.

That which totally Excuseth a Fact, and takes away from it the nature of a Crime, can be none but that, which at the same time, taketh away the obligation of the Law. For the Fact committed once against the Law, if he that committed it be obliged to the Law, can be no other than a Crime.

The want of means to know the Law, totally Excuseth: For the Law whereof a man has no means to enforme himselfe, is not obligatory. But the want of diligence to enquire, shall not be considered as a want of means; Nor shall any man, that pretendeth to reason enough for the Government of his own affairs, be supposed to want means to know the Lawes of Nature; because they are known by the reason he pretends to: only Children, and Madmen are Excused from offences against the Law Naturall.

Where a man is captive, or in the power of the enemy, (and he is then in the power of the enemy, when his person, or his means of living, is so,) if it be without his own fault, the Obligation of the Law ceaseth; because he must obey the enemy, or dye; and consequently such obedience is no Crime: for no man is obliged (when the protection of the Law faileth,) not to protect himself, by the best means he can.

If a man by the terrour of present death, be compelled to doe a fact against the Law, he is totally Excused; because no Law can oblige a man to abandon his own preservation. And supposing such a Law were obligatory; yet a man would reason thus, *If I doe it not I die presently* ; *if I doe it, I die afterwards* ; *therefore by doing it, there is time of life gained*; Nature therefore compells him to the fact.

When a man is destitute of food, or other thing necessary for his life, and cannot preserve himselfe any other way, but by some fact against the Law; as if in a great famine he take the food by force, or stealth, which he cannot obtaine for mony, nor charity; or in defence of his life, snatch away another mans Sword, he is totally Excused, for the reason next before alledged.

Again, Facts done against the Law, by the authority of another, are by that authority Excused against the Author; because no man ought to accuse his own fact in another, that is but his instrument: but it is not Excused against a third person thereby injured; because in the violation of the Law, both the Author, and Actor are Criminalls. From hence it followeth that when that Man, or Assembly, that hath the Soveraign Power, commandeth a man to do that which is contrary to a former Law, the doing of it is totally Excused: For he ought not to condemn it himselfe, because he is the Author; and what cannot justly be condemned by the Soveraign, cannot justly be punished by any other. Besides, when the Soveraign commandeth any thing to be done against his own former Law, the Command, as to that particular fact, is an abrogation of the Law.

If that Man, or Assembly, that hath the Soveraign Power, disclaime any Right essentiall to the Soveraignty, whereby there accrueth to the Subject, any liberty inconsistent with the Soveraign

Power, that is to say, with the very being of a Common-wealth, if the Subject shall refuse to obey the Command in any thing, contrary to the liberty granted, this is neverthelesse a Sinne, and contrary to the duty of the Subject: for he ought to take notice of what is inconsistent with the Soveraignty, because it was erected by his own consent, and for his own defence; and that such liberty as is inconsistent with it, was granted through ignorance of the evill consequence thereof. But if he not onely disobey, but also resist a publique Minister in the execution of it, then it is a Crime; because he might have been righted, (without any breach of the Peace,) upon complaint.

The Degrees of Crime are taken on divers Scales, and measured, First, by the malignity of the Source, or Cause: Secondly, by the contagion of the Example: Thirdly, by the mischiefe of the Effect; and Fourthly, by the concurrence of Times, Places, and Persons.

The same Fact done against the Law, if it proceed from Presumption of strength, riches, or friends to resist those that are to execute the Law, is a greater Crime, than if it proceed from hope of not being discovered, or of escape by flight: For Presumption of impunity by force, is a Root, from whence springeth, at all times, and upon all temptations, a contempt of all Lawes; whereas in the later case, the apprehension of danger that makes a man fly, renders him more obedient for the future. A Crime which we know to be so, is greater than the same Crime proceeding from a false perswasion that it is lawfull: For he that committeth it against his own conscience, presumeth on his force, or other power, which encourages him to commit the same again: but he that doth it by errour, after the errour shewn him, is conformable to the Law.

Hee, whose errour proceeds from the authority of a Teacher, or an Interpreter of the Law publiquely authorised, is not so faulty, as he whose errour proceedeth from a peremptory pursute of his own principles, and reasoning: For what is taught by one that teacheth by publique Authority, the Common-wealth teacheth, and hath a resemblance of Law, till the same Authority controuleth it; and in all Crimes that contain not in them a denyall of the Soveraign Power, nor are against an evident Law, Excuseth totally: whereas he that groundeth his actions, on his private Judgement, ought according to the rectitude, or errour thereof, to stand, or fall.

The same Fact, if it have been constantly punished in other men, is a greater Crime, than if there have been many precedent Examples of impunity. For those Examples, are so many hopes of Impunity, given by the Soveraign himselfe: And because he which furnishes a man with such a hope, and presumption of mercy, as encourageth him to offend, hath his part in the offence; he cannot reasonably charge the offender with the whole.

A Crime arising from a sudden Passion, is not so great, as when the same ariseth from long meditation: For in the former case there is a place for Extenuation, in the common infirmity of humane nature: but he that doth it with præmeditation, has used circumspection,

and cast his eye, on the Law, on the punishment, and on the conse-
quence thereof to humane society; all which in committing the
Crime, hee hath contemned, and postposed to his own appetite.
But there is no suddennesse of Passion sufficient for a totall
Excuse: For all the time between the first knowing of the
Law, and the Commission of the Fact, shall be taken for a time of
deliberation; because he ought by meditation of the Law, to rectifie
the irregularity of his Passions.

Where the Law is publiquely, and with assiduity, before all the
people read, and interpreted; a fact done against it, is a greater
Crime, than where men are left without such instruction, to enquire
of it with difficulty, uncertainty, and interruption of their Callings,
and be informed by private men: for in this case, part of the fault
is discharged upon common infirmity; but in the former, there is
apparent negligence, which is not without some contempt of the
Soveraign Power.

Those facts which the Law expresly condemneth, but the Law-
maker by other manifest signes of his will tacitly approveth, are
lesse Crimes, than the same facts, condemned both by the Law, and
Law-maker. For seeing the will of the Law-maker is a Law, there
appear in this case two contradictory Lawes; which would totally
Excuse, if men were bound to take notice of the Soveraigns approbation, by other arguments, than are expressed by his command.
But because there are punishments consequent, not onely to the
transgression of his Law, but also to the observing of it, he is in part
a cause of the transgression, and therefore cannot reasonably
impute the whole Crime to the Delinquent. For example, the
Law condemneth Duells; the punishment is made capitall: On
the contrary part, he that refuseth Duell, is subject to contempt and
scorne, without remedy; and sometimes by the Soveraign himselfe
thought unworthy to have any charge, or preferment in Warre:
If thereupon he accept Duell, considering all men lawfully endeavour
to obtain the good opinion of them that have the Soveraign Power,
he ought not in reason to be rigorously punished; seeing part of
the fault may be discharged on the punisher: which I say, not
as wishing liberty of private revenges, or any other kind of
disobedience; but a care in Governours, not to countenance
any thing obliquely, which directly they forbid. The examples of
Princes, to those that see them, are, and ever have been, more
potent to govern their actions, than the Lawes themselves. And
though it be our duty to do, not what they do, but what they say;
yet will that duty never be performed, till it please God to give men
an extraordinary, and supernaturall grace to follow that Precept.

Again, if we compare Crimes by the mischiefe of their Effects,
First, the same fact, when it redounds to the dammage of many, is
greater, than when it redounds to the hurt of few. And therefore,
when a fact hurteth, not onely in the present, but also, (by example)
in the future, it is a greater Crime, than if it hurt onely in the present:
for the former, is a fertile Crime, and multiplyes to the hurt of many;

the later is barren.  To maintain doctrines contrary to the Religion
established in the Common-wealth, is a greater fault, in an authorised
Preacher, than in a private person:  So also is it, to live prophanely,
incontinently, or do any irreligious act whatsoever.  Likewise in a
Professor if the Law, to maintain any point, or do any act, that
tendeth to the weakning of the Soveraign Power, is a greater Crime,
than in another man:  Also in a man that hath such reputation for
wisedome, as that his counsells are followed, or his actions imitated
by many, his fact against the Law, is a greater Crime, than the same
fact in another:  For such men not onely commit Crime, but teach
it for Law to all other men.  And generally all Crimes are the
greater, by the scandall they give; that is to say, by becomming
stumbling-blocks to the weak, that look not so much upon the way
they go in, as upon the light that other men carry before them.

Also Facts of hostility against the present state of the Common-
wealth, are greater Crimes, than the same acts done to private
men:  For the dammage extends it selfe to all:  Such are the
betraying of the strengths, or revealing of the secrets of the Common-
wealth to an Enemy;  also all attempts upon the Representative of
the Common-wealth, be it a Monarch, or an Assembly;  and all
endeavours by word, or deed to diminish the Authority of the same,
either in the present time, or in succession:  which Crimes the Latines
understand by *Crimina læsæ Majestatis*, and consist in designe, or
act, contrary to a Fundamentall Law.

Likewise those Crimes, which render Judgements of no effect, are
greater Crimes, than Injuries done to one, or a few persons;  as to
receive mony to give False judgement, or testimony, is a greater
Crime, than otherwise to deceive a man of the like, or a greater
summe;  because not onely he has wrong, that falls by such judgements;  but all Judgements are rendered uselesse, and occasion
ministred to force, and private revenges.

Also Robbery, and Depeculation of the Publique treasure, or
Revenues, is a greater Crime, than the robbing, or defrauding of a
Private man;  because to robbe the publique, is to robbe many at
once.

Also the Counterfeit usurpation of publique Ministery, the
Counterfeiting of publique Seales, or publique Coine, than counterfeiting of a private mans person, or his seale;  because the fraud
thereof, extendeth to the dammage of many.

Of facts against the Law, done to private men, the greater Crime,
is that, where the dammage in the common opinion of men, is most
sensible.  And therefore

To kill against the Law, is a greater Crime, than any other injury,
life preserved.

And to kill with Torment, greater, than simply to kill.

And Mutilation of a limbe, greater, than the spoyling a man of
his goods.

And the spoyling a man of his goods, by Terrour of death, or
wounds, than by clandestine surreption.

And by clandestine Surreption, than by consent fraudulently obtained.

And the violation of chastity by Force, greater, than by flattery.

And of a woman Married, than of a woman not married.

For all these things are commonly so valued; though some men are more, and some lesse sensible of the same offence. But the Law regardeth not the particular, but the generall inclination of mankind.

And therefore the offence men take, from contumely, in words, or gesture, when they produce no other harme, than the present griefe of him that is reproached, hath been neglected in the Lawes of the Greeks, Romans, and other both antient, and moderne Commonwealths; supposing the true cause of such griefe to consist, not in the contumely, (which takes no hold upon men conscious of their own vertue,) but in the Pusillanimity of him that is offended by it.

Also a Crime against a private man, is much aggravated by the person, time, and place. For to kill ones Parent, is a greater Crime, than to kill another: for the Parent ought to have the honour of a Soveraign, (though he have surrendred his Power to the Civill Law,) because he had it originally by Nature. And to Robbe a poore man, is a greater Crime, than to robbe a rich man; because 'tis to the poore a more sensible dammage.

And a Crime committed in the Time, or Place appointed for Devotion, is greater, than if committed at another time or place: for it proceeds from a greater contempt of the Law.

Many other cases of Aggravation, and Extenuation might be added: but by these I have set down, it is obvious to every man, to take the altitude of any other Crime proposed.

Lastly, because in almost all Crimes there is an Injury done, not onely to some Private men, but also to the Common-wealth; the same Crime, when the accusation is in the name of the Common-wealth, is called Publique Crime; and when in the name of a Private man, a Private Crime; And the Pleas according thereunto called Publique, *Judicia Publica*, Pleas of the Crown; or Private Pleas. As in an Accusation of Murder, if the accuser be a Private man, the plea is a Private plea; if the accuser be the Soveraign, the plea is a Publique plea.

## CHAP. XXVIII

### *Of* Punishments, *and* Rewards

A Punishment, *is an Evill inflicted by publique Authority, on him that hath done, or omitted that which is Judged by the same Authority to be a Transgression of the Law ; to the end that the will of men may thereby the better be disposed to obedience.*

Before I inferre any thing from this definition, there is a question to be answered, of much importance; which is, by what door the Right, or Authority of Punishing in any case, came in. For by that which has been said before, no man is supposed bound by Covenant, not to resist violence; and consequently it cannot be intended, that he gave any right to another to lay violent hands upon his person. In the making of a Common-wealth, every man giveth away the right of defending another; but not of defending himselfe. Also he obligeth himselfe, to assist him that hath the Soveraignty, in the Punishing of another; but of himselfe not. But to covenant to assist the Soveraign, in doing hurt to another, unlesse he that so covenanteth have a right to doe it himselfe, is not to give him a Right to Punish. It is manifest therefore that the Right which the Common-wealth (that is, he, or they that represent it) hath to Punish, is not grounded on any concession, or gift of the Subjects. But I have also shewed formerly, that before the Institution of Common-wealth, every man had a right to every thing, and to do whatsoever he thought necessary to his own preservation; subduing, hurting, or killing any man in order thereunto. And this is the foundation of that right of Punishing, which is exercised in every Common-wealth. For the Subjects did not give the Soveraign that right; but onely in laying down theirs, strengthned him to use his own, as he should think fit, for the preservation of them all: so that it was not given, but left to him, and to him onely; and (excepting the limits set him by naturall Law) as entire, as in the condition of meer Nature, and of warre of every one against his neighbour.

From the definition of Punishment, I inferre, First, that neither private revenges, nor injuries of private men, can properly be stiled Punishment; because they proceed not from publique Authority.

Secondly, that to be neglected, and unpreferred by the publique favour, is not a Punishment; because no new evill is thereby on any man Inflicted; he is onely left in the estate he was in before.

Thirdly, that the evill inflicted by publique Authority, without precedent publique condemnation, is not to be stiled by the name of Punishment; but of an hostile act; because the fact for which a man is Punished, ought first to be Judged by publique Authority, to be a transgression of the Law.

Fourthly, that the evill inflicted by usurped power, and Judges without Authority from the Soveraign, is not Punishment; but an act of hostility; because the acts of power usurped, have not for Author, the person condemned; and therefore are not acts of publique Authority.

Fifthly, that all evill which is inflicted without intention, or possibility of disposing the Delinquent, or (by his example) other men, to obey the Lawes, is not Punishment; but an act of hostility; because without such an end, no hurt done is contained under that name.

Sixthly, whereas to certain actions, there be annexed by Nature, divers hurtfull consequences; as when a man in assaulting another, is himselfe slain, or wounded; or when he falleth into sicknesse by the doing of some unlawfull act; such hurt, though in respect of

God, who is the author of Nature, it may be said to be inflicted, and therefore a Punishment divine; yet it is not contaned in the name of Punishment in respect of men, because it is not inflicted by the Authority of man.

Seventhly, If the harm inflicted be lesse than the benefit, or contentment that naturally followeth the crime committed, that harm is not within the definition; and is rather the Price, or Redemption, than the Punishment of a Crime: Because it is of the nature of Punishment, to have for end, the disposing of men to obey the Law; which end (if it be lesse than the benefit of the transgression) it attaineth not, but worketh a contrary effect.

Eighthly, If a Punishment be determined and prescribed in the Law it selfe, and after the crime committed, there be a greater Punishment inflicted, the excesse is not Punishment, but an act of hostility. For seeing the aym of Punishment is not a revenge, but terrour; and the terrour of a great Punishment unknown, is taken away by the declaration of a lesse, the unexpected addition is no part | of the Punishment. But where there is no Punishment at all determined by the Law, there whatsoever is inflicted, hath the nature of Punishment. For he that goes about the violation of a Law, wherein no penalty is determined, expecteth an indeterminate, that is to say, an arbitrary Punishment.

Ninthly, Harme inflicted for a Fact done before there was a Law that forbad it, is not Punishment, but an act of Hostility: For before the Law, there is no transgression of the Law: But Punishment supposeth a fact judged, to have been a transgression of the Law; Therefore Harme inflicted before the Law made, is not Punishment, but an act of Hostility.

Tenthly, Hurt inflicted on the Representative of the Commonwealth, is not Punishment, but an act of Hostility: Because it is of the nature of Punishment, to be inflicted by publique Authority, which is the Authority only of the Representative it self.

Lastly, Harme inflicted upon one that is a declared enemy, fals not under the name of Punishment: Because seeing they were either never subject to the Law, and therefore cannot transgresse it; or having been subject to it, and professing to be no longer so, by consequence deny they can transgresse it, all the Harmes that can be done them, must be taken as acts of Hostility. But in declared Hostility, all infliction of evill is lawfull. From whence it followeth, that if a subject shall by fact, or word, wittingly, and deliberatly deny the authority of the Representative of the Common-wealth, (whatsoever penalty hath been formerly ordained for Treason,) he may lawfully be made to suffer whatsoever the Representative will: For in denying subjection, he denyes such Punishment as by the Law hath been ordained; and therefore suffers as an enemy of the Common-wealth; that is, according to the will of the Representative. For the Punishments set down in the Law, are to Subjects, not to Enemies; such as are they, that having been by their own act Subjects, deliberately revolting, deny the Soveraign Power.

The first, and most generall distribution of Punishments, is into *Divine*, and *Humane*.   Of the former I shall have occasion, to speak, in a more convenient place hereafter.

*Humane*, are those Punishments that be inflicted by the Commandement of Man; and are either *Corporall*, or *Pecuniary*, or *Ignominy*, or *Imprisonment*, or *Exile*, or mixt of these.

*Corporall Punishment* is that, which is inflicted on the body directly, and according to the intention of him that inflicteth it: such as are stripes, or wounds, or deprivation of such pleasures of the body, as were before lawfully enjoyed.

And of these, some be *Capitall*, some *Lesse* than *Capitall*.   Capitall, is the Infliction of Death; and that either simply, or with torment.   Lesse than Capitall, are Stripes, Wounds, Chains, and any other corporall Paine, not in its own nature mortall.   For if upon the Infliction of a Punishment death follow not in the intention of the Inflicter, the Punishment is not to bee esteemed Capitall, though the harme prove mortall by an accident not to be foreseen; in which case death is not inflicted, but hastened.

*Pecuniary Punishment*, is that which consisteth not only in the deprivation of a Summe of Mony, but also of Lands, or any other goods which are usually bought and sold for mony.   And in case the Law, that ordaineth such a punishment, be made with design to gather mony, from such as shall transgresse the same, it is not properly a Punishment, but the Price of priviledge, and exemption from the Law, which doth not absolutely forbid the fact, but only to those that are not able to pay the mony: except where the Law is Naturall, or part of Religion; for in that case it is not an exemption from the Law, but a transgression of it.   As where a Law exacteth a Pecuniary mulct, of them that take the name of God in vaine, the payment of the mulct, is not the price of a dispensation to sweare, but the Punishment of the transgression of a Law undispensable.   In like manner if the Law impose a Summe of Mony to be payd, to him that has been Injured; this is but a satisfaction for the hurt done him; and extinguisheth the accusation of the party injured, not the crime of the offender.

*Ignominy*, is the infliction of such Evill, as is made Dishonorable; or the deprivation of such Good, as is made Honourable by the Common-wealth.   For there be some things Honourable by Nature; as the effects of Courage, Magna[ni]mity, Strength, Wisdome, and other abilities of body and mind: Others made Honorable by the Common-wealth; as Badges, Titles, Offices, or any other singular marke of the Soveraigns favour.   The former, (though they may faile by nature, or accident,) cannot be taken away by a Law; and therefore the losse of them is not Punishment.   But the later, may be taken away by the publique authority that made them Honorable, and are properly Punishments: Such are degrading men condemned, of their Badges, Titles, and Offices; or declaring them uncapable of the like in time to come.

*Imprisonment*, is when a man is by publique Authority deprived of liberty; and may happen from two divers ends; whereof one is the safe custody of a man accused; the other is the inflicting of paine on a man condemned. The former is not Punishment; because no man is supposed to be Punisht, before he be Judicially heard, and declared guilty. And therefore whatsoever hurt a man is made to suffer by bonds, or restraint, before his cause be heard, over and above that which is necessary to assure his custody, is against the Law of Nature. But the later is Punishment, because Evill, and inflicted by publique Authority, for somewhat that has by the same Authority been Judged a Transgression of the Law. Under this word Impriso[n]ment, I comprehend all restraint of motion, caused by an externall obstacle, be it a House, which is called by the general name of a Prison; or an Iland, as when men are said to be confined to it; or a place where men are set to worke, as in old time men have been condemned to Quarries, and in these times to Gallies; or be it a Chaine, or any other such impediment.

*Exile*, (Banishment) is when a man is for a crime, condemned to depart out of the dominion of the Common-wealth, or out of a certaine part thereof; and during a prefixed time, or for ever, not to return into it: and seemeth not in its own nature, without other circumstances, to be a Punishment; but rather an escape, or a publique commandement to avoid Punishment by flight. And *Cicero* sayes, there was never any such Punishment ordained in the City of *Rome*; but cals it a refuge of men in danger. For if a man banished, be nevertbelesse permitted to enjoy his Goods, and the Revenue of his Lands, the meer change of ayr is no Punishment; nor does it tend to that benefit of the Common-wealth, for which all Punishments are ordained, (that is to say, to the forming of mens wils to the observation of the Law;) but many times to the dammage of the Common-wealth. For a Banished man, is a lawfull enemy of the Common-wealth that banished him; as being no more a Member of the same. But if he be withall deprived of his Lands, or Goods, then the Punishment lyeth not in the Exile, but is to be reckoned amongst Punishments Pecuniary.

All Punishments of Innocent subjects, be they great or little, are against the Law of Nature: For Punishment is only for Transgression of the Law, and therefore there can be no Punishment of the Innocent. It is therefore a violation, First, of that Law of Nature, which forbiddeth all men, in their Revenges, to look at any thing but some future good: For there can arrive no good to the Common-wealth by Punishing the Innocent. Secondly, of that, which forbiddeth Ingratitude: For seeing all Soveraign Power, is originally given by the consent of every one of the Subjects, to the end they should as long as they are obedient, be protected thereby; the Punishment of the Innocent, is a rendring of Evill for Good, And thirdly, of the Law that commandeth Equity; that is to say, an equall distribution of Justice; which in Punishing the Innocent is not observed.

But the Infliction of what evill soever, on an Innocent man, that

is not a Subject, if it be for the benefit of the Common-wealth, and
without violation of any former Covenant, is no breach of the Law
of Nature. For all men that are not Subjects, are either Enemies,
or else they have ceased from being so, by some precedent covenants.
But against Enemies, whom the Commonwealth judgeth capable
to do them hurt, it is lawfull by the originall Right of Nature to
make warre; wherein the Sword Judgeth not, nor doth the Victor
make distinction of Nocent, and Innocent, as to the time past;
nor has other respect of mercy, than as it conduceth to the good of
his own People. And upon this ground it is, that also in Subjects,
who deliberatly deny the Authority of the Common-wealth established, the vengeance is lawfully extended, not onely to the Fathers,
but also to the third and fourth generation not yet in being, and
consequently innocent of the fact, for which they are afflicted:
because the nature of this offence, consisteth in the renouncing of
subjection; which is a relapse into the condition of warre, commonly
called Rebellion; and they that so offend, suffer not as Subjects,
but as Enemies. For *Rebellion*, is but warre renewed.

REWARD, is either of *Gift*, or by *Contract*. When by Contract, is
called *Salary*, and *Wages*; which is benefit due for service performed, or promised. When of Gift, it is benefit proceeding from the
*grace* of them that bestow it, to encourage, or enable men to do
them service. And therefore when the Soveraign of a Common-
wealth appointeth a Salary to any publique Office, he that receiveth
it, is bound in Justice to performe his office; otherwise, he is bound
onely in honour, to acknowledgement, and an endeavour to requitall.
For though men have no lawfull remedy, when they be commanded
to quit their private businesse to serve the publique, without
Reward, or Salary; yet they are not bound thereto, by the Law of
Nature, nor by the Institution of the Common-wealth, unlesse the
service cannot otherwise be done; because it is supposed the
Soveraign may make use of all their means, insomuch as the most
common Souldier, may demand the wages of his warrefare, as a
debt.

The benefits which a Soveraign bestoweth on a Subject, for fear
of some power, and ability he hath to do hurt to the Common-
wealth, are not properly Rewards; for they are not Salaryes;
because there is in this case no contract supposed, every man being
obliged already not to do the Common-wealth disservice: nor are
they Graces; because they be extorted by fear, which ought not to
be incident to the Soveraign Power: but are rather Sacrifices, which
the Soveraign (considered in his naturall person, and not in the person
of the Common-wealth) makes, for the appeasing the discontent of
him he thinks more potent than himselfe; and encourage not to
obedience, but on the contraty, to the continuance, and increasing
of further extortion.

And whereas some Salaries are certain, and proceed from the
publique Treasure; and others uncertain, and casuall, proceeding
from the execution of the Office for which the Salary is ordained;

the later is in some cases hurtfull to the Common-wealth; as in
the case of Judicature. For where the benefit of the Judges, and
Ministers of a Court of Justice, ariseth for the multitude of Causes
that are brought to their cognisance, there must needs follow two
Inconveniences: One, is the nourishing of sutes; for the more
sutes, the greater benefit: and another that depends on that, which
is contention about Jurisdiction; each Court drawing to it selfe,
as many Causes as it can. But in offices of Execution there are not
those Inconveniences; because their employment cannot be encreased by any endeavour of their own. And thus much shall
suffice for the nature of Punishment, and Reward; which are, as it
were, the Nerves and Tendons, that move the limbes and joynts
of a Common-wealth.

Hitherto I have set forth the nature of Man, (whose Pride and
other Passions have compelled him to submit himselfe to Government;) together with the great power of his Governour, whom I
compared to *Leviathan*, taking that comparison out of the two last
verses of the one and fortieth of *Job*; where God having set forth
the great power of *Leviathan*, called him King of the Proud. *There
is nothing*, saith he, *on earth, to be compared with him. He is made
so as not to be afraid. Hee seeth every high thing below him ; and is
King of all the children of pride.* But because he is mortall, and
subject to decay, as all other Earthly creatures are; and because
there is that in heaven, (though not on earth) that he should stand
in fear of, and whose Lawes he ought to obey; I shall in the next
following Chapters speak of his Diseases, and the causes of his
Mortality; and of what Lawes of Nature he is bound to obey.


## CHAP. XXIX

### *Of those things that Weaken, or tend to the* DISSOLUTION *of a Common-wealth*

THOUGH nothing can be immortall, which mortals make; yet,
if men had the use of reason they pretend to, their Common-wealths
might be secured, at least, from perishing by internall diseases. For
by the nature of their Institution, they are designed to live, as long
as Man-kind, or as the Lawes of Nature, or as Justice it selfe, which
gives them life. Therefore when they come to be dissolved, not
by externall violence, but intestine disorder, the fault is not in men,
as they are the *Matter*; but as they are the *Makers*, and orderers of
them. For men, as they become at last weary of irregular justling,
and hewing one another, and desire with all their hearts, to conforme
themselves into one firme and lasting edifice; so for want, both of
the art of making fit Lawes, to square their actions by, and also of
humility, and patience, to suffer the rude and combersome points of

their present greatnesse to be taken off, they cannot without the help of a very able Architect, be compiled, into any other than a crasie building, such as hardly lasting out their own time, must assuredly fall upon the heads of their posterity.

Amongst the *Infirmities* therefore of a Common-wealth, I will reckon in the first place, those that arise from an Imperfect Institution, and resemble the diseases of a naturall body, which proceed from a Defectuous Procreation.

Of which, this is one, *That a man to obtain a Kingdome, is sometimes content with lesse Power, than to the Peace, and defence of the Common-wealth is necessarily required.* From whence it commeth to passe, that when the exercise of the Power layd by, is for the publique safety to be resumed, it hath the resemblance of an unjust act; which disposeth great numbers of men (when occasion is presented) to rebell; In the same manner as the bodies of children, gotten by diseased parents, are subject either to untimely death, or to purge the ill quality, derived from their vicious conception, by breaking out into biles and scabbs. And when Kings deny themselves some such necessary Power, it is not alwayes (though sometimes) out of ignorance of what is necessary to the office they undertake; but many times out of a hope to recover the same again at their pleasure: Wherein they reason not well; because such as will hold them to their promises, shall be maintained against them by forraign Common-wealths; who in order to the good of their own Subjects let slip few occasions to *weaken* the estate of their Neighbours. So was *Thomas Becket* Archbishop of *Canterbury,* supported against *Henry* the Second, by the Pope; the subjection of Ecclesiastiques to the Common-wealth, having been dispensed with by *William the Conquerour* at his reception, when he took an Oath, not to infringe the liberty of the Church. And so were the *Barons,* whose power was by *William Rufus* (to have their help in transferring the Succession from his Elder brother, to himselfe,) encreased to a degree, inconsistent with the Soveraign Power, maintained in their Rebellion against King *John,* by the French.

Nor does this happen in Monarchy onely. For whereas the stile of the antient Roman Common-wealth, was, *The Senate, and People of Rome;* neither Senate, nor People pretended to the whole Power; which first caused the seditions, of *Tiberius Gracchus, Caius Gracchus, Lucius Saturninus,* and others; and afterwards the warres between the Senate and the People, under *Marius* and *Sylla;* and again under *Pompey* and *Cæsar,* to the Extinction of their Democraty, and the setting up of Monarchy.

The people of *Athens* bound themselves but from one onely Action; which was, that no man on pain of death should propound the renewing of the warre for the Islands of *Salamis;* And yet thereby, if *Solon* had not caused to be given out he was mad, and afterwards in gesture and habit of a mad-man, and in verse, propounded it to the People that flocked about him, they had had an enemy perpetually in readinesse, even at the gates of their Citie;

such dammage, or shifts, are all Common-wealths forced to, that have their Power never so little limited.

In the second place, I observe the *Diseases* of a Common-wealth, that proceed from the poyson of seditious doctrines; whereof one is, *That every private man is Judge of Good and Evill actions.* This is true in the condition of meet Nature, where there are no Civill Lawes; and also under Civill Government, in such cases as are not determined by the Law. But otherwise, it is manifest, that the measure of Good and Evill actions, is the Civill Law; and the Judge the Legislator, who is alwayes Representative of the Common-wealth. From this false doctrine, men are disposed to debate with themselves, and dispute the commands of the Common-wealth; and afterwards to obey, or disobey them, as in their private judgements they shall think fit. Whereby the Common-wealth is distracted and *Weakened.*

Another doctrine repugnant to Civill Society is, that *whatsoever a man does against his Conscience, is Sinne*; and it dependeth on the presumption of making himself judge of Good and Evill. For a mans Conscience, and his Judgement is the same thing; and as the Judgement, so also the Conscience may be erroneous. Therefore, though he that is subject to no Civill Law, sinneth in all he does against his Conscience, because he has no other rule to follow but his own reason; yet it is not so with him that lives in a Common-wealth; because the Law is the publique Conscience, by which he hath already undertaken to be guided. Otherwise in such diversity, as there is of private Consciences, which are but private opinions, the Common-wealth must needs be distracted, and no man dare to obey the Soveraign Power, farther than it shall seem good in his own eyes.

It hath been also commonly taught, *That Faith and Sanctity, are not to be attained by Study and Reason, but by supernaturall Inspiration or Infusion,* which granted, I see not why any man should render a reason of his Faith; or why every Christian should not be also a Prophet; or why any man should take the Law of his Country, rather than his own Inspiration, for the rule of his action. And thus wee fall again into the fault of taking upon us to Judge of Good and Evill; or to make Judges of it, such private men as pretend to be supernaturally Inspired, to the Dissolution of all Civill Government. Faith comes by hearing, and hearing by those accidents, which guide us into the presence of them that speak to us; which accidents are all contrived by God Almighty; and yet are not supernaturall, but onely, for the great number of them that concurre to every effect, unobservable. Faith, and Sanctity, are indeed not very frequent; but yet they are not Miracles, but brought to passe by education, discipline, correction, and other naturall wayes, by which God worketh them in his elect, at such time as he thinketh fit. And these three opinions, pernicious to Peace and Government, have in this part of the world, proceeded chiefly from the tongues, and pens of unlearned Divines; who joyning the words of Holy Scripture together, otherwise than is agreeable to reason, do what they can, to make men think, that Sanctity and Natural Reason, cannot stand together.

A fourth opinion, repugnant to the nature of a Common-wealth, is this, *That he that hath the Soveraign Power, is subject to the Civill Lawes*. It is true, that Soveraigns are all subject to the Lawes of Nature; because such lawes be Divine, and cannot by any man, or Common-wealth be abrogated. But to those Lawes which the Soveraign himselfe, that is, which the Common-wealth maketh, he is not subject. For to be subject to Lawes, is to be subject to the Common-wealth, that is to the Soveraign Representative, that is to himselfe; which is not subjection, but freedome from the Lawes. Which errour, because it setteth the Lawes above the Soveraign, setteth also a Judge above him, and a Power to punish him; which is to make a new Soveraign; and again for the same reason a third, to punish the second; and so continually without end, to the Confusion, and Dissolution of the Common-wealth.

A Fifth doctrine, that tendeth to the Dissolution of a Common-wealth, is, *That every private man has an absolute Propriety in his Goods ; such, as excludeth the Right of the Soveraign.* Every man has indeed a Propriety that excludes the Right of every other Subject: And he has it onely from the Soveraign Power; without the protection whereof, every other man should have equall Right to the same. But if the Right of the Soveraign also be excluded, he cannot performe the office they have put him into; which is, to defend them both from forraign enemies, and from the injuries of one another; and consequently there is no longer a Common-wealth.

And if the Propriety of Subjects, exclude not the Right of the Soveraign Representative to their Goods; much lesse to their offices of Judicature, or Execution, in which they Represent the Soveraign himselfe.

There is a Sixth doctrine, plainly, and directly against the essence of a Common-wealth; and 'tis this, *That the Soveraign Power may be divided.* For what is it to divide the Power of a Common-wealth, but to Dissolve it; for Powers divided mutually destroy each other. And for these doctrines, men are chiefly beholding to some of those, that making profession of the Lawes, endeavour to make them depend upon their own learning, and not upon the Legislative Power.

And as False Doctrine, so also often-times the Example of different Government in a neighbouring Nation, disposeth men to alteration of the forme already setled. So the people of the Jewes were stirred up to reject God, and to call upon the Prophet *Samuel*, for a King after the manner of the Nations: So also the lesser Cities of *Greece*, were continually disturbed, with seditions of the Aristocraticall, and Democraticall factions; one part of almost every Common-wealth, desiring to imitate the Lacedæmonians; the other, the Athenians. And I doubt not, but many men, have been contented to see the late troubles in *England*, out of an imitation of the Low Countries; supposing there needed no more to grow rich, than to change, as they had done, the forme of their Government. For the constitution of mans nature, is of it selfe subject to desire novelty: When therefore they are provoked to the same, by the neighbourhood also of those that have been enriched by it, it is almost impossible for them, not to be content with those that solicite them to change; and love the first beginnings, though they be grieved with the continuance of disorder; like hot blouds, that having gotten the itch, tear themselves with their own nayles, till they can endure the smart no longer.

And as to Rebellion in particular against Monarchy; one of the most frequent causes of it, is the Reading of the books of Policy, and Histories of the antient Greeks, and Romans; from which, young men, and all others that are unprovided of the Antidote of solid Reason, receiving a strong, and delightfull impression, of the great exploits of warre, atchieved by the Conductors of their Armies, receive withall a pleasing Idea, of all they have done besides; and imagine their great prosperity, not to have proceeded from the æmulation of particular men, but from the vertue of their popular forme of government: Not considering the frequent Seditions, and Civill warres, produced by the imperfection of their Policy. From the reading, I say, of such books, men have undertaken to kill their Kings, because the Greek and Latine writers, in their books, and discourses of Policy, make it lawfull, and laudable, for any man so to do; provided before he do it, he call him Tyrant. For they say not *Regicide*, that is, killing of a King, but *Tyrannicide*, that is, killing of a Tyrant is lawfull. From the same books, they that live under a Monarch conceive an opinion, that the Subjects in a Popular Common-wealth enjoy Liberty; but that in a Monarchy they are all Slaves. I say, they that live under a Monarchy conceive such an opinion; not they that live under a Popular Government: for they find no such matter. In summe, I cannot imagine, how any thing can be more prejudiciall to a Monarchy, than the allowing of such books to be publikely read, without present applying such correctives of discreet Masters, as are fit to take away their Venime: Which Venime I will not doubt to compare to the biting of a mad Dogge, which is a disease the Physicians call *Hydrophobia*, or *fear of Water*. For as he that is so bitten, has a continuall torment of thirst, and yet abhorreth water; and is in such an estate, as if the poyson endeavoureth to convert him into a Dogge: So when a Monarchy is once bitten to the quick, by those Democraticall writers, that continually snarle at that estate; it wanteth nothing more than a strong Monarch, which neverthelesse out of a certain *Tyrannophobia*, or feare of being strongly governed, when they have him, they abhorre.

As there have been Doctors, that hold there be three Soules in a man: so there be also that think there may be more Soules, (that is, more Soveraigns,) than one, in a Common-wealth; and set up a *Supremacy* against the *Soveraignty*; *Canons* against *Lawes*; and a *Ghostly Authority* against the *Civill*; working on mens minds, with words and distinctions, that of themselves signifie nothing, but bewray (by their obscurity) that there walketh (as some think invisibly) another Kingdome, as it were a Kingdome of Fayries, in the dark. Now seeing it is manifest, that the Civill Power, and the Power of the Common-wealth is the same thing; and that Supremacy, and the Power of making Canons, and granting Faculties implyeth a Common-wealth; it followeth, that where one is Soveraign, another Supreme; where one can make Lawes, and another make Canons; there must needs be two Common-wealths, of one & the same Subjects; which is a Kingdome divided in it selfe, and cannot stand. For notwithstanding the insignificant distinction of *Temporall*, and *Ghostly*, they are still two Kingdomes, and every Subject is subject to two Masters. For seeing the *Ghostly* Power challengeth the Right to declare what is Sinne it challengeth by consequence to declare what is Law, (Sinne being nothing but the transgression of the Law;) and again, the Civill Power challenging to declare what is Law, every Subject must obey two Masters, who both will have their Commands be observed as Law; which is impossible. Or, if it be but one Kingdome, either the *Civill*, which is the Power of the Common-wealth, must be subordinate to the *Ghostly*, and then there is no Soveraignty but the *Ghostly*; or the *Ghostly* must be subordinate to the *Temporall*, and then there is no *Supremacy* but the *Temporall*. When therefore these two Powers oppose one another, the Common-wealth cannot but be in great danger of Civill warre, and Dissolution. For the *Civill* Authority being more visible, and standing in the cleerer light of naturall reason, cannot choose but draw to it in all times a very considerable part of the people: And the *Spirituall*, though it stand in the dark-nesse of Schoole distinctions, and hard words; yet because the fear of Darknesse, and Ghosts, is greater than other fears, cannot want a party sufficient to Trouble, and sometimes to Destroy a Common-wealth. And this is a Disease which not unfitly may be compared to the Epilepsie, or Falling-sicknesse (which the Jewes took to be one kind of possession by Spirits) in the Body Naturall. For as in this Disease, there is an unnaturall spirit, or wind in the head that obstructeth the roots of the Nerves, and moving them violently, taketh away the motion which naturally they should have from the power of the Soule in the Brain, and thereby causeth violent, and irregular motions (which men call Convulsions) in the parts; insomuch as he that is seized therewith, falleth down some-times into the water, and sometimes into the fire, as a man deprived of his senses; so also in the Body Politique, when the spirituall power, moveth the Members of a Common-wealth, by the terrour of punishments, and hope of rewards (which are the Nerves of it,) otherwise than by the Civill Power (which is the Soule of the Common-wealth) they ought to be moved; and by strange, and hard words suffocates their understanding, it must needs thereby Distract the people, and either Overwhelm the Common-wealth with Oppression, or cast it into the Fire of a Civill warre.

Sometimes also in the meerly Civill government, there be more than one Soule: As when the Power of levying mony, (which is the Nutritive faculty,) has depended on a generall Assembly; the Power of conduct and command, (which is the Motive faculty,) on one man; and the Power of making Lawes, (which is the Rationall faculty,) on the accidentall consent, not onely of those two, but also of a third; This endangereth the Common-wealth, somtimes for want of consent to good Lawes; but most often for want of such Nourishment, as is necessary to Life, and Motion. For although few perceive, that such government, is not government, but division of the Common-wealth into three Factions, and call it mixt Monarchy; yet the truth is, that it is not one independent Common-wealth, but three independent Factions; nor one Representative Person, but three. In the Kingdome of God, there may be three Persons independent, without breach of unity in God that Reigneth; but where men Reigne, that be subject to diversity of opinions, it cannot be so. And therefore if the King bear the person of the People, and the generall Assembly bear also the person of the People, and another Assembly bear the person of a Part of the people, they are not one Person, nor one Soveraign, but three Persons, and three Soveraigns.

To what Disease in the Naturall Body of man I may exactly compare this irregularity of a Common-wealth, I know not. But I have seen a man, that had another man growing out of his side, with an head, armes, breast, and stomach, of his own: If he had had another man growing out of his other side, the comparison might then have been exact.

Hitherto I have named such Diseases of a Common-wealth, as are of the greatest, and most present danger. There be other, not so great; which neverthelesse are not unfit to be observed. At first, the difficulty of raising Mony, for the necessary uses of the Common-wealth; especially in the approach of warre. This difficulty ariseth from the opinion, that every Subject hath of a Propriety in his lands and goods, exclusive of the Soveraigns Right to the use of the same. From whence it commeth to passe, that the Soveraign Power, which foreseeth the necessities and dangers of the Common-wealth, (finding the passage of mony to the publique Treasure obstructed, by the tenacity of the people,) whereas it ought to extend it selfe, to encounter, and prevent such dangers in their beginnings, contracteth it selfe as long as it can, and when it cannot longer, struggles with the people by stratagems of Law, to obtain little summes, which not sufficing he is fain at last violently to open the way for present supply, or Perish; and being put often to these extremities, at last reduceth the people to their due temper; or else the Common-wealth must perish. Insomuch as we may compare this Distemper very aptly to an Ague; wherein, the fleshy parts being congealed, or by venomous matter obstructed; the Veins which by their naturall course empty themselves into the Heart, are not (as they ought to be) supplyed from the Arteries whereby there succeedeth at first a cold contraction, and trembling of the limbes; and afterwards a hot, and strong endeavour of the Heart, to force a passage for the Bloud; and before it can do that, contenteth it selfe with the small refreshments of such things as coole for a time, till (if Nature be strong enough) it break at last the contumacy of the parts obstructed, and dissipateth the venome into sweat; or (if Nature be too weak) the Patient dyeth.

Again, there is sometimes in a Common-wealth, a Disease, which resembleth the Pleurisie; and that is, when the Treasure of the Common-wealth, flowing out of its due course, is gathered together in too much abundance in one, or a few private men, by Monopolies, or by Farmes of the Publique Revenues; in the same manner as the Blood in a Pleurisie, getting into the Membrane of the breast, breedeth there an Inflammation, accompanied with a Fever, and painfull stitches.

Also, the Popularity of a potent Subject, (unlesse the Common-wealth have very good caution of his fidelity,) is a dangerous Disease; because the people (which should receive their motion from the Authority of the Soveraign,) by the flattery, and by the reputation of an ambitious man, are drawn away from their obedience to the Lawes, to follow a man, of whose vertues, and designes they have no knowledge. And this is commonly of more danger in a Popular Government, than in a Monarchy; because an Army is of so great force, and multitude, as it may easily be made believe, they are the People. By this means it was, that *Julius Cæsar*, who was set up by the People against the Senate, having won to himselfe the affections of his Army, made himselfe Master, both of Senate and People. And this proceeding of popular, and ambitious men, is plain Rebellion: and may be resembled to the effects of Witchcraft.

Another infirmity of a Common-wealth, is the immoderate greatnesse of a Town, when it is able to furnish out of its own Circuit, the number, and expence of a great Army: As also the great number of Corporations; which are as it were many lesser Common-wealths in the bowels of a greater, like wormes in the entrayles of a naturall man. To which may be added, the Liberty of Disputing against absolute Power, by pretenders to Politicall Prudence; which though bred for the most part in the Lees of the people; yet animated by False Doctrines, are perpetually medling with the Fundamentall Lawes, to the molestation of the Common-wealth; like the little Wormes, which Physicians call *Ascarides*.

We may further adde, the insatiable appetite, or *Bulimia*, of enlarging Dominion; with the incurable *Wounds* thereby many times received from the enemy; And the *Wens*, of united conquests, which are many times a burthen, and with lesse danger lost, than kept; As also the *Lethargy* of Ease, and *Consumption* of Riot and Vain Expence.

Lastly, when in a warre (forraign, or intestine,) the enemies get a finall Victory; so as (the forces of the Common-wealth keeping the field no longer) there is no farther protection of Subjects in their loyalty; then is the Common-wealth DISSOLVED, and every man at liberty to protect himselfe by such courses as his own discretion shall suggest unto him. For the Soveraign, is the publique Soule, giving Life and Motion to the Common-wealth; which expiring, the Members are governed by it no more, than the Carcase of a man, by his departed (though Immortall) Soule. For though the Right of a Soveraign Monarch cannot be extinguished by the act of another; yet the Obligation of the members may. For he that wants protection, may seek it any where; and when he hath it, is obliged (without fraudulent pretence of having submitted himselfe out of feare,) to protect his Protection as long as he is able. But when the Power of an Assembly is once suppressed, the Right of the same perisheth utterly; because the Assembly it selfe is extinct; and consequently, there is no possibility for the Soveraignty to re-enter.

## CHAP. XXX

### Of the OFFICE of the Soveraign Representative

THE OFFICE of the Soveraign, (be it a Monarch, or an Assembly,) consisteth in the end, for which he was trusted with the Soveraign Power, namely the procuration of *the safety of the people*; to which he is obliged by the Law of Nature, and to render an account thereof to God, the Author of that Law, and to none but him. But by Safety here, is not meant a bare Preservation, but also all other Contentments of life, which every man by lawfull Industry, without danger, or hurt to the Common-wealth, shall acquire to himselfe.

And this is intended should be done, not by care applyed to Individualls, further than their protection from injuries, when they shall complain; but by a generall Providence, contained in publique Instruction, both of Doctrine, and Example; and in the making, and executing of good Lawes, to which individuall persons may apply their own cases.

And because, if the essentiall Rights of Soveraignty (specified before in the eighteenth Chapter) be taken away, the Common-wealth is thereby dissolved, and every man returneth into the condition, and calamity of a warre with every other man, (which is the greatest evill that can happen in this life;) it is the Office of the Soveraign, to maintain those Rights entire; and consequently against his duty, First, to transferre to another, or to lay from himselfe any of them. For he that deserteth the Means, deserteth the Ends; and he deserteth the Means, that being the Soveraign, acknowledgeth himselfe subject to the Civill Lawes; and renounceth the Power of Supreme Judicature; or of making Warre, or Peace by his own Authority; or of Judging of the Necessities of the Common-wealth; or of levying Mony, and Souldiers, when, and as much as in his own conscience he shall judge necessary; or of making Officers, and Ministers both of Warre, and Peace; or of appointing Teachers, and examining what Doctrines are conformable, or contrary to the Defence, Peace, and Good of the people. Secondly, it is against his Duty, to let the people be ignorant, or mis-informed of the grounds, and reasons of those his essentiall Rights; because thereby men are easie to be seduced, and drawn to resist him, when the Common-wealth shall require their use and exercise.

And the grounds of these Rights, have the rather need to be diligently, and truly taught; because they cannot be maintained by any Civill Law, or terrour of legall punishment. For a Civill Law, that shall forbid Rebellion (and such is all resistance to the essentiall Rights of Soveraignty,) is not (as a Civill Law) any obligation, but by vertue onely of the Law of Nature, that forbiddeth the violation of Faith; which naturall obligation if men know not, they cannot know the Right of any Law the Soveraign maketh. And for the Punishment, they take it but for an act of Hostility; which when they think they have strength enough, they will endeavour by acts of Hostility, to avoyd.

As I have heard some say, that Justice is but a word, without substance; and that whatsoever a man can by force, or act, acquire to himselfe, (not onely in the condition of warre, but also in a Common-wealth,) is his own, which I have already shewed to be false: So there be also that maintain, that there are no grounds, nor Principles of Reason, to sustain those essentiall Rights, which make Soveraignty absolute. For if there were, they would have been found out in some place, or other; whereas we see, there has not hitherto been any Common-wealth, where those Rights have been acknowledged, or challenged. Wherein they argue as ill, as if the Savage people of América, should deny there were any grounds, or Principles of Reason, so to build a house, as to last as long as the materials, because they never yet saw any so well built. Time, and Industry, produce every day new knowledge. And as the art of well building, is derived from Principles of Reason, observed by industrious men, that had long studied the nature of materials, and the divers effects of figure, and proportion, long after mankind began (though poorly) to build: So, long time after men have begun to constitute Common-wealths, imperfect, and apt to relapse into disorder, there may, Principles of Reason be found out, by industrious meditation, to make their constitution (excepting by externall violence) everlasting. And such are those which I have in this discourse set forth: Which whether they come not into the sight of those that have Power to make use of them, or be neglected by them, or not, concerneth my particular interest, at this day, very little. But supposing that these of mine are not such Principles of Reason; yet I am sure they are Principles from Authority of Scriptures; as I shall make it appear when I shall come to speak of the Kingdome of God, (administred by *Moses*,) over the Jewes, his peculiar people by Covenant.

But they say again, that though the Principles be right, yet Common people are not of capacity enough to be made to under-stand them.  I should be glad, that the Rich, and Potent Subjects of a Kingdome, or those that are accounted the most Learned, were no lesse incapable than they.  But all men know, that the obstruc-tions to this kind of doctrine, proceed not so much from the difficulty of the matter, as from the interest of them that are to learn.  Potent men, digest hardly any thing that setteth up a Power to bridle their affections; and Learned men, any thing that discovereth their errours, and thereby lesseneth their Authority: whereas the Common-peoples minds, unlesse they be tainted with dependance on the Potent, or scribbled over with the opinions of their Doctors, are like clean paper, fit to receive whatsoever by Publique Authority shall be imprinted in them.  Shall whole Nations be brought to *acquiesce* in the great Mysteries of Christian Religion, which are above Reason; and millions of men be made believe, that the same Body may be in innumerable places, at one and the same time, which is against Reason; and shall not men be able, by their teach-ing, and preaching, protected by the Law, to make that received, which is so consonant to Reason, that any unprejudicated man, needs no more to learn it, than to hear it?  I conclude therefore, that in the instruction of the people in the Essentiall Rights (which are the Naturall, and Fundamentall Lawes) of Soveraignty, there is no difficulty, (whilest a Soveraign has his Power entire,) but what proceeds from his own fault, or the fault of those whom he trusteth in the administration of the Common-wealth; and consequently, it is his Duty, to cause them so to be instructed; and not onely his Duty, but his Benefit also, and Security, against the danger that may arrive to himselfe in his naturall Person, from Rebellion.

And (to descend to particulars) the People are to be taught, First, that they ought not to be in love with any forme of Govern-ment they see in their neighbour Nations, more than with their own, nor (whatsoever present prosperity they behold in Nations that are otherwise governed than they,) to desire change.  For the prosperity of a People ruled by an Aristocraticall, or Democraticall assembly, commeth not from Aristocracy, nor from Democracy, but from the Obedience, and Concord of the Subjects: nor do the people flourish in a Monarchy, because one man has the right to rule them, but because they obey him.  Take away in any kind of State, the Obedience, (and consequently the Concord of the People,) and they shall not onely not flourish but in short time be dissolved.  And they that go about by disobedience, to doe no more than reforme the Common-wealth, shall find they do thereby destroy it; like the foolish daughters of *Peleus* (in the fable;) which desiring to renew the youth of their decrepit Father, did by the Counsell of *Medea*, cut him in pieces, and boyle him, together with strange herbs, but made not of him a new man.  This desire of change, is like the breach of the first of Gods Commandements:  For there God sayes, *Non habebis Deos alienos*; Thou shalt not have the

Gods of other Nations; and in another place concerning *Kings*, that they are *Gods*.

Secondly, they are to be taught, that they ought not to be led with admiration of the vertue of any of their fellow Subjects, how high soever he stand, nor how conspicuously soever he shine in the Common-wealth; nor of any Assembly, (except the Soveraign Assembly,) so as to deferre to them any obedience, or honour, appropriate to the Soveraign onely, whom (in their particular stations) they represent; nor to receive any influence from them, but such as is conveighed by them from the Soveraign Authority. For that Soveraign, cannot be imagined to love his People as he ought, that is not Jealous of them, but suffers them by the flattery of Popular men, to be seduced from their loyalty, as they have often been, not onely secretly, but openly, so as to proclaime Marriage with them *in facie Ecclesiæ* by Preachers; and by publishing the same in the open streets: which may fitly be compared to the violation of the second of the ten Commandements.

Thirdly, in consequence to this, they ought to be informed, how great a fault it is, to speak evill of the Soveraign Representative, (whether One man, or an Assembly of men;) or to argue and dispute his Power, or any way to use his Name irreverently, whereby he may be brought into Contempt with his People, and their Obedience (in which the safety of the Common-wealth consisteth) slackened. Which doctrine the third Commandement by resemblance pointeth to.

Fourthly, seeing people cannot be taught this, nor when 'tis taught, remember it, nor after one generation past, so much as know in whom the Soveraign Power is placed, without setting a part from their ordinary labour, some certain times, in which they may attend those that are appointed to instruct them; It is necessary that some such times be determined, wherein they may assemble together and (after prayers and praises given to God, the Soveraign of Soveraigns) hear those their Duties told them, and the Postiive Lawes, such as generally concern them all, read and expounded, and be put in mind of the Authority that maketh them Lawes. To his end had the *Jewes* every seventh day, a *Sabbath*, in which the Law was read and expounded; and in the solemnity whereof they were put in mind, that their King was God; that having created the world in six dayes, he rested the seventh day; and by their resting on it from their labour, that that God was their King, which redeemed them from their servile, and painfull labour in *Egypt*, and gave them a time, after they had rejoyced in God, to take joy also in themselves, by lawfull recreation. So that the first Table of the Commandements, is spent all, in setting down the summe of Gods absolute Power; not onely as God, but as King by pact, (in peculiar) of the Jewes; and may therefore give light, to those that have Soveraign Power conferred on them by the consent of men, to see what doctrine they Ought to teach their Subjects.

And because the first instruction of Children, dependeth on the

care of their Parents; it is necessary that they should be obedient
to them, whilest they are under their tuition; and not onely so, but
that also afterwards (as gratitude requireth,) they acknowledge
the benefit of their education, by externall signes of honour. To
which end they are to be taught, that originally the Father of every
man was also his Soveraign Lord, with power over him of life and
death; and that the Fathers of families, when by instituting a
Common-wealth, they resigned that absolute Power, yet it was
never intended, they should lose the honour due unto them for their
education. For to relinquish such right, was not necessary to the
Institution of Soveraign Power; nor would there by any reason,
why any man should desire to have children, or take the care to
nourish, and instruct them, if they were afterwards to have no other
benefit from them, than from other men. And this accordeth with
the fifth Commandement.

Again, every Soveraign Ought to cause Justice to be taught,
which (consisting in taking from no man what is his,) is as much as
to say, to cause men to be taught not to deprive their Neighbours,
by violence, or fraud, of any thing which by the Soveraign Authority
is theirs. Of things held in propriety, those that are dearest to a
man are his own life, & limbs; and in the next degree (in most
men,) those that concern conjugall affection; and after them riches
and means of living. Therefore the People are to be taught, to
abstain from violence to one anothers person, by private revenges;
from violation of conjugall honour; and from forcible rapine, and
fraudulent surreption of one anothers goods. For which purpose
also it is necessary they be shewed the evill consequences of false
Judgement, by corruption either of Judges or Witnesses, whereby
the distinction of propriety is taken away, and Justice becomes of
no effect: all which things are intimated in the sixth, seventh,
eighth, and ninth Commandements.

Lastly, they are to be taught, that not onely the unjust facts, but
the designes and intentions to do them, (though by accident hindred,)
are Injustice; which consisteth in the pravity of the will, as well as
in the irregularity of the act. And this is the intention of the tenth
Commandement, and the summe of the second Table; which is
reduced all to this one Commandement of mutuall Charity, *Thou shalt
love thy neighbour as thy selfe:* as the summe of the first Table is
reduced to *the love of God;* whom they had then newly received
as their King.

As for the Means, and Conduits, by which the people may receive
this Instruction, wee are to search, by what means so many Opinions,
contrary to the peace of Mankind, upon weak and false Principles,
have neverthelesse been so deeply rooted in them. I mean those,
which I have in the precedent Chapter specified: as That men shall
Judge of what is lawfull and unlawfull, not by the Law it selfe,
but by their own Consciences; that is to say, by their own private
Judgements: That Subjects sinne in obeying the Commands of the
Common-wealth, unlesse they themselves have first judged them to

be lawfull: That their Propriety in their riches is such, as to exclude the Dominion, which the Common-wealth hath over the same: That it is lawfull for Subjects to kill such, as they call Tyrants: That the Soveraign Power may be divided, and the like; which come to be instilled into the People by this means. They whom necessity, or covetousnesse keepeth attent on their trades, and labour; and they, on the other side, whom superfluity, or sloth carrieth after their sensuall pleasures, (which two sorts of men take up the greatest part of Man-kind,) being diverted from the deep meditation, which the learning of truth, not onely in the matter of Naturall Justice, but also of all other Sciences necessarily requireth, receive the Notions of their duty, chiefly from Divines in the Pulpit, and partly from such of their Neighbours, or familiar acquaintance, as having the Faculty of discoursing readily, and plausibly, seem wiser and better learned in cases of Law, and Conscience, than themselves. And the Divines, and such others as make shew of Learning, derive their knowledge from the Universities, and from the Schooles of Law, or from the Books, which by men eminent in those Schooles, and Universities have been published. It is therefore manifest, that the Instruction of the people, dependeth wholly, on the right teaching of Youth in the Universities. But are not (may some man say) the Universities of *England* learned enough already to do that? or is it you will undertake to teach the Universities? Hard questions. Yet to the first, I doubt not to answer; that till towards the later end of *Henry the eighth*, the Power of the Pope, was alwayes upheld against the Powei of the Common-wealth, principally by the Universities; and that the doctrines maintained by so many Preachers, against the Soveraign Power of the King, and by so many Lawyers, and others, that had their education there, is a sufficient argument, that though the Universities were not authors of those false doctrines, yet they knew not how to plant the true. For in such a contradiction of Opinions, it is most certain, that they have not been sufficiently instructed; and 'tis no wonder, if they yet retain a relish of that subtile liquor, wherewith they were first seasoned, against the Civill Authority. But to the later question, it is not fit, nor needfull for me to say either I, or No: for any man that sees what I am doing, may easily perceive what I think.

The safety of the People, requireth further, from him, or them that have the Soveraign Power, that Justice be equally administred to all degrees of People; that is, that as well the rich, and mighty, as poor and obscure persons, may be righted of the injuries done them; so as the great, may have no greater hope of impunity, when they doe violence, dishonour, or any Injury to the meaner sort, than when one of these, does the like to one of them: For in this consisteth Equity; to which, as being a Precept of the Law of Nature, a Soveraign is as much subject, as any of the meanest of his People. All breaches of the Law, are offences against the Commonwealth: but there be some, that are also against private Persons. Those that concern the Common-wealth onely, may without breach of Equity be pardoned; for every man may pardon what is done against himselfe, according to his own discretion. But an offence against a private man, cannot in Equity be pardoned, without the consent of him that is injured; or reasonable satisfaction.

The Inequality of Subjects, proceedeth from the Acts of Soveraign Power; and therefore has no more place in the presence of the Soveraign; that is to say, in a Court of Justice, then the Inequality between Kings, and their Subjects, in the presence of the King of Kings. The honour of great Persons, is to be valued for their beneficence, and the aydes they give to men of inferiour rank, or not at all. And the violences, oppressions, and injuries they do, are not extenuated, but aggravated by the greatnesse of their persons; because they have least need to commit them. The consequences of this partiality towards the great, proceed in this manner. Impunity maketh Insolence; Insolence Hatred; and Hatred, and Endeavour to pull down all oppressing and contumelious greatnesse, though with the ruine of the Common-wealth.

To Equall Justice, appertaineth also the Equall imposition of Taxes; the Equality whereof dependeth not on the Equality of riches, but on the Equality of the debt, that every man oweth to the Common-wealth for his defence. It is not enough, for a man to labour for the maintenance of his life; but also to fight, (if need be,) for the securing of his labour. They must either do as the Jewes did after their return from captivity, in re-edifying the Temple, build with one hand, and hold the Sword in the other; or else they must hire others to fight for them. For the Impositions, that are layd on the People by the Soveraign Power, are nothing else but the Wages, due to them that hold the publique Sword, to defend private men in the exercise of severall Trades, and Callings. Seeing then the benefit that every one receiveth thereby, is the enjoyment of life, which is equally dear to poor, and rich; the debt which a poor man oweth them that defend his life, is the same which a rich man oweth for the defence of his; saving that the rich, who have the service of the poor, may be debtors not onely for their own persons, but for many more. Which considered, the Equality of Imposition, consisteth rather in the Equality of that which is consumed, than of the riches of the persons that consume the same. For what reason is there, that he which laboureth much, and sparing the fruits of his labour, consumeth little, should be more charged, then he that living idlely, getteth little, and spendeth all he gets; seeing the one hath no more protection from the Common-wealth, then the other? But when the Impositions, are layd upon those things which men consume, every man payeth Equally for what he useth: Nor is the Common-wealth defrauded, by the luxurious waste of private men.

And whereas many men, by accident unevitable, become unable to maintain themselves by their labour; they ought not to be left to the Charity of private persons; but to be provided for, (as farforth as the necessities of Nature require, by the Lawes of the

Common-wealth. For as it is Uncharitablenesse in any man, to neglect the impotent; so it is in the Soveraign of a Common-wealth, to expose them to the hazard of such uncertain Charity. But for such as have strong bodies, the case is otherwise: they are to be forced to work; and to avoyd the excuse of not finding employ-ment, there ought to be such Lawes, as may encourage all manner of Arts; as Navigation, Agriculture, Fishing, and all manner of Mani-facture that requires labour. The multitude of poor, and yet strong people still encreasing, they are to be transplanted into Countries not sufficiently inhabited: where neverthelesse, they are not to exterminate those they find there; but constrain them to inhabit closer together, and not range a great deal of ground, to snatch what they find; but to court each little Plot with art and labour, to give them their sustenance in due season. And when all the world is overcharged with Inhabitants, then the last remedy of all is Warre; which provideth for every man, by Victory, or Death.

To the care of the Soveraign, belongeth the making of Good Lawes. But what is a good Law? By a Good Law, I mean not a Just Law: for no Law can be Unjust. The Law is made by the Soveraign Power, and all that is done by such Power, is warranted, and owned by every one of the people; and that which every man will have so, no man can say it unjust. It is in the Lawes of a Common-wealth, as in the Lawes of Gaming: whatsoever the Gamesters all agree on, is Injustice to none of them. A good Law is that, which is *Needfull*, for the *Good of the People*, and withall *Perspicuous*.

For the use of Lawes, (which are but Rules Authorised) is not to bind the People from all Voluntary actions; but to direct and keep them in such a motion, as not to hurt themselves by their own impetuous desires, rashnesse, or indiscretion; as Hedges are set, not to stop Travellers, but to keep them in the way. And therefore a Law that is not Needful, having not the true End of a Law, is not Good. A Law may be conceived to be Good, when it is for the benefit of the Soveraign; though it be not Necessary for the People; but it is not so. For the good of the Soveraign and People, cannot be separated. It is a weak Soveraign, that has weak Subjects; and a weak People, whose Soveraign wanteth Power to rule them at his will. Unnecessary Lawes are not good Lawes; but trapps for Mony: which where the right of Soveraign Power is acknowledged, are superfluous; and where it is not acknowledged, unsufficient to defend the People.

The Perspicuity, consisteth not so much in the words of the Law it selfe, as in a Declaration of the Causes, and Motives, for which it was made. That is it, that shewes us the meaning of the Legislator; and the meaning of the Legislator known, the Law is more easily understood by few, than many words. For all words, are subject to ambiguity; and therefore multiplication of words in the body of the Law, is multiplication of ambiguity: Besides it seems to imply, (by too much diligence,) that whosoever can evade the words, is without the compasse of the Law. And this is a cause of many unnecessary Processes. For when I consider how short were the Lawes of antient times; and how they grew by degrees still longer; me thinks I see a contention between the Penners, and Pleaders of the Law; the former seeking to circumscribe the later; and the later to evade their circumscriptions; and that the Pleaders have got the Victory. It belongeth therefore to the Office of a Legislator, (such as is in all Common-wealths the Supreme Representative, be it one Man, or an Assembly,) to make the reason Perspicuous, why the Law was made; and the Body of the Law it selfe, as short, but in as proper, and significant termes, as may be.

It belongeth also to the Office of the Soveraign, to make a right application of Punishments, and Rewards. And seeing the end of punishing is not revenge, and discharge of choler; but correction, either of the offender, or of others by his example; the severest Punishments are to be inflicted for those Crimes, that are of most Danger to the Publique; such as are those which proceed from malice to the Government established; those that spring from contempt of Justice; those that provoke Indignation in the Multitude; and those, which unpunished, seem Authorised, as when they are committed by Sonnes, Servants, or Favorites of men in Authority: For Indignation carrieth men, not onely against the Actors, and Authors of Injustice; but against all Power that is likely to protect them; as in the case of *Tarquin*; when for the Insolent act of one of his Sonnes, he was driven out of *Rome*, and the Monarchy it selfe dissolved. But Crimes of Infirmity; such as are those which proceed from great provocation, from great fear, great need, or from ignorance whether the Fact be a great Crime, or not, there is place many times for Lenity, without prejudice to the Common-wealth; and Lenity when there is such place for it, is required by the Law of Nature. The Punishment of the Leaders, and teachers in a Commotion; not the poore seduced People, when they are punished, can profit the Common-wealth by their example. To be severe to the People, is to punish that ignorance, which may in great part be imputed to the Soveraign, whose fault it was, they were no better instructed.

In like manner it belongeth to the Office, and Duty of the Soveraign, to apply his Rewards alwayes so, as there may arise from them benefit to the Common-wealth: wherein consisteth their Use, and End; and is then done, when they that have well served the Common-wealth, are with as little expence of the Common Treasure, as is possible, so well recompenced, as others thereby may be encouraged, both to serve the same as faithfully as they can, and to study the arts by which they may be enabled to do it better. To buy with Mony, or Preferment, from a Popular ambitious Subject, to be quiet, and desist from making all impressions in the mindes of the People, has nothing of the nature of Reward; (which is ordained not for disservice, but for service past;) nor a signe of Gratitude, but of Fear: nor does it tend to the Benefit, but to the Dammage of the Publique. It is a contention with Ambition,

like that of *Hercules* with the Monster *Hydra*, which having many
heads, for every one that was vanquished, there grew up three. For
in like manner, when the stubbornnesse of one Popular man, is
overcome with Reward, there arise many more (by the Example)
that do the same Mischiefe, in hope of like Benefit: and as
all sorts of Manifacture, so also Malice encreaseth by being
vendible. And though sometimes a Civill warre, may be dif-
ferred, by such wayes as that, yet the danger growes still the greater,
and the Publique ruine more assured. It is therefore against the
Duty of the Soveraign, to whom the Publique Safety is committed,
to Reward those that aspire to greatnesse by disturbing the Peace of
their Country, and not rather to oppose the beginnings of such men,
with a little danger, than after a longer time with greater.

Another Businesse of the Soveraign, is to choose good Counsellours; I mean such, whose advice he is to take in the Government
of the Common-wealth. For this word Counsell, *Consilium*,
corrupted from *Considium*, is of a large signification, and comprehendeth all Assemblies of men that sit together, not onely to
deliberate what is to be done hereafter, but also to judge of Facts
past, and of Law for the present. I take it here in the first sense
onely: And in this sense, there is no choyce of Counsell, neither in a
Democracy, nor Aristocracy; because the persons Counselling are
members of the person Counselled. The choyce of Counsellours
therefore is proper to Monarchy; In which, the Soveraign that
endeavoureth not to make choyce of those, that in every kind are
the most able, dischargeth not his Office as he ought to do. The
most able Counsellours, are they that have least hope of benefit
by giving evill Counsell, and most knowledge of those things that
conduce to the Peace, and Defence of the Common-wealth. It is a
hard matter to know who expecteth benefit from publique troubles;
but the signes that guide to a just suspicion, is the soothing of the
people in their unreasonable, or irremediable grievances, by men
whose estates are not sufficient to discharge their accustomed
expences, and may easily be observed by any one whom it concerns
to know it. But to know, who has most knowledge of the Publique
affaires, is yet harder; and they that know them, need them a great
deale the lesse. For to know, who knowes the Rules almost of any
Art, is a great degree of the knowledge of the same Art; because
no man can be assured of the truth of anothers Rules, but he that is
first taught to understand them. But the best signes of Knowledge
of any Art, are, much conversing in it, and constant good effects
of it. Good Counsell comes not by Lot, nor by Inheritance; and
therefore there is no more reason to expect good Advice from the
rich, or noble, in matter of State, than in delineating the dimensions
of a fortresse; unlesse we shall think there needs no method in the
study of the Politiques, (as there does in the study of Geometry,)
but onely to be lookers on; which is not so. For the Politiques is
the harder study of the two. Whereas in these parts of *Europe*,
it hath been taken for a Right of certain persons, to have place in

the highest Councell of State by Inheritance; it is derived from the Conquests of the antient Germans; wherein many absolute Lords joyning together to conquer other Nations, would not enter in to the Confederacy, without such Priviledges, as might be marks of difference in time following, between their Posterity, and the Posterity of their Subjects; which Priviledges being inconsistent with the Soveraign Power, by the favour of the Soveraign, they may seem to keep; but contending for them as their Right, they must needs by degrees let them go, and have at last no further honour, then adhæreth naturally to their abilities.

And how able soever be the Counsellours in any affaire, the benfit of their Counsell is greater, when they give every one his Advice, and the reasons of it apart, than when they do it in an Assembly, by way of Orations; and when they have præmeditated, than when they speak on the sudden; both because they have more time, to survey the consequences of action; and are lesse subject to be carried away to contradiction, through Envy, Emulation, or other Passions arising from the difference of opinion.

The best Counsell, in those things that concern not other Nations, but onely the ease, and benefit the Subjects may enjoy, by Lawes that look onely inward, is to be taken from the generall informations, and complaints of the people of each Province, who are best acquainted with their own wants, and ought therefore, when they demand nothing in derogation of the essentiall Rights of Soveraignty to be diligently taken notice of. For without those Essentiall Rights, (as I have often before said,) the Common-wealth cannot at all subsist.

A Commander of an Army in chiefe, if he be not Popular, shall not be beloved, nor feared as he ought to be by his Army; and consequently cannot performe that office with good successe! He must therefore be Industrious, Valiant, Affable, Liberall, and Fortunate, that he may gain an opinion both of sufficiency, and of loving his Souldiers. This is Popularity, and breeds in the Souldiers both desire, and courage, to recommend themselves to his favour; and protects the severity of the Generall, in punishing (when need is) the Mutinous, or negligent Souldiers. But this love of Souldiers, (if caution be not given of the Commanders fidelity,) is a dangerous thing to Soveraign Power; especially when it is in the hands of an Assembly not popular. It belongeth therefore to the safety of the People, both that they be good Conductors, and faithful Subjects, to whom the Soveraign Commits his Armies.

But when the Soveraign himselfe is Popular; that is, reverenced and beloved of his People, there is no danger at all from the Popularity of a Subject. For Souldiers are never so generally unjust, as to side with their Captain; though they love him, against their Soveraign, when they love not onely his Person, but also his Cause. And therefore those, who by violence have at any time suppressed the Power of their lawfull Soveraign, before they could settle themselves in his place, have been alwayes put to the trouble of contriving their Titles, to save the People from the shame of receiving them. To have a known Right to Soveraign Power, is so popular a quality, as he that has it needs no more, for his own part, to turn the hearts of his Subjects to him, but that they see him able absolutely to govern his own Family: Nor, on the part of his enemies, but a disbanding of their Armies. For the greatest and most active part of Mankind, has never hetherto been well contented with the present.

Concerning the Offices of one Soveraign to another, which are comprehended in that Law, which is commonly called the *Law of Nations*, I need not say any thing in this place; because the Law of Nations, and the Law of Nature, is the same thing. And every Soveraign hath the same Right, in procuring the safety of his People, that any particular man can have, in procuring the safety of his own Body. And the same Law, that dictateth to men that have no Civil Government, what they ought to do, and what to avoyd in regard of one another, dictateth the same to Common-wealths, that is, to the Consciences of Soveraign Princes, and Soveraign Assemblies; there being no Court of Naturall Justice, but in the Conscience onely; where not Man, but God raigneth; whose Lawes, (such of them as oblige all Mankind,) in respect of God, as he is the Author of Nature, are *Naturall*; and in respect of the same God, as he is King of Kings, are *Lawes*. But of the Kingdome of God, as King of Kings, and as King also of a peculiar People, I shall speak in the rest of this discourse.

## CHAP. XXXI

### *Of the* KINGDOME OF GOD BY NATURE

THAT the condition of meer Nature, that is to say, of absolute Liberty, such as is theirs, that neither are Soveraigns, nor Subjects, is Anarchy, and the condition of Warre: That the Præcepts, by which men are guided to avoyd that condition, are the Lawes of Nature: That a Common-wealth, without Soveraign Power, is but a word, without substance, and cannot stand: That Subjects owe to Soveraigns, simple Obedience, in all things, wherein their obedience is not repugnant to the Lawes of God, I have sufficiently proved, in that which I have already written. There wants onely, for the entire knowledge of Civill duty, to know what are those Lawes of God. For without that, a man knows not, when he is commanded any thing by the Civill Power, whether it be contrary to the Law of God, or not: and so, either by too much civill obedience, offends the Divine Majesty, or through feare of offending God, transgresses the commandements of the Common-wealth. To avoyd both these Rocks, it is necessary to know what are the Lawes Divine. And seeing the knowledge of all Law, dependeth on the knowledge of the Soveraign Power; I shall say something in that which followeth, of the KINGDOME OF GOD.

*God is King, let the Earth rejoyce,* saith the Psalmist. And again, *God is King though the Nations be angry; and he that sitteth on the Cherubins, though the earth be moved.* Whether men will or not, they must be subject alwayes to the Divine Power. By denying the Existence, or Providence of God, men may shake off their Ease, but not their Yoke. But to call this Power of God, which extendeth it selfe not onely to Man, but also to Beasts, and Plants, and Bodies inanimate, by the name of Kingdome, is but a metaphoricall use of the word. For he onely is properly said to Raigne, that governs his Subjects, by his Word, and by promise of Rewards to those that obey it, and by threatning them with Punishment that obey it not. Subjects therefore in the Kingdome of God, are not Bodies Inanimate, nor creatures Irrationall; because they understand no Precepts as his: Nor Atheists; nor they that believe not that God has any care of the actions of mankind; because they acknowledge no Word for his, nor have hope of his rewards, or fear of his threatnings. They therefore that believe there is a God that governeth the world, and hath given Præcepts, and propounded Rewards, and Punishments to Mankind, are Gods Subjects; all the rest, are to be understood as Enemies.

To rule by Words, requires that such Words be manifestly made known; for else they are no Lawes: For to the nature of Lawes belongeth a sufficient, and clear Promulgation, such as may take away the excuse of Ignorance; which in the Lawes of men is but of one onely kind, and that is, Proclamation, or Promulgation by the voyce of man. But God declareth his Lawes three wayes; by the Dictates of *Naturall Reason,* by *Revelation,* and by the *Voyce* of some *man,* to whom by the operation of Miracles, he procureth credit with the rest. From hence there ariseth a triple Word of God, *Rational, Sensible,* and *Prophetique :* to which Correspondeth a triple Hearing; *Right Reason, Sense Supernaturall,* and *Faith.* As for Sense Supernaturall, which consisteth in Revelation, or Inspiration, there have not been any Universall Lawes so given, because God speaketh not in that manner, but to particular persons, and to divers men divers things.

From the difference between the other two kinds of Gods Word, *Rationall,* and *Prophetique,* there may be attributed to God, a twofold Kingdome, Naturall, and *Prophetique :* Naturall, wherein he governeth as many of Mankind as acknowledge his Providence, by the naturall Dictates of Right Reason; And Prophetique, wherein having chosen out one peculiar Nation (the Jewes) for his Subjects, he governed them, and none but them, not onely by naturall Reason, but by Positive Lawes, which he gave them by the mouths of his holy Prophets. Of the Naturall Kingdome of God I intend to speak in this Chapter.

The Right of Nature, whereby God reigneth over men, and punisheth those that break his Lawes, is to be derived not from his

Creating them, as if he required obedience, as of Gratitude for his benefits; but from his *Irresistible Power.* I have formerly shewn, how the Soveraign Right ariseth from Pact: To shew how the same Right may arise from Nature, requires no more, but to shew in what case it is never taken away. Seeing all men by Nature had Right to All things, they had Right every one to reigne over all the rest. But because this Right could not be obtained by force, it concerned the safety of every one, laying by that Right, to set up men (with Soveraign Authority) by common consent, to rule and defend them: whereas if there had been any man of Power Irresistible; there had been no reason, why he should not by that Power have ruled, and defended both himselfe, and them, according to his own discretion. To those therefore whose Power is irresistible, the dominion of all men adhæreth naturally by their excellence of Power; and consequently it is from that Power, that the Kingdome over men, and the Right of afflicting men at his pleasure, belongeth Naturally to God Almighty; not as Creator, and Gracious; but as Omnipotent. And though Punishment be due for Sinne onely, because by that word is understood Affliction for Sinne; yet the Right of Afflicting, is not alwayes derived from mens Sinne, but from Gods Power.

This question, *Why Evill men often Prosper, and Good men suffer Adversity,* has been much disputed by the Antient, and is the same with this of ours, *by what Right God dispenseth the Prosperities and Adversities of this life*; and is of that difficulty, as it hath shaken the faith, not onely of the Vulgar, but of Philosophers, and which is more, of the Saints, concerning the Divine Providence. *How Good* (saith *David*) *is the God of Israel to those that are Upright in Heart ; and yet my feet were almost gone, my tradeings had well-nigh slipt ; for I was grieved at the Wicked, when I saw the Ungodly in such Prosperity.* And *Job,* how earnestly does he expostulate with God, for the many Afflictions he suffered, notwithstanding his Righteousnesse? This question in the case of *Job,* is decided by God himselfe, not by arguments derived from *Job's* Sinne, but his own Power. For whereas the friends of *Job* drew their arguments from his Affliction to his Sinne, and he defended himselfe by the conscience of his Innocence, God himselfe taketh up the matter, and having justified the Affliction by arguments drawn from his Power, such as this, *Where wast thou when I layd the foundations of the earth,* and the like, both approved *Job's* Innocence, and reproved the Erroneous doctrine of his friends. Conformable to this doctrine is the sentence of our Saviour, concerning the man that was born Blind, in these words, *Neither hath this man sinned, nor his fathers ; but that the works of God might be made manifest in him.* And though it be said, *That Death entred into the world by sinne,* (by which is meant that if *Adam* had never sinned, he had never dyed, that is, never suffered any separation of his soule from his body,) it follows not thence, that God could not justly have Afflicted him, though he had not Sinned, as well as he afflicteth other living creatures, that cannot sinne.

Having spoken of the Right of Gods Soveraignty, as grounded onely on Nature; we are to consider next, what are the Divine Lawes, or Dictates of Naturall Reason; which Lawes concern either the naturall Duties of one man to another, or the Honour naturally due to our Divine Soveraign. The first are the same Lawes of Nature, of which I have spoken already in the 14. and 15. Chapters of this Treatise; namely, Equity, Justice, Mercy, Humility, and the rest of the Morall Vertues. It remaineth therefore that we consider, what Præcepts are dictated to men, by their Naturall Reason onely, without other word of God, touching the Honour and Worship of the Divine Majesty.

Honour consisteth in the inward thought, and opinion of the Power, and Goodnesse of another: and therefore to Honour God, is to think as Highly of his Power and Goodnesse, as is possible. And of that opinion, the externall signes appearing in the Words, and Actions of men, are called *Worship*; which is one part of that which the Latines understand by the word *Cultus*: For *Cultus* signifieth properly, and constantly, that labour which a man bestowes on any thing, with a purpose to make benefit by it. Now those things whereof we make benefit, are either subject to us, and the profit they yeeld, followeth the labour we bestow upon them, as a naturall effect; or they are not subject to us, but answer our labour, according to their own Wills. In the first sense the labour bestowed on the Earth, is called *Culture*; and the education of Children a *Culture* of their mindes. In the second sense, where mens wills are to be wrought to our purpose, not by Force, but by Compleasance, it signifieth as much as Courting, that is, a winning of favour by good offices; as by praises, by acknowledging their Power, and by whatsoever is pleasing to them from whom we look for any benefit. And this is properly *Worship*: in which sense *Publicola*, is understood for a Worshipper of the People; and *Cultus Dei*, for the Worship of God.

From internall Honour, consisting in the opinion of Power and Goodnesse, arise three Passions; *Love*, which hath reference to Goodnesse; and *Hope*, and *Fear*, that relate to Power: And three parts of externall worship; *Praise, Magnifying,* and *Blessing*: The subject of Praise, being Goodnesse; the subject of Magnifying, and Blessing, being Power, and the effect thereof Felicity. Praise, and Magnifying are signified both by Words, and Actions: By Words, when we say a man is Good, or Great: By Actions, when we thank him for his Bounty, and obey his Power. The opinion of the Happinesse of another, can onely be expressed by words.

There be some signes of Honour, (both in Attributes and Actions,) that be Naturally so; as amongst Attributes, *Good, Just, Liberall,* and the like; and amongst Actions, *Prayers, Thanks,* and *Obedience* Others are so by Institution, or Custome of men: and in some times and places are Honourable; in others Dishonourable; in others Indifferent: such as are the Gestures in Salutation, Prayer, and

Thanksgiving, in different times and places, differently used. The former is *Naturall*; the later *Arbitrary* Worship.

And of Arbitrary Worship, there bee two differences: For sometimes it is a *Commanded*, sometimes *Voluntary* Worship: Commanded, when it is such as hee requireth, who is Worshipped: Free, when it is such as the Worshipper thinks fit. When it is Commanded, not the words, or gesture, but the obedience is the Worship. But when Free, the Worship consists in the opinion of the beholders: for if to them the words, or actions by which we intend honour, seem ridiculous, and tending to contumely; they are no Worship; because no signes of Honour; and no signes of Honour; because a signe is not a signe to him that giveth it, but to him to whom it is made; that is, to the spectator.

Again, there is a *Publique*, and a *Private* Worship. Publique, is the Worship that a Common-wealth performeth, as one Person. Private, is that which a Private person exhibiteth. Publique, in respect of the whole Common-wealth, is Free; but in respect of Particular men it is not so. Private, is in secret Free; but in the sight of the multitude, it is never without some Restraint, either from the Lawes, or from the Opinion of men; which is contrary to the nature of Liberty.

The End of Worship amongst men, is Power. For where a man seeth another worshipped, he supposeth him powerfull, and is the readier to obey him; which makes his Power greater. But God has no Ends: the worship we do him, proceeds from our duty, and is directed according to our capacity, by those rules of Honour, that Reason dictateth to be done by the weak to the more potent men, in hope of benefit, for fear of dammage, or in thankfulnesse for good already received from them.

That we may know what worship of God is taught us by the light of Nature, I will begin with his Attributes. Where, First, it is manifest, we ought to attribute to him *Existence*: For no man can have the will to honour that, which he thinks not to have any Beeing.

Secondly, that those Philosophers, who sayd the World, or the Soule of the World was God, spake unworthily of him; and denyed his Existence: For by God, is understood the cause of the World; and to say the World is God, is to say, there is no cause of it, that is, no God.

Thirdly, to say the World was not Created, but Eternall, (seeing that which is Eternall has no cause,) is to deny there is a God.

Fourthly, that they who attributing (as they think) Ease to God, take from him the care of Man-kind; take from him his Honour: for it takes away mens love, and fear of him; which is the root of Honour.

Fifthly, in those things that signifie Greatnesse, and Power; to say he is *Finite*, is not to Honour him: For it is not a signe of the Will to Honour God, to attribute to him lesse than we can; and

Finite, is lesse than we can; because to Finite, it is easie to adde more.

Therefore to attribute *Figure* to him, is not Honour; for all Figure is Finite:

Nor to say we conceive, and imagine, or have an *Idea* of him in our mind: for whatsoever we conceive is Finite:

Nor to attribute to him *Parts*, or *Totality*; which are the Attributes onely of things Finite:

Nor to say he is in this, or that *Place*: for whatsoever is in Place, is bounded, and Finite:

Nor that he is *Moved*, or *Resteth*: for both these Attributes ascribe to him Place:

Nor that there be more Gods than one; because it implies them all Finite: for there cannot be more than one Infinite:

Nor to ascribe to him (unlesse Metaphorically, meaning not the Passion, but the Effect) Passions that partake of Griefe; as *Repentance, Anger, Mercy*: or of Want; as *Appetite, Hope, Desire*; or of any Passive faculty: For Passion, is Power limited by somewhat else.

And therefore when we ascribe to God a *Will*, it is not to be understood, as that of Man, for a *Rationall Appetite*; but as the Power, by which he effecteth every thing.

Likewise when we attribute to him *Sight*, and other acts of Sense; as also *Knowledge*, and *Understanding*; which in us is nothing else, but a tumult of the mind, raised by externall things that presse the organicall parts of mans body: For there is no such thing in God; and being things that depend on naturall causes, cannot be attributed to him.

Hee that will attribute to God, nothing but what is warranted by naturall Reason, must either use such Negative Attributes, as *Infinite, Eternall, Incomprehensible*; or Superlatives, as *Most High, most Great*, and the like; or Indefinite, as *Good, Just, Holy, Creator*; and in such sense, as if he meant not to declare what he is, (for that were to circumscribe him within the limits of our Fancy,) but how much wee admire him, and how ready we would be to obey him; which is a signe of Humility, and of a Will to honour him as much as we can: For there is but one Name to signifie our Conception of his Nature, and that is, I AM: and but one Name of his Relation to us, and that is *God*; in which is contained Father, King, and Lord.

Concerning the actions of Divine Worship, it is a most generall Precept of Reason, that they be signes of the Intention to Honour God; such as are, First, *Prayers*: For not the Carvers, when they made Images, were thought to make them Gods; but the People that *Prayed* to them.

Secondly, *Thanksgiving*; which differeth from Prayer in Divine Worship, no otherwise, than that Prayers precede, and Thanks succeed the benefit; the end both of the one, and the other, being to acknowledge God, for Author of all benefits, as well past, as future.

Thirdly, *Gifts*; that is to say, *Sacrifices*, and *Oblations*, (if they be of the best,) are signes of Honour: for they are Thanksgivings.

Fourthly, *Not to swear by any but God*, is naturally a signe of Honour: for it is a confession that God onely knoweth the heart; and that no mans wit, or strength can protect a man against Gods vengeance on the perjured.

Fifthly, it is a part of Rationall Worship, to speak Considerately of God; for it argues a Fear of him, and Fear, is a confession of his Power. Hence followeth, That the name of God is not to be used rashly, and to no purpose; for that is as much, as in Vain: And it is to no purpose unlesse it be by way of Oath, and by order of the Common-wealth, to make Judgements certain; or between Common-wealths, to avoyd Warre. And that disputing of Gods nature is contrary to his Honour: For it is supposed, that in this naturall Kingdome of God, there is no other way to know any thing, but by naturall Reason; that is, from the Principles of naturall Science; which are so farre from teaching us any thing of Gods nature, as they cannot teach us our own nature, nor the nature of the smallest creature living. And therefore, when men out of the Principles of naturall Reason, dispute of the Attributes of God, they but dishonour him: For in the Attributes which we give to God, we are not to consider the signification of Philosophicall Truth; but the signification of Pious Intention, to do him the greatest Honour we are able. From the want of which consideration, have proceeded the volumes of disputation about the nature of God, that tend not to his Honour, but to the honour of our own wits, and learning; and are nothing else but inconsiderate, and vain abuses of his Sacred Name.

Sixthly, in *Prayers, Thanksgiving, Offerings*, and *Sacrifices*, it is a Dictate of naturall Reason, that they be every one in his kind the best, and most significant of Honour. As for example, that Prayers, and Thanksgiving, be made in Words and Phrases, not sudden, nor light, nor Plebeian; but beautifull, and well composed; For else we do not God as much honour as we can. And therefore the Heathens did absurdly, to worship Images for Gods: But their doing it in Verse, and with Musick, both of Voyce, and Instruments, was reasonable. Also that the Beasts they offered in sacrifice, and the Gifts they offered, and their actions in Worshipping, were full of submission, and commemorative of benefits received, was according to reason, as proceeding from an intention to honour him.

Seventhly, Reason directeth not onely to worship God in Secret; but also, and especially, in Publique, and in the sight of men: For without that, (that which in honour is most acceptable) the procuring others to honour him, is lost.

Lastly, Obedience to his Lawes (that is, in this case to the Lawes of Nature,) is the greatest worship of all. For as Obedience is more acceptable to God than Sacrifice; so also to set light by his Commandements, is the greatest of all contumelies. And these are the

Lawes of that Divine Worship, which naturall Reason dictateth
to private men.

But seeing a Common-wealth is but one Person, it ought also to
exhibite to God but one Worship; which then it doth, when it
commandeth it to be exhibited by Private men, Publiquely. And
this is Publique Worship; the property whereof, is to be *Uniforme*:
For those actions that are done differently, by different men, cannot
be said to be a Publique Worship. And therefore, where many
sorts of Worship be allowed, proceeding from the different Religions
of Private men, it cannot be said there is any Publique Worship,
nor that the Common-wealth is of any Religion at all.

And because words (and consequently the Attributes of God)
have their signification by agreement, and constitution of men;
those Attributes are to be held significative of Honour, that men
intend shall so be; and whatsoever may be done by the wills of
particular men, where there is no Law but Reason, may be done
by the will of the Common-wealth, by Lawes Civill. And because
a Common-wealth hath no Will, nor makes no Lawes, but those that
are made by the Will of him, or them that have the Soveraign Power;
it followeth, that those Attributes which the Soveraign ordaineth,
in the Worship of God, for signes of Honour, ought to be taken and
used for such, by private men in their publique Worship.

But because not all Actions are signes by Constitution; but some
are Naturally signes of Honour, others of Contumely, these later
(which are those that men are ashamed to do in the sight of them
they reverence) cannot be made by humane power a part of Divine
worship; nor the former (such as are decent, modest, humble
Behaviour) ever be separated from it. But whereas there be an
infinite number of Actions, and Gestures, of an indifferent nature;
such of them as the Common-wealth shall ordain to be Publiquely
and Universally in use, as signes of Honour, and part of Gods
Worship, are to be taken and used for such by the Subjects. And
that which is said in the Scripture, *It is better to obey God than men*,
hath place in the kingdome of God by Pact, and not by Nature.

Having thus briefly spoken of the Naturall Kingdome of God,
and his Naturall Lawes. I will adde onely to this Chapter a short
declaration of his Naturall Punishments. There is no action of man
in this life, that is not the beginning of so long a chayn of Consequences, as no humane Providence, is high enough, to give a man a
prospect to the end. And in this Chayn, there are linked together
both pleasing and unpleasing events; in such manner, as he that
will do any thing for his pleasure, must engage himselfe to suffer
all the pains annexed to it; and these pains, are the Naturall
Punishments of those actions, which are the beginning of more
Harme than Good. And hereby it comes to passe, that Intemperance, is naturally punished with Diseases; Rashnesse, with
Mischances; Injustice, with the Violence of Enemies; Pride, with
Ruine; Cowardise, with Oppression; Negligent government of
Princes, with Rebellion; and Rebellion, with Slaughter. For seeing

Punishments are consequent to the breach of Lawes; Naturall Punishments must be naturally consequent to the breach of the Lawes of Nature; and therfore follow them as their naturall, not arbitrary effects.

And thus farre concerning the Constitution, Nature, and Right of Soveraigns; and concerning the Duty of Subjects, derived from the Principles of Naturall Reason.   And now, considering how different this Doctrine is, from the Practise of the greatest part of the world, especially of these Western parts, that have received their Morall learning from *Rome*, and *Athens*; and how much depth of Morall Philosophy is required, in them that have the Administration of the Soveraign Power; I am at the point of believing this my labour, as uselesse, as the Common-wealth of *Plato*; For he also is of opinion that it is impossible for the disorders of State, and change of Governments by Civill Warre, ever to be taken away, till Soveraigns be Philosophers.   But when I consider again, that the Science of Naturall Justice, is the onely Science necessary for Soveraigns, and their principall Ministers; and that they need not be charged with the Sciences Mathematicall, (as by *Plato* they are,) further, than by good Lawes to encourage men to the study of them; and that neither *Plato*, nor any other Philosopher hitherto, hath put into order, and sufficiently or probably proved all the Theoremes of Morall doctrine, that men may learn thereby, both how to govern, and how to obey; I recover some hope, that one time or other, this writing of mine, may fall into the hands of a Soveraign, who will consider it himselfe, (for it is short, and I think clear,) without the help of any interessed, or envious Interpreter; and by the exercise of entire Soveraignty, in protecting the Publique teaching of it, convert this Truth of Speculation, into the Utility of Practice.

# GREAT BOOKS IN PHILOSOPHY PAPERBACK SERIES

## ESTHETICS

- ❑ Aristotle—*The Poetics*
- ❑ Aristotle—*Treatise on Rhetoric*

## ETHICS

- ❑ Aristotle—*The Nicomachean Ethics*
- ❑ Marcus Aurelius—*Meditations*
- ❑ Jeremy Bentham—*The Principles of Morals and Legislation*
- ❑ John Dewey—*The Moral Writings of John Dewey, Revised Edition*
  (edited by James Gouinlock)
- ❑ Epictetus—*Enchiridion*
- ❑ Immanuel Kant—*Fundamental Principles of the Metaphysic of Morals*
- ❑ John Stuart Mill—*Utilitarianism*
- ❑ George Edward Moore—*Principia Ethica*
- ❑ Friedrich Nietzsche—*Beyond Good and Evil*
- ❑ Plato—*Protagoras, Philebus*, and *Gorgias*
- ❑ Bertrand Russell—*Bertrand Russell On Ethics, Sex, and Marriage*
  (edited by Al Seckel)
- ❑ Arthur Schopenhauer—*The Wisdom of Life*
  and *Counsels and Maxims*
- ❑ Benedict de Spinoza—*Ethics* and *The Improvement of the Understanding*

## METAPHYSICS/EPISTEMOLOGY

- ❑ Aristotle—*De Anima*
- ❑ Aristotle—*The Metaphysics*
- ❑ Francis Bacon—*Essays*
- ❑ George Berkeley—*Three Dialogues Between Hylas and Philonous*
- ❑ W. K. Clifford—*The Ethics of Belief and Other Essays*
  (introduction by Timothy J. Madigan)
- ❑ René Descartes—*Discourse on Method* and *The Meditations*
- ❑ John Dewey—*How We Think*
- ❑ John Dewey—*The Influence of Darwin on Philosophy and Other Essays*
- ❑ Epicurus—*The Essential Epicurus: Letters, Principal Doctrines,*
  *Vatican Sayings, and Fragments*
  (translated, and with an introduction, by Eugene O'Connor)
- ❑ Sidney Hook—*The Quest for Being*
- ❑ David Hume—*An Enquiry Concerning Human Understanding*
- ❑ David Hume—*Treatise of Human Nature*
- ❑ William James—*The Meaning of Truth*
- ❑ William James—*Pragmatism*
- ❑ Immanuel Kant—*The Critique of Judgment*
- ❑ Immanuel Kant—*Critique of Practical Reason*
- ❑ Immanuel Kant—*Critique of Pure Reason*
- ❑ Gottfried Wilhelm Leibniz—*Discourse on Metaphysics* and the *Monadology*

- ❏ John Locke—*An Essay Concerning Human Understanding*
- ❏ George Herbert Mead—*The Philosophy of the Present*
- ❏ Charles S. Peirce—*The Essential Writings*
  (edited by Edward C. Moore, preface by Richard Robin)
- ❏ Plato—*The Euthyphro, Apology, Crito,* and *Phaedo*
- ❏ Plato—*Lysis, Phaedrus,* and *Symposium*
- ❏ Bertrand Russell—*The Problems of Philosophy*
- ❏ George Santayana—*The Life of Reason*
- ❏ Sextus Empiricus—*Outlines of Pyrrhonism*
- ❏ Ludwig Wittgenstein—*Wittgenstein's Lectures: Cambridge, 1932–1935* (edited by Alice Ambrose)

## PHILOSOPHY OF RELIGION

- ❏ Marcus Tullius Cicero—*The Nature of the Gods* and *On Divination*
- ❏ Ludwig Feuerbach—*The Essence of Christianity*
- ❏ David Hume—*Dialogues Concerning Natural Religion*
- ❏ John Locke—*A Letter Concerning Toleration*
- ❏ Lucretius—*On the Nature of Things*
- ❏ John Stuart Mill—*Three Essays on Religion*
- ❏ Friedrich Nietzsche—*The Antichrist*
- ❏ Thomas Paine—*The Age of Reason*
- ❏ Bertrand Russell—*Bertrand Russell On God and Religion*
  (edited by Al Seckel)

## SOCIAL AND POLITICAL PHILOSOPHY

- ❏ Aristotle—*The Politics*
- ❏ Mikhail Bakunin—*The Basic Bakunin: Writings, 1869–1871*
  (translated and edited by Robert M. Cutler)
- ❏ Edmund Burke—*Reflections on the Revolution in France*
- ❏ John Dewey—*Freedom and Culture*
- ❏ John Dewey—*Individualism Old and New*
- ❏ John Dewey—*Liberalism and Social Action*
- ❏ G. W. F. Hegel—*The Philosophy of History*
- ❏ G. W. F. Hegel—*Philosophy of Right*
- ❏ Thomas Hobbes—*The Leviathan*
- ❏ Sidney Hook—*Paradoxes of Freedom*
- ❏ Sidney Hook—*Reason, Social Myths, and Democracy*
- ❏ John Locke—*Second Treatise on Civil Government*
- ❏ Niccolo Machiavelli—*The Prince*
- ❏ Karl Marx (with Friedrich Engels)—*The German Ideology,* including *Theses on Feuerbach* and *Introduction to the Critique of Political Economy*
- ❏ Karl Marx—*The Poverty of Philosophy*
- ❏ Karl Marx/Friedrich Engels—*The Economic and Philosophic Manuscripts of 1844* and *The Communist Manifesto*
- ❏ John Stuart Mill—*Considerations on Representative Government*
- ❏ John Stuart Mill—*On Liberty*

- John Stuart Mill—*On Socialism*
- John Stuart Mill—*The Subjection of Women*
- Montesquieu, Charles de Secondat—*The Spirit of Laws*
- Friedrich Nietzsche—*Thus Spake Zarathustra*
- Thomas Paine—*Common Sense*
- Thomas Paine—*Rights of Man*
- Plato—*Laws*
- Plato—*The Republic*
- Jean-Jacques Rousseau—*The Social Contract*
- Mary Wollstonecraft—*A Vindication of the Rights of Men*
- Mary Wollstonecraft—*A Vindication of the Rights of Women*